KU-191-300

ROBERT BENCHLEY

A BIOGRAPHY

A Biography by
NATHANIEL BENCHLEY

ROBERT

Foreword by
ROBERT E. SHERWOOD

BENCHLEY

Eight pages of half-tone illustrations

CASSELL AND COMPANY LTD.

London

CASSELL & CO LTD
37/38 St. Andrew's Hill, Queen Victoria Street
London, E.C.4

and at

31/34 George IV Bridge, Edinburgh; 210 Queen Street, Melbourne; 26/30 Clarence Street, Sydney; 24 Wyndham Street, Auckland, New Zealand; 1068 Broadview Avenue, Toronto 6; P.O. Box 275, Cape Town; P.O. Box 11190, Johannesburg; Munsoor Building, Main Street, Colombo 11; Haroon Chambers, South Napier Road, Karachi; 13/14 Ajmeri Gate Extension, New Delhi 1; 15 Graham Road, Ballard Estate, Bombay 1; 17 Chittaranjan Avenue, Calcutta 13; Macdonald House, Orchard Road, Singapore 9; Avenida 9 de Julho 1138, São Paulo; Galeria Güemes, Escritorio 554/59 Florida 165, Buenos Aires; P.O. Box 959, Accra, Gold Coast; 25 rue Henri Barbusse, Paris 5e; Islands Brygge 5, Copenhagen; Kauwlaan 17, The Hague.

First published in Great Britain 1956

All rights reserved

Printed in Great Britain by
Lowe and Brydone (Printers) Limited, London, N.W.10

FOR GRAM

PREFACE

A biography of Robert Benchley has, by its very nature, its own special set of problems. It is something like a census of, say, the seven-year locusts. No two people remember him in exactly the same way, and the knack he had for making other people feel humorous now causes many of them, in reminiscing about him, to remember what *they* said and did, rather than what he said and did. And others, when asked about him, simply get a glassy look in their eyes and say, "God, what fun we had!" and then are unable to remember any details. He was known as a comedian—or, better, a humorist—but surprisingly few of the things he said were, by themselves, funny; they depended on the atmosphere of the moment, they were not said with conscious comic art, and they are only funny if the mood in which they were said can be recaptured. And then there are, of course, exceptions to all the above statements.

Another problem is that, after a certain point, his life lost anything that might be called a progressive pattern, and the chronological story of his later years, if followed in the same way as is the story of his earlier life, would degenerate into nothing more than a cataloguing of trips between New York and Hollywood. Once he was established as a motion-picture actor, his main interest became the making—and saving—of enough money to pay his income tax, with some left over to raise and equip a family and also to buy peanut brittle and neckties for himself whenever necessary. It was a Herculean job, and he wasn't always successful (the Federal men occasionally had to wait for their money, until he found some new source), but this is not particularly significant material for a biography.

So the detailed, chronological form had to give way to a

more diffuse, reminiscent form, in which different aspects of the character could be taken up and examined one at a time. And it is the cataloguing of these aspects that could very well become a Penelope's web, in the sense that it could go on forever. Every person who knew him knows eight other people who really knew him better, and the biographer who tries to track down all the sources is going to wind up a whimpering wreck. Therefore, since it could never be really complete, this reminiscent section has been restricted to the salient features of his character, because anything else would lead to acute mental disorder.

On the helpful side, however, is the fact that for many years he kept a remarkably complete diary, complete down to the weather for each day, as well as personal remarks, thoughts, and descriptions, far beyond the chronicle of the day's events. Without this, it would obviously have been impossible to re-create any of the earlier incidents in any detail, but with it, and with several people's memories, and with the mass of papers, letters, and memoranda that his wife saved up over the years, it has been possible to go into considerable detail where it was thought necessary. (That is noted only to forestall the suggestion that the biographer has been too imaginative—that it couldn't have been possible to know what Benchley thought. What might look like imagination has, in some cases, been taken straight out of the diaries, with little or no rewriting.)

The problem of how to refer to him was an involved one, because although he was known variously as Robert, Rob, Bob, Bobby, Gramps, Mr. Benchley, and Fred, there were times in the narrative when he could only be called "my father." By the same token, it would have been ludicrous to refer to a child or a high school student as "my father," so, as a stab at some kind of standardization, I have referred to him most often as Robert, varying it only when it seemed necessary or appropriate. His parents called him Robert, so that looked like as good a choice as any. Almost everybody else called him Bob or Bobby. Or Mr. Benchley. Or Gramps.

I honestly don't know if this is a good picture of my father or not. I know that it is as good a picture as *I* can give, and that it shows him as I learned to know him. But, after all, I could be prejudiced.

Nathaniel Benchley

ACKNOWLEDGMENT Some of the material in Chapters 1 and 13 appeared originally in *Holiday* magazine; Chapter 11 appeared in part, and in radically different form, in the magazine '*47;* a certain amount of Chapter 12 was in *Good Housekeeping;* and a slightly altered version of Chapter 15 was in *Sports Illustrated.*

The quote from Stephen Leacock is taken from his book *Humor and Humanity*, and is used with the permission of the publisher.

FOREWORD Some time after I entered Harvard College with the class of 1918 (that was in the fall of 1914 when some kind of trouble had developed in Europe, but nobody of my acquaintance suspected that this meant the end of the then known world), I attended a freshman smoker—a sort of get-together, good-will, beer-and-tobacco pep rally—which was addressed by various distinguished seniors and alumni, one of whom was Robert C. Benchley, of the class of 1912.

Harvard did not lack for heroes in those remote days. Improbable as it may seem, our football team was generally accorded top rank in the nation by the Spalding Guide; Yale was a respectable runner-up, but Notre Dame was nowhere. There were consequently plenty of Harvard Big Names to trot out for the wide-eyed, downy-chinned freshmen: Charlie Brickley, Eddie Mahan, Tack Hardwick, Lev Saltonstall (later a governor and senator), Dick Wigglesworth (long a member of Congress). Not to mention Ham Fish, an all-time all-American who also ascended Capitol Hill and did his best to give the legislative form of government a bad name.

Benchley was a different kind of hero. He was a mere writer and cartoonist and actor who had gained widespread fame as president of the *Harvard Lampoon* in its most glorious era (among his brilliant colleagues were Gluyas Williams, Frederick Lewis Allen, Paul Hollister, and Vinton Freedley) and as star and coauthor of various Hasty Pudding shows, in one of which he scored sensationally with a monologue as a telephone girl.

It gave me a particular thrill to see Benchley up there as the equal of the great athletes because I had every intention of stepping into his boots: I was already "going out" for the *Lampoon* and memorizing all the jokes I heard in Broadway musical shows for future use in the Pudding.

I've forgotten what Benchley said to us kiddies at that smoker (it has always been amazing to me how obdurately he defied quotation). But it didn't much matter. So formidable was his reputation as a merry-andrew that we started laughing at the very mention of his name. I didn't meet him then, or for some years thereafter, but he remained for me a shining objective toward which to strive as an undergraduate—and one which I never even approached.

My career on the *Lampoon* and in the Hasty Pudding was terminated when, having been tipped off that I was about to receive a notice from the dean announcing my expulsion from college, I hastily got out of town and across the border, where I enlisted in the Canadian army. When I emerged from that service, in 1919, I started looking for a job and I was given a tentative one ($25 a week) on the magazine *Vanity Fair*, whose editor, Frank Crowninshield, was a notoriously softhearted man. He gave me a desk in an office which contained the two other members of the editorial staff—Robert Benchley and Dorothy Parker. Even since then, my considered advice to young literary aspirants has been, "Merely make sure that you start out in fast company."

For some ten years, first at *Vanity Fair* and subsequently at *Life*, I shared an office with Rob Benchley, although his appearances at *Life* were largely limited to occasions when he dropped in to discuss a little matter of an advance in salary. During this *Life* period, Benchley was offered $500 a week by Irving Berlin and Sam Harris to appear briefly in the new *Music Box Revue*. He debated anxiously and piously whether he should accept an offer involving that kind of money. I advised him, easily, to take it, but I must confess that I hoped and even expected he wouldn't; somehow, I couldn't reconcile this penny-pinching puritan whom I thought I knew well with a salary of $500 for sixty-four minutes' work a week. But he took it and earned it. The *Music Box Revue* was a great success and so was he. The show had a long run. I thought, "Well, now Rob is getting rich, and he's salting away all that dough in savings bonds, and he'll be free of financial worries—free to devote himself to the serious stuff he has always wanted to write." Which shows how much I knew. On the Monday morning after the show closed, Benchley was around at the *Life* office; he was beaming and apologetic and asking for a moderate advance on his salary as drama critic with which to meet arrears on his rent.

In 1928 I left *Life*, primarily because I was fired, and became a playwright. Benchley moved over to *The New Yorker*. I don't recall that either of us shed a tear when, a couple of years later, *Life* expired, to be purchased subsequently, merely as a title, by Henry R. Luce.

From then on, I saw Rob more often on the screen than in actuality. He was always terribly funny in his own short pictures, written and played by himself. He was himself even when appearing as comedy relief in M-G-M heavy dramas. (He once took one of those obligatory advertisements in *Variety* and characterized himself as a movie actor who specialized in "Society Drunk" roles.) He became for me a sort of remote legend. When he died, masses of his friends gathered for appropriate memorial services, with cocktails, at "21" in New York and Mike Romanoff's in Beverly Hills. Two of the mourners at the Romanoff wake were Dorothy Parker and I.

I loved him, and I shall enjoy the glowing memory of him for as long as I live. His life—as recorded in this book with filial understanding and remarkable objectivity by his son Nat—represented some of the strangest reversals of moods and habits I have ever observed in one human being. Together with many others, I saw him in various contrasting characters:

As a methodical, teetotalling, nonsmoking, galosh-wearing,

penurious, homebound commuter, who didn't appear to have a worry or concern in the world beyond the precarious state of his bank balance and the effect thereof on his family in Crestwood (not to be confused with Crestview);

As a violent crusader for civil rights, a marcher in the picket lines for Sacco and Vanzetti, a passionate pacifist, and (so help me!) an ardent prohibitionist;

And, finally, as a laboriously irresponsible *flâneur* or court jester of the Café Society belt, of Hollywood or Antibes.

He could wear the motley, all right, but he always remained indelibly the same person: Benchley.

Which made him forever unique, and forever wonderful to be with, and to read about, and to remember.

Robert E. Sherwood

LIST OF ILLUSTRATIONS (following page 94)

Robert Benchley at two and five. Robert with Lillian Duryea. At Nyack, 1901. Lillian at Nyack.

Class picture, South High School, Worcester. The Discus Thrower. South High Mandolin Club.

At Harvard in 1912. *Ralph Roister Doister*, 1911. Barnum & Bailey, 1917.

Parody screen-test poses. Robert in *The Reluctant Dragon*.

Scenes from *How to Read* and *The Courtship of the Newt*.

Scenes from *Dark Magic*, *The Day of Rest*, and *A Night at the Movies*.

Robert and Jennie, 1932. Robert in *How to Figure Income Tax*. Honorary fire chief, Worcester.

Honorary mayor, Marineland. Robert and Gertrude. The boulevardier.

1

One day, when Robert Benchley was scanning a pile of newspapers in search of something about which to write, he came across a report from the American Psychiatric Association, listing the primary symptoms of dementia praecox, or schizophrenia. He almost didn't read it, but one of the symptoms caught his eye, and with growing horror he read the entire list, then put down the paper and went out for a long walk. When, two days later, he returned, he sat down and made out his own list, showing how he qualified on the various counts. A slightly abridged version of the symptoms and his comments:

(1) "Defective judgment." Well, I could keep you here all night giving examples of my defective judgment that would make your blood curdle. I couldn't even judge a sack-race. On this count I qualify hands down.

(2) "Retarded perception." I didn't even know that the fleet was in until I read *Time* ten days later.

(3) "Restriction in the field of attention." My attention can be held only by strapping me down to a cot and sitting on my chest. Even then my eyes wander.

(4) "Silly laughter." I hold the Interscholastic (New England), Intercollegiate, East Coast Amateur and Open Professional cups for silly laughter. I laugh at anything except a French clown. You can't be sillier than that.

(5) "Lack of skill in motor performance." I was asked to surrender my licence while driving an old Model T Ford in 1915 because I could not co-ordinate in time to press the clutch at just the right moment. I also had a little trouble with "right" and "left." Next to "silly laughter," "lack of skill in motor performance" is my forte.

(6) "Stupor." We need not go into this. The last thing I remember clearly is that elaborate parade for Admiral Dewey under the arch at Twenty-third Street. There are hundreds of

people willing to bet that I have *never* had my eyes open. I have no proof to the contrary.

Some of this was exaggerated, but not as much as might be supposed. Benchley was a highly subjective writer, and most of what he wrote was conditioned by his feelings about himself. Among his gifts was the ability to set these feelings down neatly and precisely, as he did in describing his self-consciousness when wearing a new white suit, saying, "In it I have the feeling of being a sky-writer who can't spell." He was willing, even eager, to make fun of himself, provided he was reasonably sure that others would know what he was talking about, but he was reluctant to do anything that appeared to be straining to make the point.

This reluctance was illustrated one time in 1944, when he was leaving a radio rehearsal, and the Inquiring Fotographer of the New York *Daily News* stopped the members of the cast and said that he had a question for them. The question was: "Do you feel any different, now that you are a success, than you did when you started your career?" The other members of the show answered with various gracious expressions of humility, saying that they always reminded themselves what it was like to be at the bottom of the ladder, but Benchley demurred, on the ground that the reporter would inevitably rephrase what he said to try to make it funny, and would only make him look silly. He knew from experience that if a man was a professional comedian the newspapers would insist that he say something funny, and there was no funny answer to this particular question. The Inquiring Fotographer replied that he had to write fifty words of *something*, so Benchley might as well give it to him as let him think it up himself.

"All right," said Benchley, who weighed about two hundred pounds and was feeling rather shaky that morning, "I'll give it to you. But if you change a word of it, I'll sue you." With that, he took an envelope from his pocket, hesitated a minute, then wrote: "When I started what you call my 'career,' I wore a size 14½ collar, did exercises to develop my chest, and had never had a drink. You ask if I feel different now?"

This insistence that he be funny was a constant irritation to him and, for the most part, he tried to combat it. There is nothing harder than to deliver humour on sudden order, and Benchley, who at one point was writing three syndicated columns a week, doing the theatre reviews for *The New Yorker*, appearing in a weekly radio show, and making shorts and full-length pictures in Hollywood, had all he could do to fulfill his contractual duties without trying to be funny on the side. What was more, he didn't really want to be funny; what he wanted more than anything else was to be a good writer, and he was frustrated because the only way he could make money was as a comedian. He summed up his dilemma once to Harold Ross, editor of *The New Yorker*, by saying, "I am not a writer and not an actor. I don't know what I am." It would not be true to say that he didn't *ever* want to be funny; what he resented was being considered a professional funny man, and as such not being taken seriously. He felt strongly about a number of subjects, and it infuriated him when people insisted on looking for a laugh in everything he said. On the other hand, he would intentionally misunderstand someone, as he did when a friend told him that the particular drink he was drinking was slow poison, and he replied, "So who's in a hurry?" He liked, when the mood was upon him, to send comical telegrams to friends, as he did to Charles Brackett, who was in Paris at the time of Lindbergh's historic flight. Six days after Lindbergh landed at Le Bourget, Benchley sent a cable to Brackett, saying, ANY TIDINGS OF LINDBERGH? LEFT HERE WEEK AGO AM WORRIED. A lesser man than Brackett might simply have said "No," or let the cable lie around while he tried to think of an involved answer. But Brackett's reply was immediate. DO YOU MEAN GEORGE LINDBERGH? he cabled.

Whether he liked it or not, Benchley was tagged as a funny man, and in order to maintain his output he had to be constantly searching for material. Since he didn't use gags in the normal, or radio-comedian, sense of the word, he had to find his material in what he saw happening around him or what he read in the daily papers. He read every New York paper every day, scanning the columns for items of minor interest that he considered funny, or about which some humorous comment could be made, and at times the search was a dismal and a frustrating one. It was epitomized by a dream he had one night, from which he awoke in a warm glow of laughter. He had, in his dream, said something that was so excruciatingly funny that as he lay there, chuckling to himself, he was undecided whether he should write it in an article, or save it and say it at just the right time, when he could relish the appreciation of his audience. It was the perfect quip, the bon mot of the century, and he knew that he had better write it down while it was still fresh in his mind, or it might fade with the other half-remembered dreams. He got up, found a piece of paper, and was just about to write the line when he came fully awake and realized what it was. He had dreamed that he and some friends were sitting in a restaurant, and that the glasses in front of them were empty. By way of asking if they should have another round of drinks, he had said, brightly, "Well! Should we refuel?" Sadly, he put the pencil down and went back to bed.

Stephen Leacock defined humour as "the kindly contemplation of the incongruities of life, and the artistic expression thereof," and that is a pretty good description of Benchley's particular form of humour. The word "kindly" is important in any definition of real humour, and Benchley's was, almost without exception, kindly. He could have moments of towering rage, often directed against an authority of some sort, or against someone who was being officious, but for the most part he went out of his way to avoid hurting people's feelings, and his humour followed the same pattern. He had an unerring knowledge of the precise word or action that would make a person feel at ease, or happy, or important, and it is those things that are remembered by people who couldn't repeat to you one funny word he ever said. One night, for instance, he ran into John O'Hara at the theatre, at a time before O'Hara was famous, and Benchley was at the peak of his Broadway, or pre-Hollywood, fame. O'Hara was escorting a young lady from Bryn Mawr, on whom he was doing his best to make an impression, and as Benchley went past them he bowed to the girl, then said, "Hello, Mr. O'Hara. I'll bet we're the only ones here wearing pumps." It was no world-shattering remark, certainly, but it was an extra touch of friendliness and perception at a time when a "hello" would have been all O'Hara could have asked for, and O'Hara's stock soared like an eagle. He never forgot it, nor did he forget the Christmas Eve of 1933, when he was writing *Appointment in Samarra* and had gone, alone, on the wagon, and dejected, into Tony's for his Christmas Eve supper of soup and coffee. He and Luigi, the waiter-bartender, were the only people there; Luigi was wishing he was home and O'Hara wasn't wishing much of anything, when, shortly after midnight, the door opened and Benchley came in with two friends. He saw O'Hara sitting there alone, and knew exactly how he felt. "You're not drinking coffee tonight," he announced. "Luigi, bring some champagne and stout." So, for the only time in two years, O'Hara went off the wagon; Benchley mixed the Black Velvets with great care and not a little ceremony; he was gay and friendly, and allied O'Hara with him as he kidded the people with whom he had come; and when, after two hours, they parted company and O'Hara went back to his hotel, O'Hara was singing and serene and his life was beautiful.

This knowledge of the precise word or action could also be used to get rid of a person, or to put someone in his place, and under those circumstances it was chilling even to watch. He could get rid of someone quickly, quietly, and—if he wanted to—without giving offence, an almost impossible task just on the face of it. There was, for instance, one afternoon when a lot of people had gathered in his Hollywood bungalow, for no other reason than that they had been going past and had decided to drop in. One of them, a writer who had been slaving all afternoon over a combination of Bourbon and Irish whiskies, was sitting on a couch next to the wife of an absent bandleader, and it was obvious that he found her charming. He had just tried a tentative grip on her right knee, when Benchley circled by and leaned over and spoke softly to the bandleader's wife. "I'm sorry," he said. "Is my friend becoming offensive?" The writer straightened up as though a bolt of electricity had shot through him, and he made his contrite adieus and was out of the bungalow within three minutes.

Benchley's remark to Ross that he was not an actor was, strictly speaking, true, although his *How to Sleep* short won the Academy Award in 1935 and in his minor roles in full-length pictures he occasionally stole the scenes—and the notices—from the stars. He was not an actor because he was not acting; he was simply behaving as he normally would, and the quality that he brought to most of his parts, a quality of good-natured fumbling, was as much a part of him as his moustache. It requires great skill to read lines as naturally as he did, but it is not what can be called interpretive acting. One of the best parts he ever played was in the radio version of James Thurber's "The Secret Life of Walter Mitty," because it was a role in which he felt completely at ease. He would have been very proud if he had been the one who wrote the story of Walter Mitty, the little man who dreams great dreams.

A great deal of the appeal of Benchley's movie shorts came from his hesitant, bewildered approach to the problems of ordinary living, and the only thing that saved him from complete annihilation at the hands of businessmen was that he confounded them more often than they confounded him.

He even acquired a modest amount of fame in this field, as became evident one time during World War II, when a secret meeting of high administration officials was held to select a man who would integrate the nation's economic resources with the war effort. The job required a man of dynamic leadership as well as sound business sense, and none of the people suggested seemed to have quite the necessary qualifications. Finally, when it was clear that the meeting was getting nowhere and the participants were becoming cross and tired, the late James Forrestal, then Secretary of the Navy, thought of a way of breaking it up.

"All right," he said. "I have the man. I nominate Robert Benchley."

It was quickly agreed that everybody ought to go home and get a little sleep, and maybe the morning would bring some clearer thinking.

Probably no other person, with the possible exception of Adm. Karl Doenitz, would have done more harm to the Allied war effort than would Benchley in the position for which Forrestal proposed him, because as a businessman he was roughly in the class with Wilkins Micawber. He had a deep-seated distrust of anything supposed to be efficient, or legal, and the mere sight of a contract caused his eyes to glaze. When, in 1940, he signed with David O. Selznick in Hollywood, he and Selznick met to decide what the terms of the contract should be, and the result was an embossed, notarized, and beribboned document which read: "Know all men by these presents: agreement indenture between David O. Selznick, Esq., Party of the First Part, and Robert Benchley, also Party of the First Part: I hereby agree. (signed) Robert Benchley—David O. Selznick."

The only businesslike thing he ever did was to hire a secretary, and with that act the resemblance to anything businesslike came to an end. His first secretary was one Charles MacGregor, a small, pleasant man with large teeth and a derby hat, whom he met one day in the rain in front of the

New York Public Library. He ran into a friend of his, who was with MacGregor. They were introduced, and after Benchley and his friend had talked for a minute or so, Benchley noticed that MacGregor was carrying a small bunch of violets, covered with wax paper. MacGregor's coat collar was turned up, and he was listening quietly to the talk and trying to shield the violets from the rain.

"I hope I'm not detaining you here," Benchley said. "You look as if you had a date, or something."

"Oh, that's all right," said MacGregor. "I'm just taking these flowers to a shirt in the shirt hospital."

Here, clearly, was a man worth knowing, and when, subsequently, the Wall Street crash wiped out MacGregor's savings, an arrangement was made whereby he came to Benchley's room every day, balanced the chequebook, handled the incoming and outgoing money, and did odd secretarial jobs, such as getting Benchley out of bed, telling him what the weather was like, and supplying him with ideas for articles. He became as nearly indispensable as a man can be. For just one thing, he was a genius at waking a person gently and inoffensively. He would walk into the bedroom and say, very quietly, "The men are here for the trunks," and Benchley would be thrown into an immediate turmoil of activity, stumbling about the room and groping for clothes to put into the nonexistent trunks. By the time he realized it was all a ruse, he was as wide-awake as a third baseman. Naturally, MacGregor didn't say the same thing every morning; he varied it with such things as, "There are some men here to flood the bed for skating."

MacGregor's greatest single coup as a secretary was achieved one day when an article was due for *Cosmopolitan*, an article that not only hadn't been written but hadn't even been conceived. Benchley had been puttering over his drama copy for *The New Yorker*, and the *Cosmopolitan* deadline had sneaked up completely unnoticed. There was, furthermore, little or no money in the till, and the *Cosmopolitan* cheque was something of a necessity. (Benchley was physically unable to save money, but he was in far better financial shape when he was making $1,500 a year than when he was making $100,000. And one year, if he had saved every penny he earned, he wouldn't have had enough to pay the income tax for the year before.) At MacGregor's suggestion, he put the *New Yorker* copy in an envelope marked "*Cosmopolitan*," and MacGregor hurried it over to that magazine's office, presented the envelope, and picked up the cheque. (In those days, they paid on delivery of the copy, something they have never done since—and for obvious reasons.) He then deposited the cheque and notified Benchley, who called *Cosmopolitan* and got in touch with one of the editors.

"I'm terribly sorry," he said, "but my secretary has made an idiotic mistake—he's sent your copy to *The New Yorker*, and the *New Yorker* copy to you. *The New Yorker* is sending your copy to you by messenger, and I wondered if you'd send theirs to them."

Obligingly, the *Cosmopolitan* editor dispatched the drama copy to *The New Yorker*, and then had to wait several weeks for the article for which he had already paid.

As a matter of fact, deadlines were always a bugaboo. He wrote slowly, and with great care, sometimes brooding and gnawing his nails for fifteen minutes before pecking in a comma, and he always had the feeling that what he was writing wasn't as good as it should have been. As he once said: "It took me fifteen years to discover that I had no talent for writing, but I couldn't give it up because by that time I was too famous." At any rate, what he wrote was single-spaced, set halfway down the page and with a left-hand margin as wide as the copy itself, so that it was almost impossible for the copyreaders and checkers to write anything between the lines, and it was equally impossible to estimate a word-count without actually counting all the words. It always came out shorter than the desk man thought it was going to, and then he had to chase Benchley all over town to get the required material to fill. And he was often testy with the queries of the checkers, who, on *The New Yorker*, will correct a man on the spelling of his mother's nickname. Once, when Benchley had started a critical remark by saying, "I don't mean to be a Cassandra about this," the copy-desk man wrote in the margin of the author's proof: "Ah, but Cassandra prophesied truly." Benchley's reply, when he returned the proof, was simple and direct. "You keep out of this," he wrote.

Over the years, the various editors with whom he worked came to learn that his copy would not be in until the last minute, if it came in at all. They accepted this, but he couldn't; he had a conscience about missing deadlines, and he always felt it necessary to dream up elaborate excuses when it became obvious that the work wasn't going to be done in time. His mother, who lived in Worcester, Massachusetts, was obliging enough to send telegrams to the editors, purportedly signed by her son, saying that she was sick and that he was in Worcester with her, and that his copy might be a day or two late. (Once, when she was visiting friends in Boston, she wired his refusal to a Banshee luncheon after he had called her and told her to send the following: SORRY I CANT ATTEND LUNCHEON TODAY BECAUSE I AM IN BOSTON STOP DONT KNOW WHY I AM IN BOSTON BUT IT MUST BE IMPORTANT BECAUSE HERE I AM.) She sent one of these "mother is sick" telegrams, collect, to Art Samuels, the editor of *Harper's Bazaar*, and after receiving the telegram Samuels happened to run into Donald Ogden Stewart, a friend of Benchley's, on the street. Samuels mentioned that Benchley was in Worcester, where his mother was sick, and asked if Stewart knew whether she was dangerously ill.

"She can't be too bad," Stewart replied. "I just left Benchley in his room a half hour ago."

Then, realizing that he had said the wrong thing, Stewart called Benchley and told him what had happened, and apologized for not having thought a little more quickly. Immediately, Benchley started sending telegrams to friends all over the country, and after an interval collect telegrams signed with his name began to trickle and then to pour into the *Harper's Bazaar* office, saying that he was in Santa Fe being inducted into a Navajo Indian tribe, that he was in Florida judging the Orange Blossom Carnival, that he was in Detroit inspecting the new Packard engines, that he was in Hollywood working on a picture with Greta Garbo, and that he was in Maine acting as a guide for a hunting party. Only the fact that the telegraph company refused to send collect cables from Europe kept him from having been in London, Chantilly, and Rome. Finally, at the end of the day, a telegram arrived for him, collect, from Samuels. It said, simply: I GATHER YOU HAVENT DONE THE PIECE.

But of all the editors, it was those at *The New Yorker* who had the hardest time. They had to get copy out of him every week. When they finally got it, it was so good and so clean that everybody in the office wanted to read it before it was sent off to Greenwich to be set in type, but it was usually so late that there was time for little more than a quick run-through before it was handed to the waiting messenger. For several years, they managed to get it more or less on time by telling him that the deadline was Saturday night, when actually it was Sunday night, but that dodge failed when a new man let the truth slip. Benchley had called, late Saturday night, to say that it might be a couple of hours before the copy was in, because he seemed to be in Philadelphia and nobody there had a typewriter, and the man told him not to worry, that Sunday would do just as well. After that, Sunday afternoon would melt into Sunday evening, and the people would sit around *The New Yorker*, waiting either for the copy or, what was more likely, a telephone call saying that there might be a delay of just an hour or two. Once he called and said that his typewriter, with the copy in it, had been stolen, and that he would have to start all over again, a prospect that seemed rather dim at the moment, since he was obviously calling from a fairly large party. Once or twice, the *New Yorker* people tried sending a messenger over to his room, in hope that this might spur him on to a quicker completion of the job, but they abandoned this after the messenger, in one case one of the managing editors, became paralyzed with drink while waiting. There was a small, handy bar in the room, and Benchley insisted that whoever was waiting for the copy should make himself completely at home.

His room in the Hotel Royalton, in midtown New York, was one in which it was impossible to be formal, and as far as he was concerned this made it an ideal place to do business. It was decorated with a mad assortment of knickknacks and horribilia, but at the same time it was comfortable to the point of being soporific, and anyone who came into it with the idea of driving a fast bargain, or of getting away with something—or, for that matter, of even being serious—usually found that within a half hour he had forgotten what he came for. Even the police couldn't remain alert in that room. One night, Benchley called the police to complain about the bell in a sidewalk elevator that was keeping him awake, and the desk sergeant sent two men over to investigate. By the time they got up to the room the bell had stopped ringing, and Benchley offered them a drink in return for their trouble. The two officers looked at each other and cleared their throats, and when, three hours later, they left the hotel, one of them skidded on the freshly washed lobby floor and did a spectacular ground loop before crashing flat on his back.

As for the Internal Revenue men who periodically came around to investigate his earnings and deductions, their reactions to the room were mixed. One time, when Benchley had been unable to meet a particularly heavy tax installment, the Federal men sent him a four-page, wildly complicated form, designed to show his assets and liabilities down to the last quarter, including the change on his dresser. He simply wrote "Don't be silly" on the form, and sent it back. The result was that an Internal Revenue man dropped around to the Royalton, and what might have been a tense situation was eased by the fact that Benchley and the Revenue man recognized each other from early-Prohibition speakeasy days. Benchley, who had his accountant standing by with a briefcase full of papers, relaxed and started to mix three whisky sours, but the Revenue man said he'd have to have a Coke; he was no longer drinking. He explained that his drinking days had ended early one morning, when he had been walking along the street and a hydrant that he was passing had burst, blasting him down the block like a cork and injuring him quite badly. When the general laughter had subsided, Benchley looked at his accountant and said that it was a pretty unlikely story, and that they'd have to watch this man more carefully than they had intended. For some reason, the man found nothing to criticize in any of Benchley's accounts, and the afternoon ended in a glow of friendship. In fact, the man had such a good time that he came back for social visits whenever he was in the neighborhood.

It was not only editors and businessmen who found Benchley something of a problem to deal with; doctors had their troubles with him too. He had a sneaking suspicion that doctors were only one step ahead of the general public as far as knowledge went, and that they could be thrown off balance by anything completely unexpected. He had a chance to test this theory in 1940 when he came down with pneumonia out on the Coast, and the doctor who attended him gave him one of the new "miracle" sulfa drugs. He took the pills as directed and then, one afternoon before the doctor was due to call, he and Charles Butterworth broke open a pillow and, with library paste, glued the feathers all over him, from the waist on down. When the doctor arrived, he examined Benchley's chest, asked him how he was feeling, and if the pills had done any good.

Benchley said he thought they had, and then added, "I don't know quite what to make of *this*, though," as he threw back the bedclothes. "Is this all right?"

The doctor to whom he gave the worst time was a psychiatrist, also on the Coast, who cornered him at a cocktail party and said he'd like to analyze him. Benchley suspected that the man was simply building up case histories for a Sunday-supplement article, so he agreed to an appointment and went around the following day. After a few of the usual preliminaries, the doctor asked if there was anything on his mind —anything that was troubling him.

"Yes," said Benchley. "Or—rather—no. It's nothing." He smiled quickly.

"Go ahead," the doctor said, his pencil poised. "You can tell me anything you wish."

"It's really nothing," Benchley protested. "You wouldn't be interested."

"I'll be the judge of that," said the doctor, gently. "Come on, now—let's have it."

Benchley took a deep breath. "Well," he said, "I live in one of those bungalows in the Garden of Allah, and in the bungalow next to mine is a sheep dog—you know, one of those great big woolly dogs, with blue eyes. Every morning this dog walks past my door and looks in at me, and when our eyes meet I get a funny kind of tingling feeling—I can't describe it any other way—and there's a kind of recognition between us. The dog knows it—I know he does, by the way he looks at me with those big blue eyes. It's got now so that I can't get to work until he comes past and looks at me, and then I feel fine all the rest of the day. That's all there is to it. . . . I told you it wouldn't interest you."

The doctor was quiet for a moment. "Are you married?" he asked.

"Certainly," said Benchley. "I've been married twenty-six years. Have two children." He looked around the office and whistled a little tune.

The doctor got up and went over to the window and stared outside. He tapped his pencil on the glass for a while, then glanced at his watch. "Look," he said. "I have another appointment that's due right now. Could we continue this some other time?"

"Certainly," said Benchley. "Any time you say." He got up, shook hands, and left the doctor staring out of the window. He never heard from him again.

Of all the people with whom he did business, lawyers probably had the least rewarding time, because he was impatient with the details of the law and reasoned that decisions should be based on common sense. He could say in a sentence what it took a lawyer ten minutes to say, and he saw no reason for wasting time with trivia. (His will, for instance, was exactly one sentence long, and it read: "Confident that she will adequately provide for our two sons, and any child hereafter born to us, I make no provision for them, but give all my property to my wife, Gertrude D. Benchley, absolutely, appointing her Executrix without security.") One time, although he did it unconsciously, he threw a lawyer into such a state of confusion that everything had to be called off. He had written a piece for *Liberty*, which he thought that magazine had decided not to use, but of which it had retained a carbon copy. Somewhat unwisely, MacGregor sent the original to *The Detroit Athletic Club News* and when *Liberty* finally ran the piece, the *D.A.C. News* entered suit against *Liberty* for one million dollars.

When word of the suit reached Benchley, he jumped into his clothes and stormed over to the office of the lawyer who was representing the *D.A.C. News*.

"Listen to me," he said to the lawyer. "*Liberty* is not at fault in this—I'm the one who is. I am completely guilty—I am so guilty that any lawyer who would take my case would be crooked. I won't even enter a defence—you can take your million dollars right now. Go ahead—find a million dollars on me, and you can have it."

The lawyer closed his eyes and pinched the bridge of his nose. "Mr. Benchley," he said slowly, "before you say anything more, would you mind buttoning your trousers?"

The suit was just quietly dropped.

Politically, Benchley referred to himself as "a confused liberal," although most of the time he was a registered Republican and voted—when he was in one place long enough to be allowed to vote—Democratic. He belonged to as many guilds and unions as was possible, and some of his closest friends were of the fox-hunting, horse-racing, polo-playing set. It was impossible to pin him down in any one category, because he overlapped so many types, and he had, as his fundamental characteristic, the kind of sympathy and understanding that defies classification. Although he deprecated his own work, he had a respect for George Ade that amounted almost to worship, and the night that Ade's death was announced on the radio, Benchley got up out of bed and went on the town. "When a great humorist dies," he said, "everybody should go to a place where there is laughter, and drink to his memory until the lights go out." He did just that; he closed the Stork Club, laughing and reminiscing about Ade, and then moved on to other places with later closing hours.

For several years prior to 1943, his writing had been coming harder and harder, and what ideas occurred to him either seemed not worth the struggle of writing them, or were vaguely reminiscent of something he had written in 1922. The more time he spent making motion pictures and doing radio shows, both of which were lucrative and at the same time intellectually numbing, the harder it was for him to sit down and grind out a piece of copy for *The New Yorker.* Once, his friend George Oppenheimer came into the room and found Benchley standing and staring down at his typewriter, in which was a piece of yellow copy paper and a single sentence.

"I'd like to know what play I thought I was reviewing last

night," Benchley said. "Take a look at this, if you will."

Oppenheimer looked at the paper, on which was the sentence: "It is more difficult to get a pig under a gate."

Finally, it began to occur to him that very few humorists remained funny much beyond the age of fifty, and he resolved to quit while he was still ahead. When, in December of 1943, at the age of fifty-four, he announced flatly that he was through with writing and was resigned to being a radio and movie comedian, the *New York Herald Tribune* carried an editorial that said, in part:

> Many of our writers, once regarded as excellent humorists, live to a great age under the amiable but often pathetic delusion that their powers to create laughs are in no way diminished with the passing years. They are not critical enough to be bored with themselves. Mr. Benchley may be wrong, but his example is salutory.

His worry about having neglected writing for the easier money was always nagging at him, and sometimes it came to the surface in strange ways. Once, around 1939, he was at a party in Hollywood that was attended by, among other people, Dorothy Parker, F. Scott Fitzgerald, and Robert E. Sherwood, all of whom were friends of Benchley's from the early 1920s. Sherwood had, at that time, just received the second of his three Pulitzer Prizes for dramatic writing, Mrs. Parker was a respected and successful script writer, and Benchley was approaching the peak of his fame as a comedian. At one point, late in the evening, Benchley was heard to say, "Those eyes—I can't stand those eyes looking at me!" Everybody stopped and turned, and saw that Benchley was backing away from Sherwood. They waited, already smiling and set to laugh at the joke that was about to come, but Benchley was serious. He pointed at Sherwood, and said, "He's looking at me and thinking of how he knew me when I was going to be a great writer. . . . And he's thinking *now* look at what I am!" There was an awkward silence, and then people began to talk again. For Sherwood, the most haunting part of the experience was not the fact that he probably *had* had something like that in his mind, but the fact that Benchley knew that if the gap that had existed between their writing in 1920 had continued as it should have, then Benchley would have been a far greater writer than anyone in the room. That wasn't what Benchley had in mind when he spoke, but Sherwood is positive that that was what motivated his anguish.

Usually, however, he was much more cheerful about the matter. His *New Yorker* copy was acute and concise, but it was also kindly and genial, and he never took the easy way out by making jokes at the expense of a bad play or actor. Probably the closest he ever came to that form of criticism was in his review of *Green Waters*, in which he wrote: "The hero (I guess he was) is a bastard in both senses of the word, and it gets on his nerves," and even the author and the actor concerned could hardly take offence at that. He was probably happier with his *New Yorker* copy than with anything else, and the only times he became introspective were when he found himself doing undignified things to make a living. In his free time, he could be as undignified as he pleased; it just galled him to *have* to do anything absurd.

The movie shorts which he wrote and acted in were of a generally high level of dignity, but there was one of them, about a man who buys a Home Magic set for his son, that had a more slapstick ending than most. In it, the man gets to fiddling with some magic disappearing bag, and there is a quick puff and the final shot shows him strung up in the telephone wires outside his house, wearing a paper hat and looking like a big, frantic owl. He wrote the scene and he had to play in it, although he became a little queasy when he saw the telephone wires that had been strung up in the studio in Astoria, where the film was being shot. There were two dummy poles, with heavy wires strung between them, and a backdrop painted to simulate the sky. Three men, lying side by side, tested the strength of the wires, and as an added precaution the floor beneath them was padded with mats. The director told Benchley to climb up and take his place. Wearing a paper party hat, he was hoisted and strung out across the wires, and as he was waiting for the final camera adjustments he looked down at a corner of the studio, where his wife Gertrude was watching.

"Remember how good in Latin I was in school?" he asked.

"I do," replied Gertrude.

"Well, look where it got me," he said.

2

If you were able to generalize about any large municipality, you might say that Worcester, Massachusetts, was a city of churches, mansard roofs, cupolas, portcullises, and heavy, red-brick Victorian architecture. Inside the older Worcester houses, dimly lit by the red, blue, amber, and green stained-glass windows at the stair landings, were statuettes known as Rogers groups, or massive steel engravings of stags, or still-life compositions that looked like ducks pressed under glass. There were cuckoo clocks, and heavy draperies, and dark panelled walls, and in the winter the light from the snow outside glared through the parlour lace curtains with the brilliance of a battery of cold, white floodlights. On a winter night, the trolleys used to give off crackling blue flashes that made the snow look briefly purple, and almost every other sound was muffled by the falling snow. In the summer, Worcester was stifling hot, and the elm and sycamore and maple trees stood motionless in the heavy air. Still speaking generally, you could say that Worcester was a piece of Victorian America that, on the surface, changed little or not at all. The iron deer that once watched over Worcester's lawns are now mostly gone, but the cupolas and the mansard roofs remain, among the glistening new apartments and the rows of old, three-decker tenements.

Worcester's early prosperity was derived from textiles and the manufacture of textile machinery. A few of its woollen mills have closed, and the distribution of the wealth has changed somewhat, but machine-tool plants do well in times of war and threats of war, and Worcester's more affluent citizens have never had much cause to worry. There were fortunes made in steel, barbed wire, envelopes, looms, emery wheels, firearms, and boots. Worcester has also produced its share of prominent men and women, among them Eli Whitney, Generals Artemas Ward and Rufus Putnam, Dr. William T. G. Morton, Dorothea Lynde Dix, S. N. Behrman, George Bancroft, and Edward Everett Hale.

The first Benchley to attract any notice in Worcester was Henry W. Benchley, the great-grandson of William, who had come to this country from Merthyr Tydfil, Glamorgan, Wales, some years before the Revolution, and had died in Smithfield, Rhode Island, in 1811. Henry went into politics, was a representative from Worcester in the Massachusetts Senate, and was one of the founders of the Republican party in the eastern section of the United States. His wife, Julia, was of no particular help to him in his career; she startled official Worcester by, among other things, standing at the top of a flight of stairs at a state ball and raising her skirts so that the metal hoops were visible, and also by willing her head to the local hospital for inspection by any medical students who might be interested. (Unfortunately, there is no record of their findings.) In spite of her, however, Henry became Lieutenant Governor of Massachusetts, serving from 1856 to 1858, and then, feeling that the slavery problem needed more personal attention than he could give it from the Statehouse, he went to Texas and set up a station for the Underground Railroad, helping slaves escape to the North. He was caught, convicted, and spent the rest of the time until Appomattox in a Texas jail. Somewhat incredibly, a small town in Brown County, Texas, was later named for him. The last time anybody counted, it had a population of seventy people, twelve of whom wanted to leave town but couldn't think of anywhere else to go.

While his father was languishing in jail, Charles Henry Benchley, who was fourteen years old, convinced the recruiting officers that he was sixteen, and he was assigned to F Company, First Battalion of Heavy Artillery of the Massachusetts Volunteer Militia. Two years later, at the end of the war, he was discharged as a corporal. Then in 1869, he signed up for a four-year hitch in the Navy, where he had a glorious time and learned that you can drown a fish by dragging it backward through the water. In 1893, after a succession of jobs in Worcester, he was appointed Mayor's clerk, a position he held through thirty years and twelve mayors, until his death in 1923. Charlie Benchley was a short, chunky man, with pince-nez glasses, a large moustache, and a shining, bald top to his head, and his derby hat always seemed to be just a little too small for him. He was quiet and gentle, and he was an easy target for any of the G.A.R. veterans who came to see him in his collateral position as Soldiers' Relief Agent for the city.

He was nominally a Republican, but he came to know so much about the organization of City Hall that he was indispensable to any incoming mayor. He was efficient, and he was courteous, and he had a sly, wispy sense of humour. The only confusion he caused in thirty years as clerk was not so much his fault as it was the fault of a system that put both his and the mayor's telephones on the same line. In addition to his other jobs, Charlie was burial officer for servicemen and their widows, and it was up to him to see that the funeral arrangements were carried out with the proper reverence and, if necessary, éclat. One time, he put through a call to a Boston undertaker about the disposition of the body of a veteran's widow, and at the same time, without his knowledge, the mayor was trying to reach a Boston lawyer. The operator called back, Charlie picked up the phone, and the operator said, "Your Boston call. Go ahead."

There was a "hello" at the other end of the line, and without preamble Charlie said, "You took the body of Joanna Hurley. What did you do with it?"

"What's *that?*" said the voice. "What did you say?"

"I said you took the body of Joanna Hurley," Charlie repeated. "What did you do with it?" He could also be firm, when he had to.

"In God's name, what are you talking about?" asked the voice, in a frightened tone.

At that point the mayor cut in, and recognized the lawyer he was calling, but it was some minutes before the lawyer could compose himself enough to make any sense. As for Charlie, he told the story at intervals for the rest of his life.

When he died of a stroke on April 20, 1923, the flag at City Hall was lowered to half staff, and in the funeral parade marched the mayor, the heads of the city departments, the former mayors whom he had served, and delegations from the G.A.R. and the United States War Veterans.

In 1874 he had married Maria Jane Moran, a stately, imposing woman who had two characteristics not often found in the same person: she was single-minded to the point of blindness on some subjects, and yet she was always able to laugh at herself. She would go into a black rage at the sight of three men in a buggy (to her, three men in a buggy were automatically drunk), but when, on an ocean liner, she wandered into the bar by mistake, she chortled gleefully over the fact that she had appeared to be staggering as she left. She was once run down by an ice truck, and her only comment from the hospital bed was, "They *say* I dented a fender." She hated trees, because they lived longer than humans, and when she was twenty-one she had all her teeth pulled out, because one or two of them had been giving her trouble. She knew to the minute how long it took Charlie to get home from the office, and if he was three minutes late, it meant that he had stopped off for a beer and was, therefore, drunk. Charlie, who had acquired a mild taste for beer in the Army, would sometimes stay downtown rather than bring a beer breath home, because he knew that, as far as Jennie was concerned, one beer was the same as thirty. These occasional defections of his (one or two a year was the average) were stopped when Jennie arranged matters so that she collected his pay cheque, out of which she gave him carfare and nothing else. "His friends don't like me," she once remarked dryly, "but his creditors love me." And she was proud of the fact that one time, when she discovered a pint of whisky that

Charlie had neglected to hide, he had watched her pour it down the sink and had not uttered a word of protest. In company, Jennie did the talking for them both, but when Charlie did manage to get a word in, it was usually something that was quietly funny. (It should be said to Jennie's credit that she encouraged his telling of the Joanna Hurley story whenever possible.) She was by no means humourless, and she was not particularly stern; but on matters about which she felt deeply there was never the smallest room for argument. Her father was a native of Protestant Northern Ireland, and one of her maternal ancestors had fought in the American Revolution, and the combination of these two strains resulted in what could most charitably be called a strong character. If she had not had a fine sense of the ridiculous, especially where it concerned herself, Charlie's home life would have been fairly dismal. As it was, they were a happily married couple, in a middle-class Victorian sort of way.

In 1876 a son, Edmund Nathaniel, was born, and when the succeeding years brought no other children, Charlie and Jennie gave all the care and affection to Edmund's upbringing that was in their combined powers. He grew to be a tall, lean-jawed, good-looking boy, with an aptitude for dramatics and a warm and somewhat pixie sense of humour, and he was extremely popular with the other students at Woodland Street School and, later, English High School. All of Jennie's fierce pride was centred on Edmund.

Then, on September 15, 1889, the year before Edmund entered high school, Robert Charles Benchley was born, and Charlie and Jennie had to reorganize their plans to accommodate an infant in the family. After more than thirteen years, and with their thinking adjusted only toward Edmund's future, they found themselves somewhat startled at the idea of beginning all over again. To a teen-ager, however, a baby brother is something of a comic miracle, and Edmund was delighted to help take care of the new arrival. He pampered him, and carried him about the house and took long walks with small Robert in his arms, and when he grew tired he would give him to Charlie, who would after a while pass him on to Jennie. The process became known as the "first, second, and third relief," and if Robert lacked anything in his early years, it certainly wasn't attention. He grew to worship Edmund with a white-hot devotion that was rivalled only by Jennie's. In fact, it was to Edmund that Robert always turned for advice and help, and when, in his first year in school, Robert was required to learn a poem for recitation in class, he went to Edmund and asked him what poem he thought would be best. Quietly, Edmund took his small brother aside, and in a matter of minutes had taught Robert a poem that ran:

> My mother-in-law has lately died;
> For her my heart doth yearn.
> I know she's with the angels now
> 'Cause she's too tough to burn.

Proudly, Robert recited the poem the next day in school, and reported to Edmund that the reception had been only fair. Charlie and Jennie were at first mystified by the note from the teacher that Robert gave them, but they were convulsed when Edmund explained what it was all about. If Edmund had proposed that Robert recite passages from *The Arabian Nights*, Robert would not only have done it, but Charlie and Jennie would have approved.

Edmund graduated from high school in 1894, and then, through the influence of Senator George Frisbie Hoar, he got an appointment to the Military Academy at West Point. The cadets were allowed no vacations plebe year, and very few after that, but at regular intervals a delegation from Worcester would descend on West Point to visit briefly with Edmund and watch him at evening parade. The delegation included Charlie, Jennie, and Robert, and sometimes Jennie's sister, Mary Elizabeth Prentice, otherwise known as Aunt Lizzie, and Aunt Lizzie's daughter, Mabelle, who was called

Dot, as well as a sprinkling of Worcester girls who were friends of Dot's and Edmund's. It made into quite an imposing group, and the trip from Worcester was a long and gritty one, but the sight of Edmund marching with the cadets (he eventually became a member of the colour guard) made it worth the trouble. Jennie was nearly strangled with pride, Charlie watched everything with the critically approving eye of an old soldier, and Robert considered the whole thing one hell of an exciting experience. His only reservation was about the sunset gun; the noise of it frightened him, and when the gun was about to be fired, he would dart away from Jennie and try to hide someplace where the concussion would be less. One time, he escaped from Jennie and nobody thought to look for him until the cadets wheeled around and started to march into the chapel; then it was discovered that Robert, tactlessly dressed in a blue sailor suit with a white whistle, was standing directly in their line of march. Jennie couldn't get to him in time; Edmund was in no position to give commands, and with brisk precision the corps of cadets bore down upon the fascinated Robert, their starched white trousers snapping louder and louder as they approached. When they reached him, they divided briefly and then closed ranks again, and flowed around him like a river around a small tree stump. Robert's only reaction was one of pride; Edmund had winked at him as he passed.

In April of 1898, Edmund's last year at West Point, the United States flexed its muscles and declared war on Spain, and Edmund's class was graduated early in order to go into action in Cuba. Edmund chose the infantry, and was given a three-day leave at home before being shipped out. The day he left Worcester, he shook hands with Charlie, and kissed Robert, and then Jennie took him into the bathroom, where she could have complete privacy for her good-bye. When his train left the station, she watched it until the last wisp of smoke had faded out of sight.

In those days, the Fourth of July celebrations were far

more violent than they are now. There was the usual run of firecrackers, but there were also cannon crackers—eight-, ten-, and twelve-inchers—and there were a few detonating contraptions that approached the power of a land mine. The entire day, from early dawn until far into the night, was a series of cracklings, explosions, fountains of fire, and frantic calls to the doctor, and the sharp smell of powder permeated the grass and hung in the air. July 4, 1898, was hot and muggy, and in the afternoon heavy bunches of clouds began to gather on the horizon, promising the rain that everybody said was caused by the explosions, which disturbed the air.

Robert didn't like the loud firecrackers, but Charlie took him on the lawn and set off a few strings of Chinese lady crackers for him, and also let him throw some torpedoes, which went off with a noise like a cap pistol when they landed on something hard. In the street out front, a hurdy-gurdy ground out its frantic, tinny music, but nobody paid much attention to it. From the porch, Jennie watched contentedly, and when a man with a newspaper in his pocket turned off the street and came slowly up the walk, she surveyed him with mild curiosity, hoping only that he wasn't one of Charlie's friends from downtown.

The man was a newspaper reporter, bringing the news that Edmund had been killed in Cuba on July 1. Although all the facts weren't known immediately, what had happened was that Edmund's company had crossed the San Juan River under heavy artillery and small-arms fire, and Edmund's regimental colonel had ordered him to recross the river and pass the word for the other companies to come up and form a line of attack. Edmund waded back, and had given the instructions to two of the company commanders when a Spanish sniper, perched high among the tangled trees, had shot him neatly through the heart. He was buried on the spot, under a cross made from an ammunition crate, and a mule's shoe was hung on the cross.

Jennie's anguish was terrible in its ferocity. She went into a state of shock, and when she became coherent, her first words were "*Oh, why couldn't it have been Robert?*" Then she screamed for somebody to stop the noise of the hurdy-gurdy, and Charlie went out and gave the man a dollar to move off. The man passed the word that there was a soft touch at 3 Shepard Street, and it later cost Charlie a great deal more to buy off the other hurdy-gurdy men who came flocking noisily to the address.

When the rest of the family had been notified, Aunt Lizzie's daughter, Dot, came over and took Robert home with her, and he stayed at Aunt Lizzie's for several days, until Jennie's control began to return. Nobody knows how the word got around, but a good part of the city of Worcester, including the children in Robert's class in school, knew what his mother had said.

Edmund's death provided Jennie with a new phobia. Not only did she become so antiwar that, in the 1914–1918 fracas, she disapproved of the Red Cross (because it kept people alive so that they could return to the front), but she also developed a deep-seated distrust of all uniformed government officials—and that included postmen. Thirty-four years later, when she was seventy-nine, she was applying for a passport for a trip to Europe, and, since her birth certificate was unavailable, she was required to substitute the oath of allegiance for proof of citizenship. She went to the town clerk of Nantucket, Massachusetts, where she was staying at the time, and Orin Coffin, the clerk, asked her to raise her right hand. She did.

"Do you swear to defend the Constitution of the United States against all enemies, domestic and foreign?" Coffin asked.

Jennie snapped her hand down. "Do I have to?" she said.

"If you want to get a passport, you do," Coffin replied.

Jennie glowered at him for several seconds. "Well, there are days when I wouldn't," she said.

Coffin shrugged, and after another pause she raised her hand and took the oath.

She was equally waspish with anyone even remotely connected with the Army. At the end of the Spanish-American War, a group went down to Cuba and, with some difficulty, located Edmund's grave in the thorny underbrush and brought his remains back for burial at West Point. They also brought the wooden cross, which was put in a glass frame and attached to the new headstone. It was Jennie's custom, if possible on Memorial Day or about the first of July, to take flowers to the grave, but about West Point itself she felt not the slightest trace of nostalgia. One time, when the automobile in which she was riding pulled up to a military policeman for instructions as to how to reach the cemetery, Jennie leaned across the driver (her daughter-in-law) and pointed a finger at the MP.

"Young man," she said, "I am the daughter of a soldier, the widow of a soldier, and the mother of a soldier, and I want you to know that no grandson of mine is ever coming here."

The driver of the car winked at the MP, and with as straight a face as possible, the MP snapped to attention, said, "Yes, ma'am," and saluted.

Her phobia obviously resulted in the banning of all guns, swords, toy uniforms, firecrackers, and even loud noises, but it also had a corollary in a set of superstitions that grew up around Edmund's last departure from Worcester. Forever afterward, no member of the family could say good-bye to anybody, or kiss anybody, in the bathroom (of all known superstitions, this one is probably the easiest to observe); the very word "good-bye" was forbidden, and "good morning" or "good night" was substituted when terminating a telephone call; and it was further forbidden to watch a train, or any other form of transportation, out of sight. July 1 was considered the family bugaboo day, and this had an odd fulfillment when, in various succeeding years, Jennie was hit by the ice wagon, Robert fell down a flight of phantom stairs and permanently damaged one knee, Dot died of a stroke, and Robert's wife was in an automobile accident involving a Georgian prince—all on July 1.

When Jennie had recovered from the initial shock of Edmund's death, Robert returned home from Aunt Lizzie's, and Jennie set about trying to atone for the awful words she had spoken. She waited on Robert literally hand and foot; until he was ready to go to high school, she tied his shoes for him every morning. It was flatly impossible for him to do any wrong, and any teacher who reprimanded him felt the full force of Jennie's wrath. Once, he reported to her that Miss Ella Drury, his Sunday-school teacher, had chided him for being too gay, and therefore irreverent, and Jennie took off in a cloud of indignation and collared the unfortunate Miss Drury.

"Don't you *dare* ever do anything to make my Robert unhappy—even for a *moment!*" Jennie stormed.

Somewhat shaken, Miss Drury protested that Robert had marked up the hymnbook, and produced a page to show that, on the line "Mercy drops 'round us are falling," he had emended it to read "Lemon drops."

"Well, it sounds more cheerful that way," Jennie said, and whirled around and stamped off.

Strangely enough, it was Jennie who first made Robert aware of the fact that there were children in Worcester less fortunate than he, and this awareness developed later into a strong interest in social service work. Each Christmas she would, with Robert's help, get up a batch of presents and take them to the visiting nurse, for distribution among those children who would otherwise have had nothing, and her insistence on this ritual made a deep impression on him. She also took him to the Community Tree, where presents were handed out by a local Santa Claus, but this practice was discontinued when, one year, Robert's present fell down behind the tree, and his name was never called. When the last name had been called, and Robert was mournfully silent, Jennie descended on Santa Claus like a troop of cavalry. The present was found, but by that time it was too late. The sight of Robert's anxious face, and his quiet anguish when it appeared that there was nothing for him, left such a scar on Jennie's soul that she never again took him to a Community Tree, nor would she later go to one with her grandchildren. Just as she felt keenly about war and whisky, Jennie felt even more keenly about the big and little sorrows of childhood, and she would have no part in anything that had been proved a potential cause of grief.

There was one other person who played an important part in Robert's upbringing. Lillian Duryea, a forceful, large-eyed, titian-haired young lady, used occasionally to go to West Point from her family's home in Nyack, and at West Point she met, and fell in love with, Edmund. After Edmund's death, Lillian announced that they had been secretly engaged, and she determined to do for Robert all that she would have done if she and Edmund had been married. She had the resources of the prosperous Duryea's Starch business behind her, and she did everything but legally adopt Robert, in return for which she insisted that he write to her once a week and that he come to Nyack every year on the anniversary of Edmund's death. The house in Nyack was large and ornate and forbidding, and every July 1 the curtains were pulled during the period of mourning, while Robert and the members of the Duryea family made obeisance to Edmund's memory. Robert also went at other times, when things were somewhat more cheerful, and Lillian showed him the sights, the restaurants, and the theatres of New York.

In Worcester, his life followed a pattern similar to Edmund's, and he grew to look a great deal like Edmund, except that he was thinner. (At the age of seventeen, he stood five feet eleven inches, and weighed 135 pounds.) He was gay and comical, and he delighted his classmates by illustrating the Latin texts with drawings that made all the Romans look Irish. The drawings were passable, but the pencils he used were atrocious; he was so bereft of talent at anything mechanical that it was impossible for him to sharpen a pencil into anything more than a gnarled stub. He always had a pencil in his hand, but it was usually a pencil that nobody else could have used. Like Edmund, he had a flair for dramatics; he was treasurer of the high school dramatic club and appeared in its plays and minstrel shows (he was fairly adept at the mandolin, banjo, and guitar), and every now and then he and some of the other high school boys would sign on as extras when the various repertory companies played Worcester. The pay was twenty-five cents a night, but Robert's career as a repertory extra was cut short when, dressed as a medieval guard and wearing a brass collar with long spikes protruding all around it, he leaned against the backstage switch panel and blew out every fuse in the house. Only the fact that he had been improperly grounded saved him from being electrocuted. After that, his participation in the local theatre was restricted to ushering at showings of stereopticon views of Oberammergau, and similar items of a nonhazardous nature. The rest of his social life consisted of whist parties, reading and swimming at the YMCA, pouring coffee at church suppers, and watching the high school basketball and baseball teams. He was manager of the South High track team, and did a little noncompetitive running, and that, plus some tennis, completed his athletic activities. Most of the time, he was either studying, working on a Dramatic Club show, playing his mandolin, or reading. He read everything he could lay his hands on.

His Sundays were something to behold. Every Sunday until he went away to school, and even after that, when he came home on vacation from school and college, he went to church in the morning (usually sitting in the last row), and then to Sunday school; late in the afternoon came Christian Endeavor, and finally, after supper, evening services. Christian Endeavor was a sort of afternoon Sunday school, held in Piedmont Church, at which the young people sang Moody and Sankey hymns, and took turns leading the prayer and giving short moral speeches. There were also occasional guest speakers, such as Carrie Nation, who gave what Robert confided to his diary was a "red-hot" talk. The Christian Endeavor meetings were vaguely social, in a proper sort of way, in that they offered the boys a chance to escort the girls home. More often than not, Robert escorted Gertrude Darling, the daughter of a prosperous woollen manufacturer, to her home on May Street. They had known each other since they both were eight, when she attended a Punch-and-Judy show he was giving; they were in the same class in school and high school, and they belonged to the same group of whist and Up Jenkins players. They both saw, and went around with, a lot of other people, but Robert's feelings came clearly into focus one day, when he and a friend were standing on a street corner, and Gertrude walked past. She was all of five feet tall, and her dark hair was braided in pigtails down her back.

"See that girl?" said his friend. "She's my brother's new girl."

"Like hell she is," Robert replied, and the subject was dropped.

In the spring of 1907, Robert's junior year in high school, Lillian decided that something should be done about his education. She came up to Worcester, and at a meeting of the Benchley and Prentice families (at which, incidentally, Robert was not present) she offered to stake him to a year at Exeter and, after that, to four years at whatever college he might choose. Flatly, Jennie rejected the idea. If his family couldn't pay for it, she said, then Robert would work his own way through; she wasn't going to have him be in debt to anybody. Lillian was just as adamant, and the two women sparred for more than an hour until, finally, Jennie gave in, on the condition that the money be considered an outright gift, and not a loan. Triumphantly, Lillian took Robert to Exeter, made application for him to take the entrance examinations, and supervised his selection of a room. Robert's participation in the proceedings was limited to playing a game of pool with Joseph Ford, the assistant to the principal.

The Exeter exams presented something of a problem, because Robert was having trouble with both Latin and physics, and he spent several hours a week doing extra work in both subjects. But by dint of frantic cramming and a certain amount of prayer, he completed the necessary preparatory work, and took the exams with a slight feeling of confidence. Only the Latin exam seemed unnaturally hard; he whimpered and sweated his way through the nightmare of trying to answer questions that meant absolutely nothing to him, and it wasn't until he had finished the exam and, quivering with exhaustion, had handed it in, that he found that he had taken the Latin 4, instead of the Latin 3 for which he had prepared. As it turned out, he passed in everything except French.

At Exeter, however, they felt that the failure in French could be overlooked, largely because of the recommendation that the principal of South High made out on Robert's behalf. In a letter to Lillian, Professor Ford of Exeter said of the recommendation: "I don't remember that we have ever received one which spoke so enthusiastically of a boy's character and ability. Mr. Woodard calls him one of the best boys he has known in twenty-one years of high school work. You may imagine, therefore, that we are more than ever anxious to have him with us next year. The room which you ask for him in Gilman House is reserved, and we shall do anything else that we can to make him comfortable."

That summer, he spent most of his time with Lillian. He stayed in Nyack all of July, and, once the July 1 obsequies were over, things were fairly pleasant. There were three Duryea sisters, the house was continually full of guests, and the Hudson River provided a convenient escape from the heat. An excerpt from Robert's diary of July 23 gives a nice, if somewhat compressed, picture of a typical evening. He wrote: "Then Lucy, Miss Jean, Jessie, Miss Ida and I went on the river in the moonlight in the two canoes. Sang and drifted. Took my mandolin. Slick."

At Exeter he was, for the first time, in predominantly

masculine company. In Worcester, he spent a great deal of time talking, playing his mandolin, and singing with Jennie, Aunt Lizzie, and Dot, and in Nyack the proportion of females to males was roughly three to one, so it wasn't until he got to Exeter that there wasn't at least one woman hovering around him most of the time. His discovery of the prep-school pastime of horsing around was a glorious one, and he took great delight in the shirt-ripping contests, the wrestling matches, and the general insanity that brighten the leisure moments of a boarding-school student's life. The following excerpts from his diary give a fairly representative picture of Robert's extracurricular life at Exeter:

Nov. 22—Played football in the moonlight until nearly 11 o'clock. Came back to the room and fooled around.

Dec. 10—Had a peach of a rough-house up in John's room trying to put Fat on one bed.

Jan. 21—The room is on study hours for rough-house last night.

Feb. 25—Fat and I went to the Town Hall and heard Jacob Riis lecture on "The Battle with the Slums." Illustrated. Very interesting.

Mar. 19—Smelt a little smoke but it was the chimney.

He joined the Mandolin Club and the Dramatic Club, and did illustrations for the yearbook and the literary magazine. His marks were good, although not spectacular.

About the only unusual thing he did during his year at Exeter was write an essay for English on embalming. Frank Cushwa, his English instructor, had specified that the students should write an essay on a practical subject, so Robert, after some thought on the matter, went to the local undertaker and requested the low-down on embalming. Undertakers' apprentices are not easy to find in rural New Hampshire; the Exeter man's arthritis had been bothering him for several years, and Robert was the first person who had shown the slightest interest in taking up the trade. With almost paternal care, the man showed him around the shop, introduced him to the ins and outs of embalming, and gave him a book to take home and study. The resulting essay was a masterpiece of colourful precision, and Mr. Cushwa, who was young and rather shy, had a little trouble getting through it. He could not deny, however, that it was practical. He cleared his throat, wiped his glasses, and gave it an A.

At various times during the year, Lillian came to Boston, where Robert met her, and they discussed his choice of college. He was, at one point, interested in Yale, but for a variety of reasons (some of them Lillian's) he finally settled on Harvard, and after graduating from Exeter he took the Harvard entrance exams. Then, on July 1, he went to Nyack.

Lillian arranged it so that the summer of 1908 was a busy one. On July 10, she and Robert boarded a Fall River Line boat, which in those days provided a luxurious, overnight trip up Long Island Sound and around Point Judith to Fall River. There was a string ensemble, which played in the mirrored salon during and after dinner, and for added background music there was the rhythmic splashing of sidewheeler's paddles as they churned the quiet, moonlit waters of the Sound. Robert and Lillian sat on deck and talked until late at night, and Lillian told him all that she hoped and expected he would accomplish during his four years in college. The next morning they transferred to a boat for Nantucket Island, where they spent a week of relaxation, dancing at the Sea Cliff Inn, sailing in the harbour, and swimming in the cold, bright surf along the south shore.

After a summer of travel, most of it spent with Lillian, he had just time to go to Worcester and see Gertrude Darling off for her freshman year at Smith before he, too, had to leave for college. And before he left Nyack, he signed an IOU to Lillian, promising to repay her for everything she spent on his college education. At Lillian's request, he did not tell Jennie, and as long as she lived she never knew about it.

3 His freshman year at Harvard, Robert roomed in a house at the corner of Plympton and Mt. Auburn Streets, known to its inmates as the Plympton Pleasure Palace. Across from him on the ground floor was H. Towner Deane, of Chicago, and on the second floor were Huntington Faxon, from nearby Brookline; Frederic Gooding, of Portsmouth, New Hampshire; and Sherman Bowles, of Springfield, Massachusetts. The five became acquainted more quickly than might be expected of Harvard men on the first Monday of the term, commonly called "Bloody Monday," when, on returning from a freshman reception at Phillips Brooks House, they were met by a group of upperclassmen who herded them up into Faxon's room, and they spent the evening doing foolish stunts at the command of the sophomores. At eleven o'clock, when the sophomores left, the residents of the Pleasure Palace knew each other fairly well.

At first, there wasn't much to distinguish Robert from any other freshman. He bought a Harvard banner and hung it in his room, he tried out for the Mandolin Club and the Dramatic Club, and he became a candidate for the art board of the *Lampoon;* as often as possible, he went to the theatre in Boston, sitting high in the stuffy gloom of the twenty-five-cent seats, and on nearly every Saturday he went out and gave vocal support to the Harvard team. On some weekends, he took the two-hour trolley ride back to Worcester (the fare was ninety cents), and he went occasionally up to Exeter to visit his friends there, but most of his time was spent in Cambridge, for the simple reason that he couldn't afford to do much else. The twenty-five dollars he received every month didn't leave a great deal of room for philandering. To get to Northampton, where Gertrude was, he had to wait until the Mandolin Club made the trip for a joint concert with the Smith College Glee Club.

Gradually, his student associates and then various members of the faculty came to realize that this thin, quiet young man was not quite as nondescript as he seemed. His first theme for English, on the assigned subject of "Who and Why I Am," was as prosaic as it deserved to be, but as soon as he got the chance to choose his own subject, he did an illustrated, extended version of his Exeter embalming theme, on the reasonable assumption that the instructor would not know enough about embalming to be able to criticize it. He even went in to the Massachusetts General Hospital and watched an operation, in order to check himself on a few of the anatomical points. The freshman English instructor was bemused, and decided to retain a little more control over the choice of subject, at least while young Benchley was in his class.

As for his friends, they could never be sure as to precisely what was going to happen when they were out with him. Once, on the way into Boston with his classmates Frederick L. Allen and Laurence McKinney, the three of them passed the terminal of the nearly completed subway in Harvard Square. They decided to inspect it, and got well down into the cavernous tunnel before they were stopped by a burly Irish guard, who told them they could go no farther without a pass. Robert took a piece of paper from his pocket, went over against a tiled wall, and wrote, "Please pass these three nice boys. Robert C. Benchley." He gave it to the guard, who took it without a murmur and let them into the rest of the subway.

Another time, he and a friend were walking on Beacon Hill, and when they reached Louisburg Square, with its neat, facing rows of eighteenth-century brick houses and its atmosphere of Old World elegance, Robert had an idea. "Come on," he said. "Let's get the davenport." Picking a house at random, they went up the front steps and tapped on the silver knocker. A maid answered the door, and Robert said, "We've come for the davenport." The maid paused a second, then said, "Which one?" and Robert, who by this time could see into the hall, replied, "That one." The maid let them in, and they picked up the davenport, carried it out and across the square, and brought it to the door of another house. Robert rang the bell, and when the maid answered he said, "We've brought the davenport. Where should we put it?" The maid looked around in bewilderment, then said, "There, I guess," pointing into the sitting room. They deposited it where she said, and left. The matter wasn't straightened out for several months, when the owner of the davenport went to the other house for tea and recognized her property. The explanation that "two men just left it here" was accepted graciously, albeit a little coldly.

Robert tried several drawings for the *Lampoon*, and the first one that was printed was of two Irish biddies standing near a reeking garbage can, and one of them was saying, "Ain't it offal, Mabel?" From then on his drawings were accepted with some regularity, although the *Lampoon* editors kept requesting that he practise a little harder on drawing hands and feet, both of which he did quite badly. It didn't matter that all of the characters looked Irish, because at that time a joke wasn't considered funny unless it was about an Irishman, a Negro, or a German.

Where he had his most immediate success was with his acting. By the end of freshman year, he had been in three Dramatic Club plays and one Delta Upsilon play, the D.U. being an organization that specialized in Elizabethan drama. He was a natural at comic parts, either with or without a wig, and he often practised facial expressions in the mirror, jotting down notes as to which ones were the most effective. His extracurricular activities were rounded out by work with the social service committee of Phillips Brooks House. He was also called on a great deal to speak at club dinners, and in 1910 he gave a talk to the Harvard Club of Boston on "Through the Alimentary Canal with Gun and Camera," using only a blank screen and pointer as props. It reduced the staid Harvard Club to a quivering shambles.

The "Alimentary Canal" speech was an outgrowth of the mock travelogues he did for his D.U. friends, during which he would use a handkerchief for a screen. Oscar W. Haussermann, who was a witness to many of these lectures, has described them in some detail. "The handkerchief," he wrote, "served as the map of the region explored by Benchley, the head of an adventurous expedition which presumably had, before his lecture at the D.U. Club, already received worldwide acclaim. Benchley's manner was that of a gentle but quietly-pleased-with-himself explorer, not unwilling to talk about himself and his achievements, and assuming as a matter of course that his prosaic, stay-at-home listeners were interested in every detail of planning and of actual operation that led to the ultimate exciting success of the dangerous and intricate expedition. So, using the long pointer, he would spot on the blank white surface of the handkerchief the starting point of the trip; and then, with slow, painstaking care, trace the exact route followed by his party, interrupting himself frequently with rather confusing asides describing, in pseudoscientific jargon, the nature and amount of his curious equipment, or repeating some quaint or amusing remark of a native or of a member of his group."

He was called on so often to do the travelogue that he alternated it with a take-off on a politician, which Haussermann describes by saying that:

Bob's little, off-the-record, informal speeches about "what we are doing down there in Washington" parodied the type of pompous Washington official engaged in some movement or work which was in the public eye. At the request of his clubmates to tell him about his work in Washington, he would take a stand in front of the group, pull out his watch and, holding the timepiece in his hand so that he wouldn't be "late in catching his train back to Washington," he would then launch forth on what "we" were trying to do "down there in Washington," and the progress "we" had made to date. He was always unctuous, kindly, jovially condescending, and ready to chuckle (with a falsely deprecating or modestly boastful chuckle) over the little human touches that sometimes cropped up in the great enterprise. We never knew exactly what the enterprise was, and we felt in our "little man" way that the great man was a little muddled and obscure, but we were inclined to attribute all this to the protesting warning of the watch in his hand, which was telling him intimately that he ought not to be wasting his valuable time on us yokels, but ought to be getting back to Washington in a hurry to resume the great work which he was now so lithesomely and modestly outlining. Sometimes, the over-all aim of the intricate, extensive, and profound work "we" were doing "down there in Washington" was "to make men out of boys—or girls. . . . I mean, vice versa, as the case may be." Sometimes the ultimate aim was "to build strong bodies" or to make for "a better understanding of things" or for "a better appreciation of the great out-of-doors" or to enable "our boys and girls to see things as they should be seen."

It does not take an acute analyst to spot the style that blossomed out in the Treasurer's Report, some ten or twelve years later.

Briefly, for one term during junior year, Robert conducted a Bible class, although nobody was ever quite sure why. The best explanation was that the undergraduate head of Phillips Brooks House, a massive, profane, lumberjack type of man, decided that there were too few Harvard "undergraduate sons-of-bitches who knew anything about the Bible," and that he, as student head of religion, would goddamn well see that this was corrected. So he corralled a few of the more prominent students, and informed them that they were either going to hold Bible class or they were going to get their goddamn noses broken. So Robert held a Bible class, and kept it up all term. One postcard which he sent to his students read: "Bible

Class Meeting in Room 4, Fairfax Hall, Thursday at 5:30 P.M. Penny ante limit."

According to Haussermann, Robert's position in college was unique, because he was accepted by all of the three roughly-separated classifications into which the Harvard undergraduates could be divided. Perhaps "accepted" is not the exact word, for Haussermann says that

> . . . all his classmates subconsciously sensed that Bob was *sui generis* and was not to be classified or judged after the fashion other classmates were classified or judged. His chuckling friendliness, his catholic tolerance, and his fun-loving nature made it impossible for any of the "fast set" to regard him as a prig. His intelligence and understanding and his gift for articulating his humorous observations of the passing show precluded the great middle class of dull, good boys from claiming him as one of their own, notwithstanding the fact that he didn't drink or smoke or play around with luscious ladies. And his quality of mind and his gift of expression were recognized by his scholarly classmates and precluded *them* from regarding him as a low-brow deserving their disdain. In other words, to his classmates Bob was the one and only Bob Benchley, and as such had a common and happy appeal to *all* of them.

Other classmates who have since defined his humour have agreed only on the fact that he was never unkind, and that he seemed spontaneously to appreciate the efforts of others, which made them feel that they were a great deal funnier than they actually were. (Things like that can lead to a reaction strangely akin to love, especially in people who have never been known as being particularly funny.) If he kidded anybody, it was either himself or some generalized type—like the politician and the explorer—and his parody was the quiet, fumbling kind, rather than the slapstick kind.

Some of his early written parody was, in fact, so quiet as to be almost unnoticeable. In the summer of his junior year, Lillian took him to Europe, and he and a *Lampoon* friend who was on board decided to do a take-off on the S.S. *Caronia's* daily newspaper. With the permission of the ship's officers, they put out one edition, imitating the style and format of *The Cunard Daily Bulletin*, and they called it *The Cunard Daily Gelatin*, which floored them when they thought of it but didn't seem quite so hysterical the next day. Like its model, their paper had a "Wireless" column and a "News in Brief" column, and sprinkled throughout these columns were such items as:

All jelly-fish with blue eyes are blind.

If human beings had legs like a crab, it would take them ninety-two years and seven days to reach the sun.

The cow, an animal found in North America and Paraguay, gives milk, which is often used for cream.

There was also an instalment on a serial story, a supplement to the passenger list, and, under the heading of "Local Intelligence," the simple word "None." The *Caronia's* passengers, most of whom were British anyway, were puzzled but otherwise unmoved by the parody.

He had considerably more luck his senior year when, as president of the *Lampoon*, he organized a parody of *Life*, the then humorous magazine. The *Lampoon* had never attempted a parody before, and this issue, springing from Robert's rage at a particularly bad issue of *Life*, was not only an artistic but also a financial success, something the *Lampoon* had not known for a long time.

Senior year brought a lot of things to Robert, none of which he had expected. Being elected president of the *Lampoon* was his greatest surprise, since he considered himself an artist and the president was usually a writer, but there were also lesser surprises in his being elected to the Hasty Pudding, made a member of the Student Council, and being elected president of the Signet Society, a literary club. His main reaction to the honours, aside from the initial disbelief, was of nervous optimism. After being notified of his presidency of the *Lampoon*, he confided to his diary:

> It will mean a lot of work and a lot of worry and responsibility for it is a responsible position, yet I am very happy to be given it—not least of all because Mother will be so proud—and Gertrude too—and maybe my course will seem a little more worth while to Lillian. I never dreamed when I was a struggling freshman toiling over bum jokes that I would some day be the dreaded censor of the jokes of others—I trust I remember enough of how I felt, to be as nice as Hallowell was to me then. It is the biggest thing so far in my college course, but it doesn't seem so big now that I've got it—I can see lots bigger things that I ought to do, a "cum laude," for instance.

It was in the spring of senior year, and to nobody's surprise, that he and Gertrude Darling announced their engagement. He had managed to make the trip to Northampton more and more often, and his roommates, who included Deane and Faxon since freshman year, and Parker Blair and Howard Isham since the year after, were well aware that he wasn't going there for the skiing. They all knew Gertrude; they had even had excerpts from her letters read to them (albeit slightly distorted, as when she had written, "I left the window open, and so had to chase oranges all over the porch roof," and Robert, pretending to misread her handwriting, substituted the word "ovaries" for "oranges"), and it was therefore something of an anticlimax when the engagement was officially announced, at a time when the Harvard Musical Clubs were in Northampton for a concert. Mrs. Charles Downer Hazen, a sister of Lillian's who was married to a Smith professor, came to congratulate Gertrude and, after a few minutes of pleasant talk, remarked: "You must understand it if Lillian isn't enthusiastic about this. Robert is her one ewe lamb, you know."

As a matter of hard practicality, the only thing the engagement accomplished was to allow Robert and Gertrude to use the private sitting room of the housemother at Haven House. Any idea of their getting married had to wait first on his getting a job, and second on his making enough money to set up housekeeping. There was also the matter of what kind of job he should try to get. He had no idea what he wanted to do.

The first nagging suspicion that he ought to start looking around for a vocation came early in 1912, when the editor of the Boston *Journal* wrote and asked him if he wanted to try writing humorous comments, or articles on current topics, for a daily column in the paper. Robert turned the idea down, with the unconsciously prophetic remark that he'd hate to have to be humorous every day. It started him thinking, however, and about a week later he decided that the ideal life, as far as he was concerned, was that of a college professor. He resolved that he would be a teacher of English, and he immediately sat down and wrote Lillian to this effect, thereby clearing up a subject on which she had been ominously silent for some time. He then went to LeBaron Russell Briggs, dean of the Faculty of Arts and Sciences, and told him of his decision, and Dean Briggs, who knew Robert's work, was only partially encouraging. As gently as possible, he said he thought it would be better if Robert started out teaching at some boys' school, and—this he added almost as an afterthought—wherever Robert went, he would have to learn to spell a great deal better than he was spelling at the moment.

Then Charles Townsend Copeland, for whom he had great respect, advised him to go to New York and try to earn a living there, and if he didn't like it to come back to Boston. Then the publishing business began to appeal to him, and the idea of teaching was momentarily put aside. At Dean Briggs's suggestion, he sent a story that he had written—a whimsical little fable about "The Doodlebugs Who Eat Grapes"—to *St. Nicholas Magazine*, not so much with the idea of taking up writing as a career as of making a little extra money on the side. (The Doodlebugs story was never bought, but it somehow—and inexplicably—turned up in the *Lampoon* in the fall of 1954. The forty-two years between its inception and its appearing in print may very well set some kind of record.)

For the next couple of months, Robert was in a turmoil of indecision. He wrote to Andover and applied for a teaching job, and he was told by Harlan Amen of Exeter that there was a good chance he might be asked to teach there. On the other side, his friend Jack Reed, to whom he had written in New York for advice, recommended that he come there, and Copey not only advised him to go to New York, but remarked further that he ought to go into business, "so that you may buy your wife a hat as good as the next man's." He wrote to Bliss Perry for advice about publishing, and then, on April 6, he got a letter of introduction to a Mr. Leckner, of the advertising department of the Curtis Publishing Company's Boston office, but that proved a dead end. Four days later, by appointment, he went to the Union Club and met the Reverend Dr. Endicott Peabody, who offered him a position teaching French at Groton. Robert replied that he was in no way qualified to teach French, and that he was beginning to weaken in his zeal for teaching, and they parted with only one thing definite—that if he did teach, it would not be at Groton.

Then, at a meeting at the Harvard Union on May 16, Bliss Perry and Oliver Cutts spoke about the work of the Civic Service League, which had its headquarters in Philadelphia, and it occurred to Robert that social service might be the thing he was best fitted for. He had done settlement work for Phillips Brooks House, and was aware of the urgent need for social workers of all kinds, so after the meeting he went up to Cutts and asked for further information on the work. Cutts spent the rest of the evening answering questions for him, and Robert came away with the feeling that, for the first time, he might be able to make a living and also do some good at the same time. He felt that, with a social service job, he could look any man in the eye and say that his job was just as good, and that it would give him the necessary time to look around and settle on something permanent.

Throughout his four years in college, he had had no particular troubles with his studies, although his extracurricular activities had cut sharply into his study hours. Once, when he found that he was about twelve books behind in an English course, he made up the deficit by one night of concentrated studying of the chapter summaries. He even had time for a little extra studying, and every night before retiring he would learn ten words from the dictionary, going through it alphabetically. His favourite studying costume was a silk hat, and nothing else. With International Law, however, he found that he had a course that completely defied him. Partially because he couldn't get interested enough in it to do much studying, and partially because what he did study always seemed to be the wrong thing, he came to the final exam with a very shaky record behind him, and with no hope of passing the course if he didn't do well on the exam. On June 10, too sick with grippe to get out of bed, he had a proctor come to his room and bring the exam to him, and for three hours he wrote what he could remember of International Law. The main essay question was a discussion of the Newfoundland Fisheries dispute, between the United States and Great Britain, and with his ears ringing and his vision blurred, Robert took a long chance and answered that question from the point of view of the fish.

The instructor who read the exam shook his head and, laughing, gave him a flat F. The Government Department at Harvard is still laughing at that exam, but they neglect to mention that because of it, Robert did not get his degree with the rest of his class. The impression is that he got an A on it.

He stayed around for the Commencement exercises, however, because he had to give the Ivy Oration, a humorous address that is part of Harvard's Class Day ceremonies. It automatically fell to the president of the *Lampoon* to give the Ivy Oration (in later years, the safer and more practical system of having tryouts was adopted), and Robert was required to stand in the middle of Soldiers' Field and give a funny speech to the assembled classmates, graduates, and families. There were no microphones, and the humour had to be put across by sheer lung power, which robbed the speech of its more subtle nuances. Robert spent a great deal of time writing, rewriting, revising, and practising his speech, and when the time came for him to go on, he threw most of the prepared text aside and ad-libbed his way through the ordeal.

A kind of protective coma settles around anyone who gives a speech in Soldiers' Field; the faces of the audience blur into one massive curtain, which shuts the speaker off from any sensation of reality, and he moves with a cold detachment that is beyond nervousness or any fear of failure. Robert started his speech by screaming "Surprise!" and then, after a pause, he continued, "is not the name for the emotion with which I am overcome at being just now called upon to speak to you at this meeting. It is nothing short of confusion." He then launched into a combination of a political and an academic address, parodying the salient features of both types, and wound up in a blaze of beautifully meaningless rhetoric. Coming, as it did, as the climax of two days of oratory, the speech was received with wild applause.

Back in May, when he was running down every possible lead for a job, he had seen a Dr. Fairbanks about the possibility of a secretarial position at the Boston Museum of Fine Arts. At that time, it hadn't seemed like much; the pay was $800 a year to start, and the man who was leaving was making only $1,500, after six years. Now, however, it looked like about the only thing. The people at the Curtis Publishing Company had said that it would be six months or more before they might have anything; he had rejected all the teaching jobs that had been offered; the Civic Service job in Philadelphia had been too vague; and his one trip to New York, for which he had been armed with letters to Dodd, Mead & Company, Ralph Pulitzer of the *World*, and Mark Sullivan of *Collier's*, had resulted in a big, fat zero. On June 29, he wrote Dr. Fairbanks and said he would take the art-museum job.

That same day, Gertrude left to take a position as a private tutor in Lewistown, Pennsylvania, and Robert mooned around Worcester for a couple of days before starting his first work for the museum, which consisted of making an English translation of M. Guiffrey's French catalogue of paintings. All during July, in the sweltering heat of Worcester and on the cooler beaches of Webhannet, where he went briefly with Jennie, Charlie, and Aunt Lizzie, he worked over the literal translation of Guiffrey's description of the works of American, German, French, Dutch, and English painters. At certain intervals, his Doodlebugs story would come back from one editor or another, and he finally came to the conclusion that Dean Briggs's enthusiasm had overbalanced his editorial judgment. After a number of rejections, he put it aside and concentrated on his translation.

An unexpected break in the monotony came at the end of July, when he got a letter from Richard Walsh, of the Curtis Publishing Company, asking if he would like to write some advertising copy on the side, on a piecework basis. He immediately replied that he would. The Curtis Company, it appeared, was starting a campaign to induce textile manufacturers to advertise in Curtis publications, and it was Robert's job to write copy that would make the idea appealing to them. During most of August, when he wasn't rewriting his museum translation into more fluent English, he worked on the Curtis ads, sending them off and getting new assignments and comment from Walsh.

He had a rather ominous experience the end of August, when he went in to the museum to discuss something about his translation, and a man there named Carter asked him to stay for lunch. They were joined by two other men, who spent most of the lunch hour studying Robert, exchanging glances with one another, and asking him frankly why he was coming to the museum, since it was obviously no place for him. They implied further that it was no place for anybody, and when Robert told them that he was motivated by the simple desire to earn a living, they smiled grimly and said an eloquent nothing. He had little choice, however, and on September 3 he moved his belongings into the D.U. house in Cambridge and reported for his first full day's work at the museum. He hadn't been at work three days before various members of the staff began taking him aside and, on the pretext of showing him an exhibit, a filing system, or a report, began to pour into his ears their hatred of the museum, of each other, and of conditions in general. When he wasn't listening to the intramural feuds, his work consisted of reading brochures, dictating letters, and pottering around among the files. Once, he had to take a group of seventeen school children through the Egyptian department, and he managed to crib enough out of the catalogue as he walked to keep them from asking too many questions. At night, he would return to the gloomy, echoing D.U. house, and try to brighten up his room by hanging pictures of last year's clubs, organizations, and friends, but, as he admitted, "It's no fun hanging college pictures alone when you're out of college—it kind of made me sick to my stomach."

There were two things that kept him from going crazy, and one was Mrs. Jack Gardner, the vivacious, erudite seventy-two-year-old patroness of the arts. The second day that Robert was at work, Mrs. Gardner arrived at the museum in an open landau, was introduced to him, and whisked him off to the Red Sox–Senators baseball game, during which she loudly encouraged all the Boston players by name, somewhat to Robert's embarrassment. She then took him, in the landau, to the trolley for Cambridge, and let him out after making him promise that he would have dinner with her sometime soon. A little stunned, Robert agreed, and two weeks later he climbed nervously into his tuxedo, put a copy of Keats's *Endymion* in his pocket, and boarded the trolley for Chestnut Hill. It was a *diner à deux,* in a dark, high-ceilinged dining room, and the main course was fish balls, with string beans on a side dish. After dinner, they repaired to the library, where they sat in front of the fire until 9:30, and Mrs. Gardner talked about art, literature, and travel in a way that made Robert's head swim in admiration. He then signed the guestbook, climbed aboard the trolley for Cambridge, and read *Endymion* all the way back. When he got home, he found that he was achingly hungry, so before going to bed he ducked into a Childs restaurant and had a full-course dinner.

Once again, before he left Boston, he went out to Mrs. Gardner's for dinner, and the routine was the same except that the second time there were preserved cherries instead of string beans. When he left, she urged him to come back to Boston and asked him to remember that they were friends, "now and forever." It was, to say the least, a change of pace from his lonely life in the D.U. house. He couldn't understand what it was all about, but he was certainly not one to complain.

The other thing that saved his sanity was the fact that, almost as soon as he had started work at the museum, the people at Curtis said that a job might be opening up there sooner than they had expected. It was, they said, something of an experiment, in that they wanted to start a house organ called *Obiter Dicta,* and needed someone to edit it, and it would also require moving to New York, but at that point Robert would have gone to Moose Jaw and dug postholes, if it would have got him away from the museum. Curtis men of gradually increasing rank interviewed him, both in Boston and in New York, and finally, on October 2, he got a note from Walsh, saying that the job was his. The people at the museum were pleasant, in fact almost relieved, when he told them of his new job. It was generally understood by all hands that his month at the museum had been a ghastly mistake. On October

15 he turned his keys over to his successor, packed his clothes and put his furniture in storage, and caught the five o'clock for Worcester.

The next day, with a lot of sample house organs for reading material, he took the train for New York and a serious start on his career. He tested his reactions on arriving and concluded that coming to New York to live didn't seem any different from coming there for a visit. He went to the Belmont Hotel, and wrote a letter to Gertrude containing this information, and then he took the Flier to Nyack, where he spent the night in his old room in the Duryea house. The house was comparatively deserted, since only Mrs. Duryea and two elderly house guests were there, and Robert retired at 9:30, to look out over the darkened Hudson toward New York, and to consider his chances of a successful career.

So here we are [he wrote], taking a second start in the Big Game. I don't know whether I'll like the new work or whether I can do it, but somehow I'm not much worried. I'm glad to come to New York after a taste of Boston, but someday I want to go back there, some day when I'm old. When I read this in twenty-five years let me bear in mind that right now I have every helpful influence behind me and every advantage before me and if I don't make good it will be thru my own fault, for I've got as good a chance as a man ever had.

4

His first day on the job, he arrived late. It was a clear, cool October morning, and he took the 8:13 train from Nyack, a train which, as it turned out, arrived in New York too late for him to get to the eighteenth floor of the Metropolitan Building by 9. But he was so invigorated by the brisk morning air, and by the autumn foliage along the banks of the Hudson, that his tardiness was all but unnoticed in the general enthusiasm of his arrival. (*His* enthusiasm, that is; to everyone else, it was just another day.) Dick Walsh, who was to be his immediate superior, took him into a vacant office, showed him a pile of possible material for the first issue of *Obiter Dicta,* and then they spent the rest of the morning discussing the arrival of Walsh's household furniture from Boston. He came in on the 8:13 all the next week, until he finally took a five-dollar-a-week room in a YMCA on 23d Street, and then, for the first time, arrived at the office with the rest of the staff. Nobody noticed the difference, one way or the other.

Since *Obiter Dicta* was an experiment, and since nobody knew exactly what it should be—except, rather vaguely, "a house organ with a punch"—Robert had no specific instructions and no definite schedule. To make use of his spare time, of which there was a great deal, he was put to work writing advertising copy, for which he had almost no talent whatsoever. His first assignment was to do the copy for Columbia Cufturn Shirts ("A Shirt Is No Cleaner than Its Spotted Cuff"), and his copy was rejected. He next tried the copy for several textile ads, with the same result, and then was given a typewriter company to plug. He slaved all one afternoon over the typewriter copy, and finally wound up by doing a wild parody on the whole thing. He had a little better luck—if such it could be called—writing letters to various merchants, luring them into placing advertisements in the Curtis Style

Book and the Home Pattern Book. There is no record of how many ads he brought in, but at least his letters were passed by Edward W. Hazen and Stanley R. Latshaw, the heads of the departments concerned. Typical letters were headed "If You Were a Manufacturer of Sugar" and "What Is Given Away for Nothing Is Usually Worth It," and his comparative success in this field led to his being assigned to write letters to headmasters and headmistresses of private schools, advising them of the advantages of advertising in Curtis publications. He was next assigned to think up a campaign for Stein Bloch Clothes, but his idea—that the clothes be advertised to fit either thin or fat men, instead of the square-jawed Lyendecker gods—was rejected as heresy.

His main problem at this time, and one on which he asked all his friends and acquaintances for advice, was how much money he needed to get married and live in New York. The consensus seemed to be that $2,000 a year was the absolute minimum, and that $2,500 was preferable, and, since Robert was making $1,500, he couldn't find much encouragement. Gertrude, who was still in Lewistown, agreed that, if he were to be raised to $1,800 and if he had $500 in the bank, it would be worth taking the chance. But both possibilities seemed rather dim, and the idea of getting $500 ahead was almost fantastic. He lunched at places that served a thirty-cent table-d'hôte plate, and he either walked or subwayed every place he went, but he was invariably behind in his payment of his Harvard Club bill, and his credit rating was such that Rogers Peet refused to let him open a charge account.

He spent almost all his spare time at the Harvard Club, eating supper there when he was not posted (friends would occasionally extend their credit to him when his was cut off), and using the reading room whenever he possibly could. He was reading for two half-year courses, Comparative Literature 6a and English 29, in order to make up for his failure in International Law, and in addition he was slowly grinding his way through Dr. Eliot's Five-foot Shelf of the classics. The Public Library supplied what books the Harvard Club couldn't. His room at the YMCA was bleak and cheerless, and the Harvard Club was therefore his home, where he met friends and classmates, and where he could read and nap and write letters to home and to Gertrude. Its dark, oak-panelled rooms and dim green reading lamps provided a certain amount of comfort and cheer, and it saw him through an otherwise desolate period in his life. More than once, on rainy winter afternoons, he sat in a far corner of the writing room and worked on his letters while his left sock, wet from the hole in the shoe, dried across the top of the reading light. There were, however, occasional moments of cheer, and the five-dollar bonus the Curtis Company gave him for Christmas made the difference in his being able to get back to Worcester for the holiday. He arrived in Worcester with twenty cents, but harvested enough in his stocking to return to New York the next day.

After much fussing, preparation, and revision, he completed the dummy for the first copy of *Obiter Dicta* by the middle of January, and had enough material left over to make up the dummy for Number 2. Number 1 was sent to Mr. Hazen for his approval before being set in type, but when, after a week of no comment, Robert found that it was still lying deep in Mr. Hazen's "in" basket, he took it out, replaced it with the dummy of Number 2, and gave Number 1 to the printer. Number 1, when it finally came out, was criticized by the powers in Philadelphia as being "too technical, too scattering, and wholly lacking in punch," but there was never any word from Mr. Hazen about his not having seen the dummy. Walsh volunteered to help Robert with subsequent issues, and see if they could be given "a little more life."

The first issue led off with a piece called "What Is a House Organ?" written by Robert, and the opening paragraph went as follows:

Conceptions of a house organ vary in picturesqueness from that of Someone's Sister, who connects it hazily with a parlor melodeon, to that of the man who considers it his own literary mouth-organ in which to air his personal views on the lightweight championship or a good one that a friend of his told him the other day. The Sister has a sneaking suspicion that her idea is not quite right, and consequently avoids giving it definite utterance. This constitutes one of the chief advantages of her view over the mouth-organ idea—it doesn't clutter up the desk.

Later issues had such features as "The Farmer-Businessman," "Sex Education," "Intensive Typography," "From Cider-press to Rotary," "Sentiment in Business," "Cultivating the Jobber," and "Selling through Boys." How the "Sex Education" item crept in is a little vague, except that the *Ladies' Home Journal* had for several years been conducting a crusade to get parents to tell their children the hows and the whys and the wherefores of procreation. The *Obiter* article on the subject commended the *Ladies' Home Journal* for its courage, but beyond that was unspecific.

The end of January, he went up to Cambridge and took the examination in English 29, which he barely passed, and the one in Comp Lit 6a, which he passed a little more handily, thanks to a last-minute study of Freddy Allen's lecture notes from the year before. Being thus assured of his Bachelor of Arts degree (it was mailed to him on March 8), and discovering that he had $14.05 that he had forgotten about in the Cambridge bank, he bought a silk hat and a hatbox with a red lining, and then he and Allen went in to the Bijou Dream Theater in Boston, to splurge on some movies.

When he got back to New York, he found, to his amazement, that Mr. Hazen had O.K.'d two of his textile ads, and that he had been designated to head up an information bureau, the function of which was to send out weekly newsletters and monthly printed leaves for notebooks. Feeling a little heady with all this success, he decided that he could buy Gertrude an engagement ring at the earliest possible moment.

He didn't get a chance until March 24, when he went to Philadelphia on Curtis business, and she came up from Lewistown and met him. They walked down Chestnut Street, talking and window shopping, and in the window of Harburger Brothers jewellery store they saw a solitaire that appealed to them. They went inside and priced it, and it was $210, of which Robert had $60 in his pocket, so he hurried back to the Curtis building, where he got an advance of $150 against his future pay. He agreed that if he was unable to establish credit with the jeweller, his pay would be withheld until the $150 was paid back; if he could get credit, he would return the money as soon as the credit was established. When he got back, the jeweller said that the ring had been sent out to be reset, so Gertrude went off to do some other shopping, and Robert waited for the ring, all the while watching as the time for Gertrude's train back to Lewistown crept closer. Finally, he had to leave, in order to meet Gertrude at the station, and the jeweller said that he would send the ring over by messenger as soon as it was ready.

While they stood in the station, Gertrude's train, the 4:30, came steaming in, but there was no sign of the man with the ring. The 4:30 pulled out, and the 4:37 came and went, and still they stood there, while the platform filled and emptied and people hurried past. Just as the 4:50 came into the station, the perspiring messenger arrived, and they snatched the package from him and jumped aboard the train. In the dark, sooty vestibule of a Pullman car, Robert unwrapped the package and slid the tiny ring onto her finger, and then they went into the dining car and had supper. Robert stayed in Lewistown until eleven o'clock that night, when he caught the sleeper for New York.

As it turned out, the jeweller did not extend credit to him, and he was not paid again until May 23.

The only activity from which he derived any real

pleasure in New York was his work with the Intercollegiate Social Service Committee, which organized boys' clubs on the lower East Side. Every Wednesday night, he went down to the East Side House, at the corner of Sixteenth Street and the East River, and ran a meeting of eight fourteen-year-olds, who called themselves the Seagull A.C. Actually, his job was more or less that of silent supervisor; the boys handled all the club business and the parliamentary procedure, such as the election (and, often, the impeachment) of officers, and Robert's part consisted of refereeing their games, putting on the gloves and sparring with them when they asked him to, and occasionally taking them to a movie or a soda fountain. Once, he made the mistake of letting it be known that he could draw, and he spent the entire time of the meeting, until 9:40, drawing Indians, Pilgrims, and cowboys for them. He developed a deep affection for the boys of the Seagull A.C., and at the last meeting before they disbanded for the summer, they reciprocated by giving him a banquet. It was a hot, filthy day in July, and Robert almost hadn't gone to the meeting. When he got there, the Seagulls had lined up a spread consisting of ham sandwiches, hot coffee, ice cream, and mouthwash, all of it supplied from the store of the brother of one of the members.

His only other recreation was reading, and the farther along he got in Eliot's Five-foot Shelf the more he began to think that a lot of it had been overrated. One night, after skimming through a few of Bacon's essays without any emotion whatsoever, he wrote:

If one adopts the Missourian attitude in reading the masters, and, laying aside their reputation, puts the burden of proof on them, many times they are not so impressive.

With this attitude, he continued to plod through the Eliot collection, and when, about a year later, he finished the last book, he concluded that it hadn't been worth the effort. As far as he was concerned, there was nothing in the Five-foot

Shelf that was as inspiring as the words, which he read in an English paper, of the man Oates, in the disastrous Scott Antarctic expedition, who went out of the tent to his death and said simply, "I'm just going outside, and I may be some time." Those ten words turned Robert into an Anglophile.

For reasons that now seem somewhat obscure, the Curtis people decided to send him on a three-week fact-finding trip, through New York, Massachusetts, Ohio, and Pennsylvania, to see how the gingham business was doing. In each one of the thirty-two cities, towns, and villages that he visited, he interviewed merchants, jobbers, and buyers on the gingham situation, and each night he wrote up a report on his findings. The gingham business, it appeared, was almost moribund in New England, but was somewhat livelier out in Ohio.

It would probably be too much to say that he became the Curtis Publishing Company's trouble shooter, or even their ace investigator, but after he returned from his gingham trip he was assigned to do a survey of the Pianola situation, and to investigate crooked magazine circulation dodges at carnivals and state fairs. By this time—late August—Gertrude had moved back to Worcester to live, so Robert's field trips were conducted in an area that made it almost impossible to avoid going to Worcester. Almost every week, either on the Curtis Company's or on his own time, he managed to think of some reason for going to Worcester, and for staying there as long as possible once he got there. Gertrude's parents had died several years before, and she spent most of her time at a farm in Millbury, near Worcester, where she had been invited by the parents of her friend Katharine Colton. The Colton farm became a home for both her and Robert.

He had given up his room at the YMCA, and during the summer he shared a house in Whitestone Landing with a group of friends. On September 22, there was a wreck on the Long Island Railroad at College Point, which tied up the line all day, and it was noon before Robert managed to get to the office. His excuse was perfectly valid and was accepted without reservation, but Walsh told him that Mr. Latshaw wanted Robert to lunch with Walsh and himself. They had lunch and talked of ominously trivial matters, and then after lunch Mr. Latshaw left, and Walsh cleared his throat. There were changes in the air, he said, and there seemed to be some doubt as to whether Robert had enough interest in his job to make him the best man for it. Robert listened, half with dread and half with relief, because he had known that sooner or later this was going to come, while Walsh said that what they wanted was some really serious *writing*, and that he thought Robert could do it if he buckled down, worked like hell, and went at it tooth and nail. Robert agreed that he hadn't been giving it all he might have, and said that, now that he knew what was wanted, he not only could do it, but would.

The next day, he plunged into an article on "Advertising and Luxuries," to prove that he was the man for the job. He wrote along on sheer momentum for a while, and then bogged down when he couldn't find the figures on the rise in price of flour. Then all the figures he had used seemed open to question, so he put the article aside and began to stare out the window, and wonder if he really *was* the best man for the job. Suddenly, he wanted very much to go back to Boston.

One by one, the articles that he had written were returned to him, either for revision or as total casualties. Mr. Latshaw demolished the "Advertising and Luxuries" story, sentence by sentence. He worked all one morning on a piece called "Advertising Anatomy," which was killed on the grounds of being too obvious; the harder he tried, the worse his copy seemed to become. It was difficult for him to concentrate on agency situations and merchandising problems, because in most cases it was a matter of complete indifference to him whether a product was sold or wasn't. He spent the entire day of Woodrow Wilson's first inauguration with Walsh, trying to think of new ways to describe the taste of peanut butter. Although he personally liked peanut butter, he was sure that there was some better way of earning a living. He took to daydreaming, and devoted one afternoon to thinking how wonderful it would be if he were dramatic critic on *Life*. Another day, when he was supposed to be working on an ad on rug and carpet production, his mind kept straining to get at the plot of a story he wanted to write. He didn't know what kind of story it would be, but he knew that it had to be about a motorman, because he couldn't remember ever having read a story about a motorman. At four o'clock, when the plot still hadn't come, he left the office, and the rug and carpet ad, and went up to the headquarters of the Urban League, where he signed up as a worker for the improvement of Negroes' living conditions.

If he had been serious about advertising, or had wanted to stay with the Curtis Company, he probably wouldn't have done the stunt he did at the annual convention in Philadelphia. As it was, however, he figured that he didn't have much to lose, so with great care he selected and rented a red wig, bought crepe hair for a matching beard, and rented a pair of eyeglasses, with which disguise he went to the Curtis Company banquet as Mr. Constantine, the president of a Seattle advertising agency. He had, earlier, tried out the disguise on Walsh, and the consensus was that he had about an even chance of getting away with it. Aside from Walsh, the only other person who knew what was going on was the toastmaster. Robert was seated next to Cyrus H. K. Curtis himself, and in the predinner small talk, Mr. Curtis said that he had recently been in Denver, and asked Robert if he knew the city.

"Denver, sir?" Robert replied. "Why, my brother lives there!"

"Indeed?" said Mr. Curtis. "May I ask his business?"

"Burlap," said Robert. "He's in the burlap game."

After some expert double talk about burlap, he was called on by the toastmaster, with which he launched into a tirade against the Curtis Publishing Company, about which he knew just enough to be able to make it sting. The gist of his talk was that the Curtis Company was not going to be able to get away with the things on the West Coast that they had in the East, and he concluded:

"I'm not representing only my agency. I'm representing the whole agency field. For years, now, you fellows have been running over us roughshod, and we're not going to stand for it any more! You give us a fair rattle and roll, and we'll shoot square with you, but keep on this way, and we'll throw our business where it's appreciated. That statement is signed John J. Constantine, and you can paste it in your hat!"

Everybody in the room, including Mr. Curtis and Mr. Latshaw, swallowed the speech whole. Mr. Curtis's irritation was increased by the fact that Robert, who didn't know that Mrs. Curtis had once helped out around the house, said at one point—in reference to Curtis censorship—that Curtis was not so particular "when the missis was doing her own washing." Mr. Curtis had to be forcibly restrained from jumping to his feet. When, at the end of the speech, Robert ripped off his beard and broke into a chorus of "Heaven Will Protect the Working Girl," * there was a scattering of laughter, and

*A village maid was leaving home; with tears her eyes was wet;
Her mother dear was standing near the spot.
She said to her, "Neuralgia, dear, be sure you don't forget
That I'm the only mother you have got.
You are going far away, so remember what I say:
When you are in the city's giddy whirl,
From temptations, crimes and follies, villains, taxicabs and trollies,
Oh, Heaven will protect the working girl."

The dear old mother's words proved true, for soon the young girl met
A man who on her ruin was intent.
He treated her respectful, as them villains always do,
And she believed he was a perfect gent.

then thunderous silence. Nervously, the toastmaster turned to Mr. Curtis.

"How did you like it, sir?" he asked. "It was pretty funny, wasn't it?"

"Yes," Mr. Curtis replied, slowly. "It's funny now. But it wasn't funny five minutes ago."

Back in New York, Robert continued to help Walsh write and edit the *Obiter Dicta*, which Mr. Latshaw still thought "lacked punch"; he kept up his running struggle with advertising copy; and he wrote free-lance pieces for outside publications, with no success. He also submitted a couple of designs for a trade-mark for St. James Waw-waw Sauce, but they weren't used. Incredibly, Walsh told him that he was off the danger list and, what was more, that he—Walsh—was going to put in for a raise for him. It might take the board of directors a little time to approve it, he said, but he felt confident that sooner or later the raise would come through. Robert, who had had to borrow money from Freddy Allen to get his laundry out of hock, immediately felt secure enough to start making plans for a wedding in June. He obviously didn't have the necessary $500 in the bank, but he told the girl in the business office to withhold $10 a week from his pay cheque, and he entered a newspaper puzzle contest, any one of the prizes from which would give him a good start toward the $500. The first prize was $1,000, and there were several lesser prizes.

As far as his social service work was concerned, he spent several lunch hours in Harlem, investigating housing con-

---

But she found different when, one night, he took her out to dine
  Into a table De Hote so bright and gay;
He said to her, "Now, after this, we'll have a demi-tasse,"
  But to him these brave words the girl did say:
"Stand back, Villain! Go your way! Here I can no longer stay,
  Although you were a marquis or an earl;
With your villainous demi-tasses you may tempt the upper classes,
  But Heaven will protect the working girl."

ditions for the Urban League, but he wasn't particularly effective because he didn't want to interview the tenants in too much detail. He said about one building on East 112th Street that "they were all such clean and respectable people that I felt that I had no call to put them through the third degree," and, since the janitors were almost never available, he got little information that was of much use. At the Seagull A.C., however, he was more at ease. Just before Christmas, he told Miss Trenholm, the secretary of the East Side House, that he wanted to give her the money he had saved for presents for his family, and have her use it to buy things for the neighbourhood children. She agreed to do this, and he gave her the money, after which he wrote to the various members of his family, telling them why they would get no presents from him that year. There wasn't a great deal of money involved, but he felt better for having disposed of it the way he did. He also, after the first of the year, suggested to the Seagulls that they all join the Boy Scouts, an organization that he regretted not having belonged to when he was young. The idea was received with considerable enthusiasm, so Robert bought a Boy Scout manual and, in order to be able to teach the Seagulls the rudiments of scouting, he spent one afternoon at the office practising tying knots, with a piece of twine on a doorknob, and also learning how to save an old lady who was drowning or intoxicated.

It was February 13, 1914, when Walsh advised him to go ahead and plan on a June wedding because the raise, although not yet confirmed, was certain to come through; and it was February 27 when Walsh took him to lunch and, in an agony of embarrassment, told him that perhaps he had better start casting about for another line of work, since a shake-up was imminent in the department and this really wasn't his work anyway. There was no hurry about it, Walsh said; he could take as long as he wanted to find something that appealed to him, and he—Walsh—would do everything he could to help. This time, Robert's only feeling was one of relief; he felt as though a heavy weight had been lifted off him, because it had become more and more evident that he was only stalling until he could find some place where he could write what he wanted. Walsh suggested the Philadelphia *Ledger* or the Boston *Herald*, but Robert thought that maybe some social service work might be better. Also, he had met Frank Crowninshield the previous summer, and Crowninshield had invited him to write some material for the "In a Lighter Vein" department in the *Century* magazine, of which he was editor. The gentle, elegant little man had impressed Robert deeply, and Robert knew that he was someone for whom he would like to work. Crowninshield had the rare gift of encouraging and inspiring young writers, and it was more through his influence than any other that Robert continued to write, into the teeth of a blizzard of rejections.

There was no full-time job at *The Century*, however, and Robert tried several different leads until the Harvard Appointments Office arranged an interview for him with Mr. Richard Russell, of the Boston paper company of William A. Russell & Bro. He went to Boston, where Mr. Russell outlined the work as being that of welfare secretary for the five Russell Company mills, with a salary of $1,800 a year. There would be time for him to do writing of his own, and his job would consist merely of editing a projected company paper, organizing employees' clubs of some sort or other in the mills, and doing general welfare and social service work. It all sounded so good to Robert—especially the social service work and the matter of being able to do outside writing—that he didn't notice the one ominous thing about the job: it was a new position; nobody had ever done it before, and nobody was quite sure as to what would be required. Like *Obiter Dicta*, it was an experiment, and all the thoughts about it were general rather than specific. He happily accepted the position, and went back to New York to pack up his things. On the way, he read with a certain grim humour, in the latest issue of *Obiter Dicta*, an article, with tables, on the ratio of Western to Eastern advertising. I'm glad I'm out of *that*, thought Robert, and he settled back and went to sleep.

5 Before he left New York, he made one last trip to Nyack to see Mrs. Duryea. The previous December, Lillian had married a recently divorced neighbor named Wilbur Baldwin, and had gone to live in Bronxville, so there weren't many people there. But Nyack was almost a second home to Robert, and he required no more than just to sit and talk with Mrs. Duryea, and occasionally to play the Victor or the Pianola. That night, in his old, blue-papered room, he looked again down the Hudson, and wrote:

> Here it was I wrote in my diary the night I came to New York to work—and now I'm going back. It hasn't been a failure, and I have enjoyed it, but I can't say that I have got very far on whatever way I am to take. And then again, maybe I have. I can't tell.

In this state of bemused relief, he wound up his last week at the Curtis office, and on April 3 he packed his bags, took them to the station, and then spent the afternoon at the office, cleaning up odds and ends, giving away the stray paper clips he found in his desk drawer, and saying cheerful good-byes to everyone he saw. He had about finished his farewells when a message arrived from Mr. Latshaw, saying that he would like to see him at the Aldine at six o'clock, so Robert hung around the office, making small talk and watching the employees as, one by one, they closed up their desks, shook hands again with him, and left. The office was empty by six o'clock, and as he went over to the Aldine, Robert remembered his first arrival, and how he had been late, and how much he had grown to like all the people whose faces had seemed so foreign and unconcerned that morning. He was glad to be leaving New York, but he had made many friends there whom he knew he was going to miss, no matter how much more he liked his work in Boston. At the Aldine, he met Mr. Latshaw, who clearly had something on his mind and didn't know how to say it. After a certain amount of uneasy manœuvring, Mr. Latshaw decoyed him into a private dining room, where almost the entire staff of the New York office was waiting at a large, gaily decorated table. After an easy, delightful dinner, various people made short speeches and gave Robert assorted presents and mementos, among them H. G. Wells's *The World Set Free* and *Social Forces in England and America.* For the first time at a banquet of any sort—except possibly that of the Seagull A.C.—Robert was speechless. He subsequently wrote that "there wasn't much that I could say, but I loved 'em all."

The next day, in Worcester, he and Gertrude made definite plans to be married on June 6. He still didn't have the required $500, although he had a start in that his withheld Curtis money came to $140, but he was about to start making $1,800 a year, and he had almost completed the $1,000 newspaper contest, which was easy enough so that he had reasonable assurance of getting some sort of prize. But the thing that made them decide to go ahead was a second contest, run by a Boston paper, which hinged on the knowledge of obscure authors, and Robert knew every one of them. The first prize was $500, and that, plus whatever he got from the other contest, would be just what they needed to get married on. They made out a budget, based on his salary of $1,800, and found that, if they paid $32 a month for rent, their budget for the year would come to $1,846. Robert decided that he could make up the extra $46 by free-lance writing (at that time, he still hadn't sold anything), and they started sending out the invitations and making reservations for the church. Robert bought a book called *Facts for the Married,* which he perused in his spare time.

He took a room at 88 Charles Street, in Boston, with his classmate George Gray, who was working at the Chamber of Commerce, and on April 6 he reported for work at the Russell Company office, at 50 State Street. His work for the first three weeks consisted of going through the files, reading and clipping trade papers, and making occasional visits to the mills, in Mount Tom, Andover, Lawrence, and Androscoggin, Maine. Mr. Russell was out of the office a lot and he was the only one who knew even faintly what Robert was supposed to do. So Robert marked time, read the papers, and learned what he could.

The first minor jolt came early in May, when he found out that by moving to Boston he had made himself ineligible for the $1,000 newspaper contest. It was, it appeared, for residents of New York only. Then, with the sixth of June practically upon them, the results of the $500 contest were announced, and Robert had every answer right. The only trouble was that his last entry had been postmarked a day too late, and he was disqualified. Frantically, he tried to sell his violin, which he seldom used and for which he had been told he could get $150, but none of the music stores he approached would offer him more than $25 for it. He and Gertrude crossed their fingers, took a deep breath, and went ahead with their plans. The one small ray of cheer came from Arthur Beane, the secretary of Phillips Brooks House, with whom Robert had worked in college, who gave them his apartment in Cambridge for the summer. They had not yet signed up for an apartment of their own, and the extra three months gave them a little time in which to look around.

Saturday, June 6, was warm and fair, and Robert spent the morning with Gertrude's elder brother, Albert, and Catharine Faulkner, who was to be her maid of honour, in the country outside Worcester, between Spencer and Paxton, gathering laurel with which to decorate the church. The rest of the day was spent with Laurence McKinney, who was to be best man, meeting incoming friends and relatives, and doing such odd jobs as insuring the wedding presents, leaving the marriage licence with the minister, and buying last-minute odds and ends. The one thing he neglected to buy—and it wasn't discovered until the participants had gathered in the vestry of Piedmont Church, at six o'clock—was enough flowers for the bridesmaids. Gertrude had two attendants, Catharine Faulkner as maid of honour, and Katharine Coes as matron of honour, and Robert had supplied only one bouquet for the two of them. The line of march was hastily reshuffled, and the maid and matron of honour walked together, both holding onto the lone bouquet, while McKinney and the ushers made out as best they could. Since their father was no longer living, Allie gave Gertrude away, and at seven o'clock the Reverend Dr. Henry S. Bradley performed the service. In spite of McKinney's terror that he would drop the ring down the hot-air register over which he was forced to stand, the ceremony went off without a hitch, and everybody repaired to Allie's house for the reception. Robert and Gertrude had planned to stay at the Copley Plaza, in Boston, for the night, but on their way to the station they were told, by the chauffeur who had been donated by a friend, that most of the wedding party planned to ride to Boston with them. They turned around and went to the Bancroft, and didn't go to Boston until the next day. With a wedding-present gold piece, they bought a tiny camera, and then headed north to the Rangeley Lakes, in Maine, for their honeymoon. The honeymoon itself, as a matter of fact, was paid for by wedding-present gold pieces.

Since before he left New York, Robert had been writing essays and short stories, all of them unsuccessful. He did an attack on New York Bohemian life, and an indictment of war, and a story about a man he once saw sleeping in Bryant Park, and all of them went the rounds of the magazines and came back to him. Then, prompted by a news story of the electrocution of four convicted murderers, he did a story called "Your Gunman," the theme of which was that gangster spirit is simply boys' spirit demoralized. Almost incredibly, a magazine called *The Independent* said they would take it. It was his first free-lance sale, and it inspired him to work even harder. He tried a *Saturday Evening Post* type of story, and after ten minutes got one word on paper—Eben, the name of the hero. Exhausted, he went to bed. Finally, after considerable prodding from Crowninshield, he started writing pieces for *Vanity Fair*, of which Crowninshield was by this time the editor. He did what he called a "story story," the title of which, ribbing the vogue for long titles of novels, was "No Matter from What Angle You Look at It, Alice Brookhausen Was a Girl Whom You Would Hesitate to Invite into Your Own Home." Crowninshield ran the story, under the title "Hints on Writing a Book." It was Robert's first published piece, and he got $40 for it. After the war had broken out in Europe, *The Independent* returned his gunman piece, saying they didn't think they could use it "until after the war."

The war was something that disturbed Robert very deeply. Partially as a result of Edmund's death, but also because of his firm belief in the stupidity of any war, he was pacifistic to the point of being, on occasion, violent. He was in favour of anything or anybody who was against war, and as a result he found himself in some embarrassing company before World War I was over. His notes just before and after the war broke out show, to some degree, how he felt on the subject.

July 30—Europe seems tottering on the brink of a general war over the Austria-Servia affair, but I can't make it seem possible that they really will fall back so far into the middle ages after having come so far.

July 31—The stock markets all closed, and Germany is on the point of declaring war on Russia. Still, I can't help feeling that things will be straightened out without a general European war.

Aug. 3—A depression seems hanging over everything that is ominous—reflected from Europe where all the progress of 100 years is going to smash. H. G. Wells wrote better than he knew. But if any one is to lose, I hope that it is Germany and Austria, on whose aggressive brutality rests the blame.

Aug. 4—Germany has declared war on England, and Turkey on Servia. It is almost ludicrous in its immensity, yet frightful.

Aug. 16—Japan has jumped in now and given Germany till

August 20 to get out of Kaeow Chow. It is something of the "kick-him-in-the-teeth-he-ain't-got-no-friends" attitude, and "come-on-in-and-get-a-piece-while-the-getting-is-good."

As the end of summer drew near, and the yellow August heat turned Boston into a smoky furnace, Robert and Gertrude spent most of their free time buying house furnishings on the instalment plan, and also, and more importantly, looking for a house in which to put them. Their ideal of $32-a-month rent seemed impossible to find outside of the tenement districts, and they discovered to their horror that they had forgotten to include a refrigerator when they estimated the cost of furnishing. Finally, with their free time in Cambridge rapidly running out, they signed a lease for a five-room apartment in Watertown, for $36 a month plus water and heating. It threw their budget badly out of kilter, but there was nothing else they could do.

The apartment, at 117 Church Street, was on the ground floor of a building that was built on three sides of a square. It had a living room, dining-room, kitchen, and two bedrooms, as well as a basement and an individual furnace. The only thing it didn't have, when Robert and Gertrude moved in on September 1, was any furniture. Robert spent the first day hanging curtain rods, and hanging them wrong, and although the dining-room set finally arrived, their bed, which they had ordered at Jordan's, did not, so they went back to Cambridge for the night. The next day, Robert rehung the curtain rods, and still didn't get them quite right, and then he went down to Jordan's to see about the bed. Jordan's said it was somewhere on the way, and that night he and Gertrude stayed with friends in Newton. On September 7, a week after they had technically moved in, a cot arrived for the bedroom that was to be used as a study, and they spent their first night in their own apartment on the cot. The bed arrived on the ninth.

The furnace at 117 Church Street was no different from most coal furnaces of that period, but there was one thing about its operation that Robert was never able to understand. That was how to keep the fire going. As the days turned brisk, and the mornings biting cold, it became necessary to have a fire to heat the house, and Robert started off with all the confidence of a man who has seen other people build fires but has never tried it himself. The first day, the fire lasted a little beyond noon before it went out. He rebuilt it that night, and by morning the furnace was black and cold. Every morning, and then, when he got a little better at it, every other morning, he started the day by tearing out the remnants of the fire, dumping what few ashes there were, and beginning all over again with paper and kindling. Once, in a fit of rage, he lit every piece of coal individually, which took him so long that he not only missed breakfast but was quite late getting to the office, a matter about which Mr. Russell spoke to him in a deceptively pleasant voice later in the day.

Except for his occasional tardiness, however, his work at the Russell Company seemed to be going quite well. After a six-month period of groping about for something concrete to do, he was given the job of organizing a clambake for sixty-five members of the Russell Club, held at Mr. Russell's farm in North Andover. He made out all the lists and took care of all the arrangements (invitations, transportation, schedule, menu, and name badges), and the clambake, which featured clams, lobsters, corn, and sweet potatoes, all baked under seaweed, was a wild success. He was elected secretary and treasurer of the Russell Club at the meeting following the meal. He was also put in charge of editing the Russell Club house organ, and, what with the experience he had from *Obiter Dicta* and the fact that the Russell Club standards were a bit more relaxed than those of the Curtis Publishing Company, his efforts were deemed satisfactory, if not spectacular.

It was during the summer that he and Gertrude were invited out to Mr. Russell's summer home, on the North Shore. There had been a disastrous fire, which had wiped out a large part of the town of Salem and had left many hundreds of people homeless. Mr. Russell asked Robert and Gertrude to come out to Salem and work with a committee of volunteers who were trying to reunite families and get people settled in temporary homes, and he invited them to spend the night at his house. Robert, who knew just enough about Mr. Russell to suspect that one might be dressing for dinner, fire or no fire, took along his tuxedo and one dress shirt. He was right; they did dress for dinner. He was wrong, however, in supposing that they would stay only one night. The next day, with a great deal of work still to be done, Mr. Russell asked them to stay for "just one more night," and they naturally consented. When, that evening, Robert looked for his dress shirt, he found that the valet had taken it and dropped it in the laundry, and he was therefore forced to follow the track of the laundry shute and recover the rumpled shirt from the hamper. They were asked to stay a third night, and again the same thing happened; no matter where Robert put that shirt, he couldn't keep it away from the valet. By the time they finally went back to Boston, his dress shirt looked like a Napoleonic battle flag.

When, the end of September, his first piece appeared in *Vanity Fair*, Robert had drawn his last $10 from the bank, and the $40 which arrived a couple of days later was therefore in the nature of a reprieve from the firing squad. He received a much-needed boost for his ego a short while later, when Crowninshield informed him that he had received a letter from Rupert Hughes, saying he suspected that Crowninshield had written the piece, but "whoever this Robert C. Benchley is, let us have more of him." But he couldn't eat his ego, and the waits between *Vanity Fair* cheques were distressingly long.

The result of all this was that by the middle of October, Robert was $75 in debt, with only the promise of one cheque to come from *Vanity Fair*, and a balance of $1.40 in the bank. He and Gertrude made up a list of the order in which they would sell personal possessions if and when it became necessary, and he wrote back to Worcester for an itemization of his belongings there. They had gone to every Harvard football game all season, but the trip to New Haven for the Yale game was obviously out of the question, so they stood in the gutter in front of the Boston *Transcript* and watched, on an animated scoreboard, the results as Harvard christened the Yale Bowl by taking the home team, 36 to 0. Then they went happily home to a supper of baked beans. They didn't know it then, but that game marked a minor turning point in Robert's career. He was already known to his classmates—and the people at the Curtis Publishing Company—as an unusually original speaker and also as something of a prankster, but at the football dinner following the Yale game he pulled off a stunt that not only got considerable play in the local newspapers but also led one writer to call him "the greatest humorist of all time at Harvard."

Robert had been invited to speak at the dinner honouring the undefeated football team, and it occurred to him that it might be more effective if he pretended to interpret a speech from some foreign language, say, for instance, Chinese. With the help of a couple of friends in the Alumni Office, a local Chinese merchant by the name of Lung Foy was rounded up and fitted out for a suit of dress clothes. Lung wasn't particularly happy at the whole idea, but he didn't have much choice, because it turned out that he was out of jail on probation, and the police had told him that they thought it might be wise for him to do as requested. Accordingly, the night of the banquet Lung showed up at a private room in the Copley-Plaza, where he got into his rented dress clothes and where he was locked, to keep him away from the liquor that was flowing all around, until time for him to go on. When that time came, Lung was escorted into the ballroom and, after much bowing, was introduced by Dean Briggs as Professor Soong, of the Imperial University of China. They were all lucky, Dean Briggs added, to have the services of Robert C. Benchley, who would translate Professor Soong's remarks as he went along. A few people may have suspected that a gag was in the making, but the majority of the diners took it seriously. And when Lung began to talk they were all impressed, except for one man, a Chinese, who realized that Lung was simply cursing, as violently and as eloquently as he knew how. After a few minutes he stopped, and Robert got up to translate.

"The professor has been giving a short history of Chinese football," he said, "with special emphasis on the development of the lateral pass." (The lateral pass had been more or less a Yale innovation that year, and it had, as the score showed, not worked out too well. The name of the Yale coach, incidentally was Hinkey.) Robert continued: "In Chinese, the play was called the *kaew chung*, or lateral pass, but as in no instance was it ever known to gain over three yards, and that in the wrong direction, it was abandoned in the year 720. Its last use was in the game between the University of Canton and the University of Tong, in which game the latter university had the unique distinction of scoring forty-four points *against* itself, entirely through safeties resulting from the use of the lateral pass." Robert then looked at Lung with interest, and Lung cursed some more, after which Robert said, "As regards the recent game with Yale, the professor says that he was amazed at the restraint displayed by the Yale men in their tackling of the Harvard runners. In the game as *he* knew it, the idea was to tackle a runner and get him down that way, but Yale seemed to pursue the moderate policy of letting a Harvard man run until he tripped himself up, or fell from utter exhaustion, and *then* to tackle him, en masse. He thinks that this good feeling shows how much farther the sport is advanced in this country." Robert then asked Lung what, in his estimation, led to the glorious showing of the Harvard team, and what he would recommend as essential to continue another year in order to make a repetition of the victory possible. Lung cursed for a good five minutes, and then Robert turned to the audience and said, "He says 'Hinkey.' "

When the uproar had subsided enough for him to be heard, he said that the professor had to catch the midnight train for

New York, and asked therefore to be excused, thanking them all for their courteous attention. As though on cue, the entire banquet rose to its feet, applauding, and the members remained standing until Lung had left the room. Those who were introduced to him in the lobby bowed low and all but clicked their heels, and one man said that he knew a friend of a friend of Lung's, in Shanghai. "He gleat man," Lung said, in his best pidgin, and the man looked gratified. As quickly as he could, Robert got Lung out of the Copley, and back to his home and his probation officer.

About a month later he gave another speech, this time to the Wardroom Club, an organization of Regular Navy officers, and he came close to being mobbed. Nobody knows why he was invited, except that possibly the secretary of the club had read of the Chinese "professor" in the papers, and thought it might be good to have a similar joke on his fellow members. At any rate, it was agreed that Robert should pretend to be Stanton Abbott, private secretary to Josephus Daniels, then Secretary of the Navy. On the warm, rainy night of January 19, 1915, he got a haircut at the Parker House, and then picked his way down to 6 Rowes Wharf, where the Wardroom Club had its rooms. He hid behind an arras until all the members were seated, and then he came out and was introduced. The beginning of his speech was prosaic enough so that nobody suspected anything. "I assure you," he said, "that I appreciate the courtesy which you have shown in asking me in this select little circle of Navy men. It is only through just such informal and intimate contact that we civilian members of the Department can ever enter into the real spirit of the Service, and feel that we are really a part of it."

The members settled back and waited to hear more. They knew that Daniels was in favour of abolishing liquor aboard Navy ships, and Robert's ingratiating opening sounded as though he might be paving the way for some bad news. He was.

"I realize," he went on, "that there has arisen in some quarters a feeling that the present policy of broadening and democratizing the Navy is ill-advised. I am sure that such a feeling can arise only from either a misunderstanding or a misrepresentation of the motives. The Secretary is, as one who knows him personally will testify, a man of sincere convictions and earnest desire to better the conditions of his fellow men, whether it be in the United States Navy or in the cotton mills of the South. He is a firm believer in the single standard of morality, as applied alike to graduates of the Naval Academy and to graduates of the school of hard knocks." This was in direct contradiction to the Navy motto that Rank Has Its Privileges, but nobody was much worried until Robert went on to elaborate: "As you all know, it has been a regulation that all enlisted men, on returning from liberty, shall undergo a physical examination and certain prophylactic treatment, to prevent the possible spread of any disease which they may have contracted on shore." Absolute silence suddenly descended on the room. "Now, aside from the obvious humiliation thrust on the men by this discrimination between them and the officers in a matter of moral suspicion, as it were, there is the point that the actual well-being of the entire ship demands that this examination and treatment be extended to the officers as well as the men." There was a low grumble and a clearing of throats, and Robert smiled and said, "I think that the action of the Secretary in this matter will receive the support of all fair-minded Navy men." The hostility in the air began to crackle like electricity.

"There are other things in the way of democratizing the service," he went on, "which may receive the censure of the hasty few at first, but which, since they are founded on such basic principles of equality, must, in the end, be matters of great pride to all who wish to see the United States Navy lead the world. For instance, there is what may be called the community mess, in which, say, every other Thursday night, the chief petty officers shall eat with the captain, and the members of the crew—of course excepting Negroes—shall take turns eating in the wardroom mess. This would make Thursday night, if Thursday be the time selected, an occasion for the promulgation of that get-together spirit which is at the core of all cooperative effort." Two officers got up and left the room. Robert was, by this time, about to enter into the realm of wild fantasy, which he intended to be the tip-off to the hoax, but he had played it so straight, and had probed such sensitive places, that he couldn't shake them loose; they insisted on believing him, and hating him. "The Secretary has said, with remarkable astuteness," said Robert, "that the Navy should be a great University. It should be a factor in the intellectual life of every man who comes within its influence." (There was nothing the matter with that; all Navy men believe that their education is as good as the next man's.) "To this end, there is being arranged a system of competitive scholarship, to stimulate among the men a zeal for those things which go to make the all-round educated man. In place of the present fleet trophy for gunnery—" and here was where he was sure they would catch on—"there will be a trophy for the ship getting the highest average in the following group of subjects: Comparative Philosophy, Anthropology, Aesthetics, Harmony, and Counterpoint. The trophy ship shall have painted on its second smokestack a little red schoolhouse—" unbelievably, they were still hanging on— "and the member of the crew getting four points in any one of the above subjects shall be allowed to wear in his sleeve the same insignia embroidered in red." Someone threw a piece of roll, someone else threw a whole roll, and the food pattered about the podium. Robert began to perspire. "Of course," he said, with a ghastly attempt at a smile, "gunnery will not be passed unnoticed, as the Secretary realizes as well as anyone else that there ought to be someone on board who can point a gun, in case the ship should be attacked before it could summon assistance from shore. Therefore, the star gun pointer will be excused from recitations in Harmony and Counterpoint, and for two weeks will receive honourable mention in the Secretary's weekly letter to the President." At last, somebody laughed, and the laughter became general as Robert finished: "There will be severer penalties for anyone caught splitting an infinitive without written permission from Washington, and the use of Latin derivatives in place of the Anglo-Saxon ones will, wherever possible, be encouraged among the men."

It must be said for the members of the Wardroom Club that, when they discovered how they had been taken in, they collapsed with laughter (and relieved laughter, what's more), and the rest of the evening was loud and friendly. From then on, Robert was invited to every dinner of the club. His reputation got to be such that he was asked—and went—to Chicago to speak at the Harvard Club dinner there, and Abbott Lawrence Lowell, president of Harvard, agreed to speak at the dinner only on the condition that he come on before, and not after, this Benchley. He knew that to follow him would be suicide.

As he rounded out his first year of work at the Russell Company, Robert felt that he hadn't accomplished much that was worthwhile, and in a report to Mr. Russell he said so. Mr. Russell replied that bad business conditions had kept the Russell Club from being more active than it might have been, but Robert still didn't feel particularly cheerful. Aside from putting out the Bulletin, his duties consisted mainly of reading trade papers, making out charts that showed the efficiency rating of each employee, compiling accident lists, and doing a survey of pulp importation for the previous year, on which latter he fell completely apart when he had to compute percentages. As far as actual welfare work went, he was doing almost none for the company, although on the side he worked with a group of boys at Ellis Memorial once a week, where his chief duty was refereeing their basketball games. His work with the boys' clubs was the only thing in which he took any pride whatsoever.

The European war had, by 1915, settled down to a more or less static form of trench warfare, and as far as Robert was concerned it was simply a monstrous tragedy about which he preferred not to think a great deal. On May 7, he and Mr. Rantoul, an associate at the Russell Company, took the afternoon off and sneaked down to the Tremont movie theatre, where they saw the much-touted *The Birth of a Nation.* When it was over they went outside, and although the afternoon was a cloudy one, it took their eyes a little time to adjust to the light. Robert thought that the picture would do more harm than good to the Negro problem, and should therefore be better not shown; they were discussing the various aspects of the question, when they heard a newsboy bawling on the street corner. His papers announced the sinking of the *Lusitania* by a German submarine, and although the first reports were that all the passengers were saved, the casualty list began to grow with later editions, and by the next day the full extent of the disaster was known. At the Russell office, nobody talked about anything else all morning, and then, since it was Saturday, they closed up shop and went home. Gertrude had come in for her weekly marketing for vegetables, which she and Robert took out to Watertown in two small suitcases, and they spent the rest of the afternoon in depressed, bewildered talk. Robert still could not believe that anyone would ever attack this country, which was the only circumstance under which he could conceive of our going to war, but he was jolted out of the attitude of strict neutrality that he had been trying to maintain. He didn't like the war any better, but he liked the Germans less.

In July, the first wisp of close-to-home, personal trouble appeared on the horizon. As casually as possible, Mr. Russell said that business was really quite slow and that it might not be a bad idea for Robert to keep an eye out for another position, just in case. In a way, things were running true to form; Robert had lost one job shortly before getting married, and now he appeared to be about to lose another shortly before Gertrude had a baby, which was scheduled for late November. The threat of unemployment was confirmed on August 26;

Mr. Russell took him into his office and said that there was a business depression, and a real need for curtailing, and that there was no question of merit involved, but if things didn't pick up by December 1, there would then be the "painful necessity," and so on. Robert didn't tell Gertrude anything about it when he got home that night; he kept it to himself, and noticed only that the apartment looked particularly homelike and Gertrude particularly dear. He spent a long time after supper staring at the wall.

His writing, at this particular point, gave him further cause for uneasiness. *Vanity Fair* was the only magazine to which he could sell anything. He wanted to write something really good, something a little more profound than what *Vanity Fair* printed, but every "really good" piece that he wrote came back to him with dismaying speed from the editors. He was trying to write something different—something about little-known or usually forgotten people—but he was trying so hard that he tied himself up in knots and got nowhere. He tried to write a piece about a man who carried drummers' cases, but couldn't think of a plot; he worked for several weeks on a story that was laid, for no particular reason, in an art museum, but every page of it was torture, and it was nothing like what he had intended. He often dreamed of starting a *real* humour magazine—one that would be independent of advertisers, and that would have stuff by Stephen Leacock, Rea Irvin, Homer Croy, Franklin P. Adams, Gelett Burgess, and others of their calibre, and under that particular form of hypnosis he could drift through a whole afternoon and get nothing else accomplished. It often occurred to him that Gertrude, who was busy making baby dresses, was the only person who was doing anything even remotely worthwhile. The only constructive thing he was doing was going through the *Encyclopaedia Britannica* in alphabetical sequence, reading up on one subject a day. (Africa and Austria took him three days apiece.)

In his determination to write something Really Good, he

kept a notebook, in which he entered ideas, thoughts, phrases, and descriptions, more or less as they occurred to him. Some actually worked their way into print; others got no farther than the first writing. They included such items as:

Two wrongs make a right—we hate someone we have wronged until they wrong us—then the air is cleared.

Leathery odour of room full of women with seal skins and hand bags.

The scuffle of feet after a steam calliope and the parade has passed on.

Outside, the wind sighed through the trees with a sound like the wind sighing in the trees.

I, pardon the personal reference, was born in . . . . .

Deserted like a street painted on a back-drop.

Now what's the use of living in a world where there are people who would call a town ———?

I raised my hat, smiled, and backed into a tree.

The ultimate reliance of all social schemes, etc., is on the individual.

When there is new snow on the ground one hears only the voices of approaching people.

Toss off a drink—up the nose.

Mr. C—— sneezed. He was a portly person, and sneezing meant a lot to him.

Smell of a 6th Avenue trolley on a rainy day.

Dull as acrobats.

Women trying to talk through car window.

Gum & weighing machine in country station one connecting link with civilization for homesick.

Seriousness with which we take quotations from foreign papers, regardless of their standing. (Moscow dispatch to Gothenberg Gazette.)

Futility of funerals.

Man who never did anything, and then, when crisis came—didn't do anything either.

Revolutionists reactionary because they go about remedying things in the old-fashioned mob way—French Revolution etc. New way the individual. They think in old terms of collective bungling.

The only obstacles to a reform are those who say it can't be done.

Early in October, he got a letter from F.P.A.—Franklin Pierce Adams—who did the "Conning Tower" column in the *New York Tribune*. The year before, when Robert had left New York, his friend Earl Derr Biggers had told Adams that Robert was a likely prospect for the *Tribune*, and now Adams wrote that he could get him on the paper, as a reporter, for $35 a week. Robert had no particular desire to be a reporter, but he was in no position to be very choosy, and Ernest Gruening, a friend of his who was managing editor of the Boston *Traveler*, said that a few months as a reporter would be essential training for almost anything he might do later. So he wrote Adams and asked if he could hold off his decision for a month or so—at least until after the baby had arrived. Adams agreed, and Robert continued to look for a nonreportorial job in Boston. Somewhat to his surprise, he sold three editorials to *Collier's* for $25; then Mr. Russell extended the deadline until January 1, and suddenly Robert began to feel that he might not have to move to New York after all. Gertrude, to whom he had shown Adams's letter, said that whatever he wanted to do, it was all right with her. (When they were married, she had privately resolved to let him make all the decisions, since Jennie or Lillian had thitherto always made them for him.)

In the November 2 election, Robert cast a futile vote for woman suffrage, and an equally futile one for Shaw, the Prohibition candidate for governor. Robert's prohibitionism was partially inherited from Jennie, and partially the result of his strict sense of righteousness, so strict that it sometimes bordered on the prudish. He, who had never had a drink, was in the Olympian position of watching the follies of those who drank, and he forgave his friends even though he felt they made idiots of themselves. He made a typical comment when, having lunch in a French restaurant in Boston (full-course lunch fifty cents), he saw eight men, standing at the bar, and each man had a fifteen-cent whisky and a glass of water. The men downed their drinks, then gulped their water. "They have to wash the taste away with water!" Robert smirked. "Imagine—a dollar twenty for eight glasses of water!" It was inconceivable to him that anyone could throw away his money and his soul in such a fashion. He, Robert, kept track of every penny that he spent every day, even down to the three cents for a newspaper; and each year on October 16, the date when he first reported for work at the Curtis Publishing Company, he wrote in his diary a summary of his achievements during the previous year, evaluating his condition financially, physically, mentally, and spiritually. He was never particularly pleased by his self-evaluation, because he considered himself much too lazy and in a spiritual vacuum, but at least he knew better than to dim what talents he had by taking to drink. And, to be fair to him, had he been a drinking man he would probably not have written, as he did in his summary of 1914–1915:

Although still on the same job I am practically fired and without definite prospects. I do not feel that it is so much my fault as that of conditions and the fact that Mr. Russell had no regular job for me. But I might have, through forcing, made myself valuable along other lines. However, I shall not mind changing. Financially, we are a little lower, owing $100 about—with no raise and heavy bills coming. Physically, I am at about par [at twenty-five, he stood six feet and weighed 143], although I don't get outdoors enough. Mentally, I have grown through experience and reading, but spiritually I am atrophied through disuse. I have found in my Wife a joy that I had never dreamed of. I still have to find myself.

At 4 A.M. on Saturday, November 13, Gertrude woke him, and he woke the doctor, and the doctor said to call back at 5. He called back at 5, and the doctor said he'd be over around 6. They got up, and Gertrude made a pot of coffee, so that Robert and the doctor could have some, and Robert tried to do something useful but wasn't much help, so he asked Gertrude how she felt and she said she felt fine, and he said he'd look out the window and see if the doctor was coming. It was dark, and he couldn't see anything. This sort of thing kept up for about a half hour, and then the doctor arrived and drove them through the greying light to Newton Hospital, where Gertrude was put to bed in a corner room. Robert stayed with her until about 8, and then he took a train to Boston and the strange unreality of the office, where he made a couple of phone calls, and then took the 9:55 back to Newton, sure that it was already late afternoon and wondering why the sun was so bright. There was a lot of sun in Gertrude's room, but she wasn't aware of it particularly, and at 11:26 they took her upstairs and Robert picked up a copy of *The Saturday Evening Post* and sat down and tried to bring the type into focus. He read a few words of a story called "A Disappearing Bridegroom," and then decided to keep a record of events as they happened. In his small, neat handwriting, he wrote the following down the margin of the page:

Decided to begin this at 12:15.

12:27—GAME CALLED. Nurse (a new one) comes in and asks my name. "Benchley." Well, Miss Erbstadt just telephoned down & said the baby has just arrived and they are both all right. She said she didn't know whether it was a boy "or what it was." I hope not a "what it was." "Both all right" is more to the point.

[There followed a wild, looping scrawl, labelled "relieved tension!"]

12:32—Another nurse says she *thinks* she said a boy, but not sure. It ought to be fairly easy to ascertain before long.

12:35—A Boy! and love from the Wife! Yea! Nurse tried to tell me "twins," but I was a sly dog and didn't bite.

The boy, who weighed in at 6 pounds 1 ounce and was conceded by everybody to be extremely plain, was named Nathaniel Goddard Benchley, after Robert's great-grandfather, Nathaniel Goddard, who had been a deacon in Millbury, Massachusetts. It was from the Deacon that Edmund's middle name had come, and an extra family tie-in was provided by the fact that Robert's cousin Mabelle—or Dot—had married C. F. Goddard, who was no relation to the other. No matter how you looked at it, there was family mixed in it somehow, and no matter how you pronounced it, it was a long name for a small child. They decided to call him Petey Dink, or, more formally, Mr. Dink. At the end of a day that had seemed like a week, Robert splurged on a steak-and-onion dinner at the Harvard Club, and then went back to the quiet and lonely apartment, and to sleep on the cot.

Within a week a telegram arrived from Adams, requesting that Robert have breakfast with him in Boston that Saturday, since "your future hangs on the result." He met Adams at the Copley at eight o'clock Saturday morning, and Adams offered him $40 a week as a reporter on the *Tribune*, with the assurance of switching to the Sunday section—and better hours—before very long. It was planned to have a supplement called *The Tribune Magazine*, over which Adams would have parental control, and he wanted Robert to work on it as soon as it got started. In the meantime, the job as city reporter would keep him alive and wouldn't be too strenuous. It meant moving, and at least temporary disruption of the family, but Robert agreed to do it, primarily because it was the only firm offer that had come along. Also, he liked Adams and admired his column, and felt that he would be a good man to work with. It was settled that he would start work January 1.

That Christmas was a lean one. The only presents were small ones for Mr. Dink, who didn't really care, and on Christmas Eve Robert brought home a bouquet of flowers for Gertrude, as his present to her. In place of a Christmas tree, they lighted candles and put them in the windows, and then read *A Christmas Carol* out loud before going to bed. Charlie and Jennie came on from Worcester for Christmas dinner, from which the turkey had been, of necessity, omitted; and after they had left, Robert and Gertrude cleaned the silver off the sideboard and put it away in a trunk, as their first move toward breaking up the apartment. Their only real expense for Christmas had been the printing of cards, which they sent to all their friends and relatives and which, in old English script, said:

What with the Tariff and the New Baby, we haven't much left to share this Christmas except Happiness. But, my Goodness, we've got more Happiness than we ever had before.

So please don't consider it a mere Christmas formula when we say that we are hoping with all our hearts that, between this Christmas and next, some great piece of Good Fortune will make you fairly glow with joy, so that, if you are superstitious, you will say, "This is the Benchleys' Wish come true."

The parents of Robert Blackall, one of Robert's classmates, had invited Gertrude and the baby to stay in their house in Cambridge, with their daughter and son-in-law, Marian and Hans Miller, while Robert was getting settled in New York. On December 30, they piled all their portable belongings into an automobile and moved, as Robert put it, "like so many fleeing Belgian peasants," out to Cambridge. He greeted the year 1916 in an upper berth en route to New York.

6

During the nearly three months that Robert was a reporter on the *Tribune*, he was, as he later put it, "the worst reporter, even for his age, in New York City." The main reason for this was that he lacked the ability, or the nerve, to ask people questions that he considered none of his business. A certain kind of newspaper story demands insistent, and sometimes impertinent, questioning, and this Robert was simply not equipped to do. There was also the fact that he disapproved highly of the *Tribune's* editorial policy, which was wildly interventionist, and he was uneasy at having any part in gathering news that he felt was being used for jingoistic purposes.

Most of the time, however, his assignments were far removed from the war or anything to do with it, and for the first month his only assignment with international implications was to see the members of the American Vigilance Committee, including George Sylvester Viereck, who had been plugging for a memorial to a German nurse named Duensing, who, they claimed, had been "killed through the refusal of the English to allow rubber gloves into Germany." It might have made an interesting story, but the members of the Vigilance Committee were unavailable for comment, and there was nobody at the *Fatherland* office when Robert went around. He called the paper with his report, and was told to go up to see a Miss Ruth Levy, on 158th Street, and ask her if she had found a dog she had reported lost. She had, so he went back to the office.

Most of his early assignments, as a matter of fact, were of the boy-loses-dog, or human-interest, variety. The policy of a "family newspaper," such as the *Tribune* was, was to soft-pedal the more violent aspects of urban existence (unless, of course, they were so sensational as to become circulation boosters), and to concentrate on the heart-warming, the unusual, and the dull. In the last category were all the conventions, banquets, meetings, luncheons, and seminars that were attended by advertisers and subscribers, potential or actual, who liked to see their names in print. It made the reporter's life a varied, if not always a stimulating, one, and it kept him busy a full six days every week.

Robert was relatively lucky on his first assignment. He reported for work at 3 P.M., New Year's Day, and found that Robert E. MacAlarney, the city editor, was away for the day. The assistant city editor rummaged around looking for something for an obviously inexperienced reporter, and finally came up with the name of Mrs. Mary J. Hartelius, of 7901 Fifth Avenue, Bay Ridge, New Jersey. Mrs. Hartelius, it appeared, had recovered her sight on her eightieth birthday, after having been blind for eight years, and Robert was sent out to get her story. He made the trip, which was almost to Sandy Hook, in about an hour, and found the woman and her son in their rickety, weather-beaten house, sitting around the stove and listening to the Victrola. Selected portions of Robert's story appeared in the paper the next day.

His second assignment was to interview a bus conductor named E. McHugh, who had written a letter to the paper saying that not all England's poets were disappointments. (Whatever had prompted such a letter has been, unfortunately, lost forever.) Robert finally cornered the astute Mr. McHugh after supper that night, and the only way to describe the interview is in his words: "I found him a rosy, honest Englisher who told me all abaht it and with whom I found a bond in receding gums."

He was next assigned to cover an affair at the Colony Club, and when he was told by the doorman that reporters were *non grata*, he went back to the paper and wrote a description of the doormat at the Colony. It was not used.

But the assignments that caused him real pain were those involving divorce, or other personal matters that he felt he shouldn't ask about. He would stall as long as possible, hoping that the person would go out, or would be unavailable until too late to get the story, and once, when he was told to see a prominent society matron about her impending divorce, he went to her home and said to the maid: "Mrs. So-and-so doesn't want to see me, does she?" The maid replied that, since he put it that way, she probably didn't, and Robert smiled gratefully and reported to the city desk that he'd been barred from the door. Two other papers ran long interviews with the lady the next day, which Robert explained to the curious desk man by saying that the reporters had probably dummied up the interviews, or else were living with the woman and getting her story on the sly.

His most painful assignment was one which took him to Freeport, Long Island, to see a Mr. and Mrs. Alexander Brown, a divorced couple who lived fifteen feet from each other. It was a ride of almost two hours, what with a change at Lynbrook and all, and when Robert got to Mr. Brown's house, he walked up and down in the street in front, trying to get up enough nerve to ring the bell. After thinking of, and rejecting, several excuses for not doing the story, he went to the door and was admitted by Mr. Brown, a hearty, voluble man who introduced him to the six or eight assorted people—including a dwarf—who were milling around the living room, and he not only told Robert all the significant details of his marriage and divorce, but also performed a few hypnotic tricks for him, more or less as a bonus. The room was crowded and noisy, and for a minute Robert had the feeling that he was going insane. As soon as he could tear himself away, he reeled next door to where Mrs. Brown lived. She was wan and sober, but she talked freely about the problem that he could, by this time, understand all too well, having seen what life with Brown was like. The gimmick to the story—the fact that they were living next door to each other—was explained by the simple fact that, at that moment, she could find no other place to live. Robert got an 8:16 train back to New York, and worked until midnight, writing and rewriting the story.

Then, five days later, the city desk called him and said they had a report that Brown had just tried to break into Mrs. Brown's house, and that he should get out to Freeport immediately. Cursing loudly, he slopped through the rain down to Pennsylvania Station, and when he got to Lynbrook he called Brown on the telephone. Yes, Brown said, he had tried to see his ex-wife; he had gone across and knocked on the door, and she hadn't answered it, so he had come back again. Robert thanked him, came back to New York, went down to the *Tribune*, did a short item about the Browns, and went to bed wishing he had never left Boston.

Probably the most frustrating day he had was a cool, rainy Friday in February, when the desk started off by sending him up to Morningside Heights, to see a girl who had been hit by a Negro. To Robert's intense relief, the girl would not talk to anybody, so he called the office and was told to come back in. There was a flood in the subway, and it took him a long time to get downtown. He arrived at the office just in time to be told to go up to 78th Street and see a Miss Ahlstrom, who had been loudly and publicly asserting that she was eugenically fit to be a mother. (The negative side of this argument has, unhappily, disappeared in the mists of time.) Robert's assignment was simply to make her prove her point, remembering only that he was a married man and the *Tribune* a family newspaper. He went up to the Harvard Club and called Miss Ahlstrom, but she was out. He was told to get down to 400 Sixth Avenue, where there had been an elevator accident. With no relish at all, he went to the given address, but the only thing he could find were two Fords that had tangled fenders near the curb. He called in with this bit of news. He spent the next few hours at the office rewriting involved legal stories from the City News ticker, and then was told to go and try Miss Ahlstrom again. She was still out, so he went to the Harvard Club and called in his report, and the night desk said to try her again in an hour. (For a family newspaper, they were damned eager to get the word on Miss Ahlstrom.) The last time he called her, she was still out—he was never even able to find out what she was *doing* all this time—so he went down to his room on East 37th Street, got undressed and got into bed, and called the paper with his latest report. At last, they gave him his good night, and the day was over.

His social life during this period was, as might be imagined, somewhat limited, and consisted mostly of having dinner at the Harvard Club. Frank Adams and his wife, Minna, took him under their wing and made him feel at home at their apartment, and occasionally he would go out with them at night. Through the influence of Murdock Pemberton, they once got Robert into a box at the Hippodrome, where he listened to the music of John Philip Sousa's band and watched Pavlova dance, after which Adams treated the group to rarebits and—in Robert's case—sarsaparilla. He was home and in bed by 12, but it had been a memorable evening, especially since he had seen Vernon and Irene Castle in the audience at the Hippodrome.

Once, he went out to Nyack to see Mrs. Duryea, and to find out what news there was about Lillian. Ever since he and Gertrude had announced their engagement, Lillian had shown an increasing coolness; in fact, when he had first mentioned the engagement to her, she had said, "We'll talk about that when you're earning your own living," and had never referred to it again. It was clear she had other plans for him, but nobody knew what they were. She had been furious when Robert had once taken Gertrude to Nyack in her absence, and although she sent them a large silver tray as a wedding present, she did not attend the wedding. Now it appeared, although Mrs. Duryea was reluctant to say it, that Lillian intended to drop Robert and Gertrude altogether. Robert was puzzled, but not particularly distressed, because it did not affect his feelings for Mrs. Duryea, nor hers for him. He continued to think of her almost as a stepmother, and of Nyack as a second home. His comment on the whole affair was, "O very well, say I, dropped it is."

His distaste for the work on the city side of the *Tribune* was mitigated by the fact that he had many good friends on the paper, and aside from Adams, who was his sponsor, father-confessor, and friend, he drew considerable comfort and cheer from his association with George S. Kaufman and Heywood Broun. Broun was drama editor, and then Kaufman succeeded him when he took over the sports desk, and they, plus Adams and a few others, made life around the *Tribune* office a genuine pleasure.

But the thing that almost made him walk off the paper, regardless of Adams and the rest, was Marjorie and Her Battleship. It was a running feature story, telling how a little girl named Marjorie Starret had thought it would be nice to buy a battleship for Uncle Sam, and who had forthwith set up a well-organized plan to get pennies from school children, dollars from adults, and columns of publicity in papers like the *Tribune*. It was Robert's assignment, day after day, to follow Marjorie and Her Battleship; to list the day's contributors to the Battleship Fund, to go to Brooklyn and see a preacher who mentioned Marjorie's Battleship in a sermon titled "The Spirit of '76," to write the lead for the Battleship story when he was on rewrite, to round up speakers from Wall Street for a Battleship Benefit, and to write up the pedigree of a bull donated to the Battleship Fund. The men on the desk may or may not have known what particular torture they were inflicting on him, but he was all set to mutiny when, on March 20, Adams told him that he would start on the Sunday section the next week. He was on rewrite when he got the news, doing the Marjorie lead on a school's contribution to the Fund, and he was so relieved by what Adams told him that he cheerfully accepted an assignment from the desk to go down to the American Ambulance office on Wall Street and see about injecting Marjorie into their tea bazaar. Ten minutes earlier, he might have jammed the whole Battleship story down over the city editor's ears; now, with relief definitely in sight, he could shrug at the whole thing.

In what spare time he had since he arrived in New York, he had been scouring the nearby suburbs—Larchmont, Pelham, White Plains, Yonkers, and New Rochelle—in search of a small house or apartment into which he could bring his family. What he saw was either too expensive or too depressing, and on his weekly Thursday visits to Boston and Worcester for his day off, he kept Gertrude informed about what he had seen and what the prospects looked like. They finally decided that if nothing should develop in the suburbs very soon he should look for a furnished room in New York, in which they could perch temporarily while looking for something else. After a great deal of shopping around, he found an apartment on East 22d Street, in Gramercy Court, which he sublet from a nurse named Miss Anderberg, who was going away for a vacation. It had a dining-room, a bedroom, and a kitchen, and three windows, one of which led onto the fire escape and two of which faced blank brick walls. The dining-room was furnished with a mission table, a red-shaded overhead light, and overstuffed furniture (and, later, Gertrude's trunks), and in the bedroom were a double bed and a crib. It was dark and dismal, and the only place to air the baby was on the fire escape; but Robert took it because it was all he could find. On March 1 he went to Worcester, and after seeing to it that Petey was officially christened, he installed himself and his family in a compartment on the afternoon train, and brought them to New York.

When, on March 27, Robert moved over to the *Tribune Magazine*, he thought back over his brief time as a reporter, and realized that, everything considered, MacAlarney had been extraordinarily kind. MacAlarney was not responsible for the paper's policy; his job was simply to get out a news-

Above, left: Ready for a frolic, age two. The bag contains spare diapers just in case

Above, right: Five years old, and secretly hating it

Centre: With Lillian Duryea

Below, left: This was probably very funny at the time. Nyack, about 1901

Below, right: Lillian, at Nyack, dressed in black for the July 1 obsequies

Above, left: Robert, next to the last row upper left, at South High School, Worcester. Gertrude, vice-president of the class, is at lower right

Above, right: Nobody has ever been able to explain this picture. However, it was taken by H. Towner Deane, Harvard '12, whose moccasins Robert is wearing

Below: End man on the South High Mandolin Club

Right: In the D.U. production of *Ralph Roister Doister,* 1911. The short, sly tomato is R. F. Duncan, '12

Above, left: The well-dressed Harvard man of 1912

Below: With the Barnum & Bailey clowns, 1917. Robert is second from the left

Above: A series of parody screen-test poses, or, How to Get Expression with a Derby Hat

Below: A hunter in Disney's *The Reluctant Dragon*

Above: The art of reading in bed, demonstrated in M-G-M's *How to Read*

Below: Explaining newt mysteries in *The Courtship of the Newt* (M-G-M)

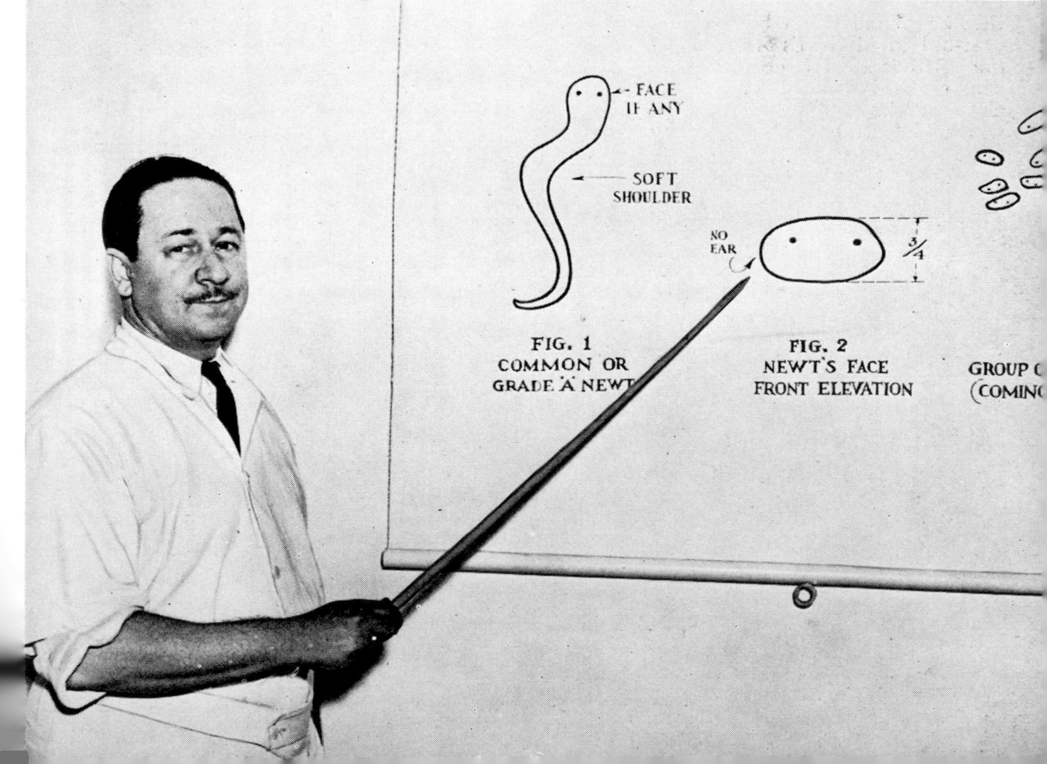

Above: It was from this position, while shooting *Dark Magic* (M-G-M), that he said, "Remember how good I was in Latin at school?"

Centre: The Coiled Spring, or Fluid Coordination method of playing badminton. From *The Day of Rest* (M-G-M)

Below: Stared down by a three-year-old in M-G-M's *A Night at the Movies.* Even after the cameras had stopped rolling, the child continued to stare at him, which did neither of them any good

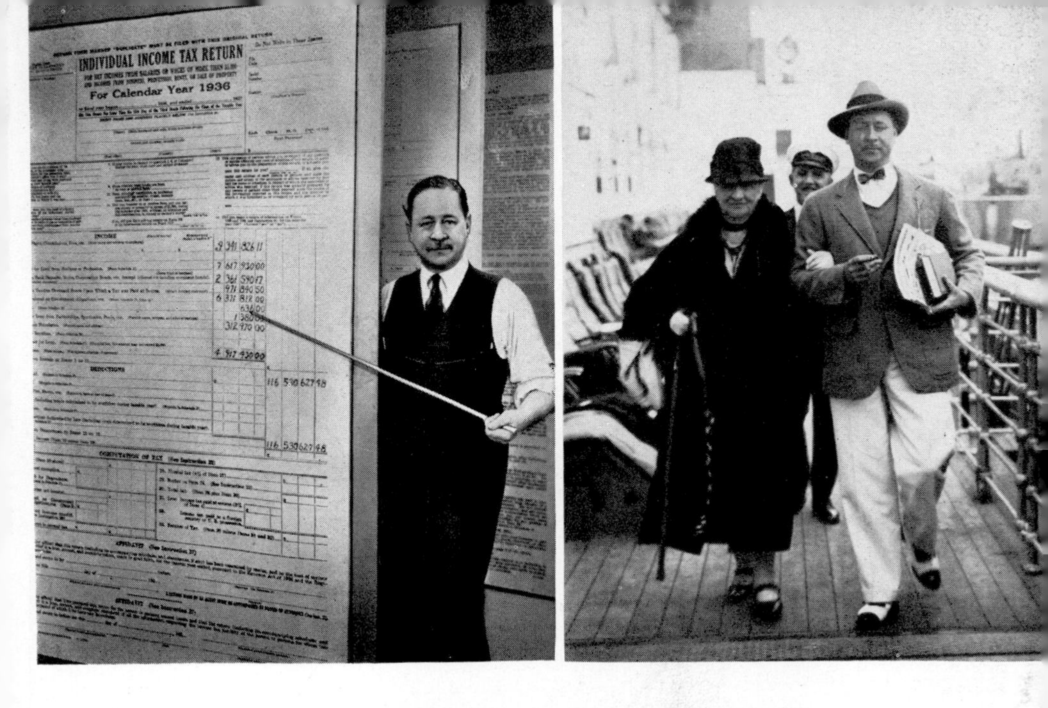

Above, left: In M-G-M's *How to Figure Income Tax*

Above, right: With Jennie in 1932, on the way to France

Below: Only honorary fire chiefs should attempt this. The picture taken a second later was damaged by water

Above With Gertrude in Nantucket, in 1942. This was the summer the terns got him

Left: One of the drawbacks of being honorary mayor of Marineland, Florida. Few men did this twice

The boulevardier

paper that pleased the owners, and Robert felt that his own contribution had been such that MacAlarney would have been justified in firing him almost from the start. He wrote MacAlarney a note, expressing his appreciation for the kindly treatment, and then, with his conscience clear, he set to work on the first job that he had ever felt really confident that he could handle.

Adams was editor of the new section, but Robert worked closely with Arthur Folwell, the former editor of *Puck* who had been imported by Adams for the *Magazine*. Robert's job was to write one feature story a week on, roughly, anything about New York or New Yorkers, and Adams also assigned him to review one book a week, the book to be selected for its phoney qualities. (Two of the books he reviewed were *Pettingell's Dream Book* and *Courtship Made Easy*.) His first feature was on the recently demolished Five Points, the murderous slum area that Dickens had written about in his *American Notes*, and he suddenly found that he had a great many ideas for stories about New York that he had never been able to write. He did pieces about subway guards, and the variety of accents heard on the street, and once he took a sampling of roast beef all over town, from the *Tribune* cafeteria to the Bowery to the Biltmore, comparing the names under which it went, the prices, and the service that accompanied it, winding up with the conclusion that the same piece of meat could be bought for 10 cents or $1.85. He also did a piece about how little New Yorkers know about the historic spots that they pass every day, and he started a parody "Popular Science" series, with such thoughtful articles as "Did Prehistoric Man Walk on His Head?" and "Do Jelly Fish Suffer Embarrassment?" None of it was particularly important, nor was it the Really Good writing that he was working toward, but at least it was fun, and he was relatively on his own. In May, Deems Taylor, who had contributed to "The Conning Tower" under the by-line "Smeed," joined the staff of the Sunday section, and he, with William E. Hill, the artist, rounded out the cheerful group. For the first time, and if only briefly, Robert was really happy with his work.

He and Gertrude continued house hunting. With them on their search were Russell Stiles, a classmate from Harvard, and his fiancée, Viola Sullivan, and the four of them combed the area around New Rochelle, Mamaroneck, Rye, Pelham, and White Plains, with even a side trip to Staten Island, but nothing satisfactory materialized. Finally, Vi Sullivan found a pair of twin houses in Crestwood that they could get for $45 a month. Robert had $10 in the bank at the time, and to cover all the costs of moving he borrowed $100 from Walsh and $100 from Adams. He also sent Gertrude and Petey back to Worcester, to wait in more congenial surroundings until the house in Crestwood should be ready. Life in the 22d Street apartment had brought Gertrude to the point where she was having nervous chills.

The Crestwood houses were small, but perfectly adequate. They were two-story, mirror-image houses, facing each other across a single walk that led in from the pavement, and each had a small garden. They were done in brown stucco and dark beams, and the interiors were pleasantly sombre, in a deep-mahogany sort of way. The afternoon sun, shining through half-pulled yellow shades, bathed the back rooms in a garish, Maxfield Parrish amber that made them unfit for any use except suicide, but the rooms were all right at morning and during the night. In the street out front, tall sycamore and maple trees all but obscured the gas street lamps, and reflected their blue-white light in a mottled, changing green. In the field directly across the street hung a massive steel loop, made from a railroad rail, and beside it was a sledge hammer, for sounding the alarm in case of fire. A few hundred yards away, the Bronx River curved lazily through the woods and fields, and the evening air rang with the sound of spring peepers.

From May 1 until May 16, Robert commuted back and

forth between New York and Crestwood in his spare time, uncrating the furniture as it arrived from Boston, opening up the cases of books and putting them away in the shelves, unpacking the china, and supervising the connection of the gas, electricity, and telephone. On May 16, Gertrude and Petey arrived on the afternoon train from Worcester, and they and Robert spent that night in the Hotel Algonquin, Petey's bed being a dresser drawer. The next morning, they went out to Crestwood, and for the first time in his life, Petey was given a room of his own. Like his first Christmas, it made little or no impression on him, but for Robert and Gertrude it was an immeasurable improvement.

At the *Tribune*, the work continued to be pleasant and life in general was cheerful. In July, Adams and his wife left for a vacation in Colorado, and Folwell and Taylor and Benchley chipped in and bought them a going-away present. In order to make sure that it went on the trip, they delivered it personally to the Adamses at the train, and it wasn't until they were well beyond 125th Street that Frank and Minna unwrapped their gift, and found that the staff had presented them with a croquet set, a sand set, and a photograph album containing the worst gag pictures that the loyal employees had been able to find.

As for his writing, Robert was working three nights a week at home on *Vanity Fair* pieces (since he was doing two a month, he used the nom de plume Brighton Perry for one of them), and was writing more serious—and less successful —pieces for other magazines. He wrote a series of editorials called "The Drinkers," and sent them to Mark Sullivan at *Collier's*, with a note volunteering his services in "the fight to smash the rummies, which *Collier's* seems to be the only magazine with guts enough to take up." Sullivan bought one of the editorials, and took an option on another, but said that the rest were too collegiate. In fact, he added, a lot of Robert's stuff was too collegiate, and he advised him to make new points of contact, in order to broaden out a bit.

About the middle of August, before Robert's annual struggle with hay fever was due to begin, Folwell assigned him to do a piece on the newly developed hay-fever serum, in the course of which he had something over a dozen free inoculations. At first it looked as though the serum might be effective—in fact, the onset of the hay fever was delayed for about a week—but by the end of August he was his usual brimming, blowing, itching self, so sensitive that the act of combing his hair or shaving his upper lip would send him into a spasm of sneezing.

Another piece, which was his idea, was to follow the page boy at any large hotel, and see if the names he was calling were just decoy names, or if someone actually answered his call. Robert suspected that there never was any such person as was always being paged, and to test his theory he followed a couple of page boys, taking notes on exactly what happened. This piece, which was titled "Call for Mr. Kenworthy!" had an opening paragraph that showed the unmistakable emergence of the Benchley method of starting a light essay. The first, feeble signs of it could be seen in the "What Is a House Organ?" piece in *Obiter Dicta*, but it didn't develop into anything like a set style until the Kenworthy piece, which began:

> A great many people have wondered to themselves, in print, just where the little black laundry-studs go after they have been yanked from the shirt. Others pass this by as inconsequential, but are concerned over the ultimate disposition of all the pencil stubs that are thrown away. Such futile rumination is all well enough for those who like it. As for me, give me a big, throbbing question like this: "Who are the people that one hears being paged in hotels? Are they real people or are they decoys? And if they are real people, what are they being paged for?"

This self-deprecating, round-the-block way of leading into a piece was, in a certain measure, Robert's way of apologizing to his audience—or to himself—for not writing something a little more important. It was advance notice that the piece was going to be fluff, and to hell with it. As a matter of fact, he wrote "Call for Mr. Kenworthy!" on the train, going to and from Mrs. Duryea's funeral in Nyack, and when Adams had read it he suggested that Robert scan the obituary notices and do *all* his work going to funerals. He had no way of knowing how moved Robert had been, and how much more final Mrs. Duryea's funeral had seemed than any other that he might attend. After the service was over, and the family had left for the cemetery, Robert roamed through the massive, empty house, and went upstairs and took a long last look at his old room and the view down the Hudson. Then he went out, and at the foot of the hill he turned back and looked up the driveway at the portcullis, at the ornate, awninged main entrance, at the wisteria-covered porch, and at the high, gabled roof, seeing for the last time all the things that he had known since he was ten years old, which would now be sold and which already had a lifeless strangeness about them. He later wrote that "if I could feel that some of Mrs. Duryea would live in me, it would be enough to assure my soul of immortality." He finished the Kenworthy piece before the ferry reached New York.

In October, Deems Taylor left for a trip to France, and his replacement was Irwin Edman, then a senior at Columbia. Edman, who later became a professor of philosophy, was a small, mild-mannered boy with rimless glasses, and although he was a stimulating person to talk to, he was also extremely gullible. Robert and Adams found this out one noon, when Robert arrived at the office and Adams, in a mock rage, threatened to fire him for being late. Robert picked up the cue and said he couldn't be fired because he'd already quit, and that Adams could try bullying someone else, and suddenly Edman plucked at Adams's sleeve and asked him to give Robert another chance, seeing as how Robert had a wife and child and all. The team of Adams and Benchley looked at each other in amazement, and from then on Edman's life around the paper was miserable. Every day, no matter what time he arrived, either Adams or Robert would look at the clock, clear his throat, and say, "Irwin, you're late," and then shake his head ominously while Edman tried to explain what had detained him. (Technically, it was impossible for Edman to be late, because he had no fixed hour at which he was to come to work.) They alternated this routine with firing one another for tardiness, and finally one day, when *Robert* told *Adams* to go to the cashier and get his money, Edman realized that the whole thing was a put-up job. In the end, his experience probably made a better philosopher of him, but it was agony at the time.

February 3, 1917, was a cold, bright Saturday, and Robert spent the morning in Crestwood reading, playing with Petey, and doing semihelpful things around the house. After lunch, he dressed against the cold by putting on a summer suit over the sweater and knickers he was wearing, and then, taking *Henry IV* to read on the train, he went down to the 3:25 for New York. He was reading on the station platform, when a neighbour came up and told him the news of the United States' having broken off relations with Germany. Then the train came in, and Robert got aboard, and all the way into New York he stared out at the bleak, brown landscape, unable to read or talk, thinking only of what had happened and what was probably coming. He knew that a diplomatic break was the only thing left, and yet he dreaded the idea because it brought war that much nearer. "Whatever comes," he wrote later, "I don't see how our actually going into the war will be the way to settle anything—war never settles anything. I am hovering between a desire to see German Prussianism buried for the good of the future world's peace, and the feeling that if war is wrong it is wrong, and no pratings of honour can justify it. The second is my real belief." When he got down to the *Tribune*, people were milling around and laughing and joking, saying things like "Well, got your gun ready?" and Robert remarked sourly to himself that, if a war should come, the entire editorial board of the *Tribune* should be drafted. He picked up the papers that carried Wilson's message, and then went downstairs and got a shave. The barber was a German, who was understandably grouchy, and as the razor scraped down toward his throat Robert had a moment of panic that he might be the unlucky American who would touch the whole thing off. But he got out of the chair unscathed, and took the 5:56 home. He thought briefly of resigning, but didn't know where else he would go.

So he stayed on the *Tribune* and, somewhat incredibly, got a raise. Less than two weeks later, a friend at the Harvard Club offered him $3,500 or $4,000 a year to go to Washington and do publicity for the Red Cross, and when he reported this to Adams, Adams said that now was the perfect time to strike for a raise. He wouldn't like the Red Cross job, Adams said, but that it was a good trump card to play, and he ought to do something about it. Robert thanked him for the advice, and went about helping Folwell make up the section. An hour or so later, Adams came back and reported that he had taken matters into his own hands, and that within a week Robert's pay would be jumped to $60. There wasn't a great deal that Robert could say, so he didn't try to say it.

He saw a chance to strike a small blow for his cause when, the end of February, he went up to Boston to gather material for a couple of Sunday features. It occurred to him that it would make a good story to go along Paul Revere's route, asking people what they thought about our getting involved in the war, and he was sure that the Middlesex Yankees would be as strongly against it as he was. He could hear them saying, "What war—you mean the war in *Europe?*" and he felt that it would be a good counteractive to the *Tribune's* foreign policy. At least *somebody* would be on record as being against a war, and the people of Lexington and Concord were as good a group as any. Gleefully, he recruited his classmate Oscar Haussermann to come with him, and the two of them started at Charlestown, walking through the streets to Sullivan Square. If Robert had been a good reporter, it might have been an interesting experience, but just as he was about to query the first citizen—a woman with a wan, harrassed look and an armful of bundles—his old shyness came over him, and it suddenly seemed like an unbearably fresh sort of thing to do. He made one or two more false starts, and then he and Haussermann boarded the trolley for Medford, and Robert decided that he could do the story just as well if he picked up some local colour and background material along the route and dummied up the people's quotes as he thought they ought to go. At Arlington, figuring that he had enough background material, Robert gave up the trek and took the five-o'clock train for Worcester. He wrote the story as he thought it should have been, and mailed it to Folwell for the next Sunday's edition. It ran as he wrote it, and if there was any official displeasure it was not immediately apparent.

It was a small blow for the cause, but by March 30 even Robert conceded that the cause was lost. On April 2, he stood in the crowd around the news ticker in the bar at the Harvard Club, and, with a feeling of numbness creeping over him, he read the President's statement that Germany's acts had brought on a state of war.

In discussing the matter of conscription with the Stileses, with whom he and Gertrude had an almost nightly visit in one house or the other, Robert said that if his services should ever be needed in the actual defence of this country he would give them willingly, but that he would never help carry the war into another country, even if they shot him for refusing. When, two months later, he registered for the draft, he decided not to tell the officials about this stipulation, reasoning that there would be time enough for that if and when he was called. As it turned out, he was automatically deferred because of Gertrude and Petey, so the problem never came up.

At the beginning of the year, Crowninshield asked him if he would substitute for P. G. Wodehouse, who wrote the drama page for *Vanity Fair* and who was going out to California for a month or two, and Robert accepted gladly. Also, in order to quiet the conscience that had been nagging him about his lack of social work, he signed up in the Big Brother movement, and on February 21 his first charge, twelve-year-old Otto Hofediener, was brought around to the paper to meet him. Robert and Otto exchanged a few cordial although uneasy words, and the next night Robert went to Otto's home, at 404 East Sixteenth Street, to be interviewed by his mother. Mrs. Hofediener was a tired, amiable German woman, whose husband had died a week before her eighth child was born, and Robert talked with her in the kitchen for a long while. When he left, he was full of determination to do as much as he could for Otto and the rest of the family, and he probably would have done more than he did, if Otto hadn't been knocked down by a *New York Sun* delivery truck, breaking his foot and sending him to the hospital and then to bed for a month. The result was that about all Robert could do was bring him small presents whenever possible, and then talk with Mrs. Hofediener in the kitchen. When he first saw Otto, Robert remarked that he was "a mighty nice kid who will probably do me more good than I him," and it distressed him to see his prediction come true so quickly. He did send his own doctor around to see Otto, and he got the Big Brother office to investigate an ambulance-chasing lawyer-doctor team that had been crowding in on Mrs. Hofediener, but beyond that there wasn't much he could do. He bought Otto a pair of roller skates for his birthday, but Otto was still in bed and so couldn't use them right away.

At the *Tribune*, he and Folwell amused themselves by thinking up new things to do for Sunday pieces. A thriller called *The Thirteenth Chair* was then running on Broadway, and at one point in the play, after the lights had gone down for a séance scene, a corpse was discovered on the sofa. It occurred to Folwell that Robert might get a good piece out of playing the corpse, so one night, with the permission of the management, he crawled through the fireplace during the séance scene, being careful not to upset the andirons as he did, and then found his way in the dark to the sofa and lay down, where he was discovered when the lights went up. Owing to the necessity for keeping his eyes closed, he wasn't able to give a very good pictorial description of his experience, but even in the darkness he felt what he called "the thrill waves from the audience," and that, plus the fact that he had met Margaret Wycherly in her dressing room before the performance, made the evening well worthwhile.

Probably the most spectacular thing he ever did in the line of duty was to play a clown in the circus, and, just as he had in his Paul Revere story, he lost his nerve at the crucial time. The circus came to New York around the middle of April, and with the willing cooperation of Harry Staton, the circus's press agent, Folwell arranged to have Robert meet Buck Baker, the one-eyed head clown. (At the same time as he met Baker, he also met Lillian Leitzle, the woman acrobat, whose conversation singed his delicate New England ears and almost frightened him away before he got started. Robert had never even heard any *men* talk the way she did, and it shook him deeply.)

After showing him around the circus, Baker told him they would put him in the act the next night. The following afternoon, Robert and Folwell and Staton picked up Baker at the Garden, and they all had dinner at the Prince George, where they talked over their plans for the evening and Baker told them of a time he had barged Grover Cleveland up a stream duck hunting. Then they went back to the Garden, having decided that Robert's "act," if such it could be called, would be to sit on the sawdust and do absolutely nothing. He would ride with the other clowns, and march with them, but when they were doing their specialties, he would just sit to one side and stare. Baker took him up to the dressing rooms and introduced him to the other clowns, all of whom were extremely friendly. Under Baker's supervision, Robert put on a pair of monstrous, flapping shoes and a ragged costume, and then Baker made him up, and he went down and into the ring with the clowns. First, Baker rode him around the ring backward in a trick Ford; then, later on, he had a ride in the fire engine. In between rides he sat on the ring edge and did nothing, and he was just becoming fond of a clown's life when Baker signalled him to come off. When he got to the entrance ramp, Robert saw to his horror that Baker wanted him to ride in the exploding jitney bus, and although his reason told him it was safe, it had always startled him when he saw it as a spectator, and he didn't feel equal to being an actual part of the explosion. This would be the time that something went wrong; somebody would have put in real dynamite instead of flash powder; he might easily break his back if he jumped the wrong way; the clowns probably practised for weeks before they rode in the bus—maybe all winter, even—and here he didn't know the first thing about it. Quickly, Robert ducked behind a team of white, spangled horses and raced up the stairs to the dressing rooms, and as fast as he could he removed his make-up and costume. Then, already feeling a little ashamed of himself, he went down and joined Folwell in a box. With a growing, gnawing feeling of guilt, he watched the rest of the circus, and the next day, when he wrote his piece for the *Tribune*, he titled it "Uneasy Lies the Head that Plays the Clown." He wrote so much that it had to be set in 8-point type to fit in the page, and even at that he trimmed a lot.

It was a long time before he dared even to see Baker, but ten days later he went back to the circus, taking with him Otto Hofediener (who had to be carried), his mother (who hadn't wanted to come, because she had no hat), and four of his seven sisters.

In Crestwood, Robert and Rus Stiles used their spare time in digging, fertilizing, and planting a Victory garden in the plot out back, which turned out to have a higher sand content than any area that side of the dunes of Long Island, and they also put down, between them, nearly fifty dozen eggs in water glass (at thirty-five cents a dozen), against the food shortage that all the papers were promising. With the coming of spring, his winter-long, losing struggle against the furnace came to an end, but new duties replaced it, and there wasn't a minute when he couldn't find something to do in or around the house. In a way, he liked these chores, because he had a theory that "anybody can do any amount of work, so long as it isn't the work he is supposed to be doing," and if he was supposed to be writing a piece for, say, *Vanity Fair*, which might make the difference between eating and going hungry, he found that he could get a great deal accomplished around the house before actually settling down to write the piece. And the nice thing was that he never felt that he was loafing, or wasting time, because the things really *had* to be done sometime, and here he was doing them. Using this philosophy, he once made labels for every jar in the pantry, whether or not it contained anything, and by the end of the day there were some three dozen, exquisitely neatly labelled jars, with signs saying, for instance: "Salt," "Pepper," "Sugar (granulated)," "Sugar (powdered)," "Sugar (brown)," "Salt," "Pepper," "Mustard (hot)," "Mustard (regular)," "Cloves," "Salt," "Thyme," "Marjoram," "Pepper," "Salt," "Mandrake Root," "Jelly (grape)," "Jelly (apple)," "Jelly (quince)," "Salt," "Pepper," and so on.

In the evenings, when the Stileses came over, they would sing old Hasty Pudding songs, with Robert playing the mandolin or guitar and Gertrude at the piano, and they would look through the 1912 class album. One night they sat in front of the fire until ten o'clock, talking about where they would build their houses when they moved back to Massachusetts to live. That was Sunday, May 27. Monday morning was cool and rainy, and Robert stayed at home until ten o'clock, working on some addenda to a *Vanity Fair* piece that Crowninshield had asked for. Then he and Vi Stiles took the train to

New York, continuing their talk of the night before. When he got to the *Tribune*, he noticed that there was an odd hush in the air, and that Edman was just sitting aimlessly at his desk, with an expression on his face as though he were trying to remember something. Robert asked him where Folwell was, and Edman said he was in with Adams, and had been for some time, and then they both sat around and talked in a desultory way, watching the door to Adams's office and trying not to wonder what was taking Folwell so long. Then the door opened, and Adams beckoned them to come in, and they went in and Folwell greeted Robert quietly, and Adams told them to sit down. Without further preamble, Adams told them that they were all fired—Folwell, Edman, and Robert—effective in two weeks, and that the *Tribune Magazine* was being discontinued as such. Adams said that George V. Rogers, the vice-president and general manager who had notified him of the move, had said that it was dictated by economy, but nobody really believed him. Many people had remarked, in recent months, that the *Magazine* seemed to be jeering at the *Tribune*, and it was logical to assume that, sooner or later, the management would come to the same conclusion. They would get vacation pay, Adams said, and that would be that.

In the two weeks that they stayed around, listlessly putting out the last couple of issues of the *Magazine*, they received a great deal of sympathy but little else, although one friend wrote to a man named Reilly, at Metro Film Corporation, suggesting Robert for a job writing movie captions. He saw Reilly, who said that there wasn't anything immediate but might be in a few days, and Robert told him to call if he ever needed him, thereby leaving it up to Reilly. He wasn't too keen about doing movie work, "not being quite reconciled to mixing up in circles which must consist of the country's most frothy and inconsequential citizens." He had notified Crowninshield of the recent developments, and Crowninshield had said "how interesting" and "we must have lunch next week," but Robert was not much more eager to work on *Vanity Fair* than he was to work in the movies.

During the last week, it became obvious that there was not going to be anything immediate at *Vanity Fair*, although Crowninshield kept muttering about a job as managing editor at $75 a week, so he said to hell with it all and decided to free-lance until forced by hunger to go out and get a job.

He started his free-lance writing on June 11, and spent most of the morning rearranging his desk so as to get better light. He then wrote a page on the old art-museum story, which he had started a long time ago, and after lunch it occurred to him that he would need some more office supplies if he was going to be working at home. He took the 2:38 to New York, where he bought a desk tray and pad in a stationery store on 42d Street, and a box of paper clips at another store, and got the 4:07 back to Crestwood, which got him there just in time to cut the lawn and trim the hedges before supper. After supper, he washed the dishes, and then he and Gertrude went across and chatted with the Stileses until 9:45, when they came back and went to bed. As he lay in bed and thought about his writing, he reasoned that no man could be expected to get more than one page done his very first day, and that some people, in fact, might not have done even that much.

That was a Monday. By Thursday, he had begun to wonder if he could ever really write at home—or anywhere else, for that matter—and by Friday, although he had finished Page 10 of the story, he had no idea whether or not it was any good. He did a quick piece for *Vanity Fair*, and then got back to the art-museum story, but it came very hard; Gertrude had gone to Northampton for a reunion, and he had to keep an eye on Petey. On Tuesday, June 19, he got up at five o'clock, dressed and packed for himself and Petey, and they went in town and took the 9:15 for Worcester. Gertrude got aboard at Springfield, and they all went on together to Millbury, to the farm of Mrs. Samuel Colton, Katharine Coes's mother. It was "Mother" Colton who had looked out for Gertrude after her parents had died, and she was the logical refuge in time of trouble. They had no idea how long they were going to stay; all Robert knew was that he needed someplace in which to recuperate from his second stab at New York, and at Red Farm in Millbury he and his family would be in congenial, homelike surroundings, and he might at last be able to do some serious writing.

7

Red Farm was two red barns and a long, two-story, white-trimmed red house, settled atop a hill outside Millbury. There was also a small but wonderfully ornate and dilapidated playhouse, hidden among a grove of gnarled apple trees, and behind one barn an ancient, lifeless sleigh stood rotting among the weeds. The sweet smell of hay, coming up from the lower fields, mingled with the musky smell of pigs and cows and horses, but there was always a slight breeze that kept any one smell from being too strong. The Colton children and grandchildren and friends' children had swarmed through and around Red Farm for so many years that the farm seemed to have adapted itself to them, and it felt as though it were more a farm for children than for farming. There was an air of enchantment about it, from the old pony Silas, on whom all the children crawled, to the view out of the long windows of the dining-room, from which you could see across the valley and watch a thunderstorm fifteen or twenty miles away.

When Robert and Gertrude and Petey arrived, the Colton clan was somewhat depleted. Kay had married Loring Coes, and was living in Worcester with him and their three children; Jim was serving aboard the U.S.S. *Vermont*, and Jack was on coastal patrol on the U.S.S. *Aztec*. That left only Sam, Syd, Rod, Sue and El at home with Mother Colton, with Henry (the chauffeur) and the farmer and the hired man to help out as needed. When Henry drove the Pope-Hartford around, and the Coltons and their friends got in to take a ride, the odds were slightly less than even that an axle would break before they returned. If the Coeses were along, it was almost a dead certainty.

After the first couple of days of showing Petey around the farm, Robert settled down and began to write in earnest. He did the usual fluff for *Vanity Fair*, and then started in on an ambitious piece to send to the *Atlantic*, a piece which he described as being about "home-made scenes in reading literature." He did a first draft, then rewrote it specifically for the *Atlantic*, taking each sentence and deliberately injecting form, culture, and euphony into it. He even managed to drag in the word "aestivation," which was no mean feat considering the subject. After almost a month of rewriting and polishing, he sent it off, and then turned his attention back to the art-museum piece, which had by this time reached a length of 7,000 words with no end in sight. He wrote another thousand words, and then put it aside to read at some later date, because he couldn't see himself rewriting 8,000 words over and again unless he was sure that the piece was going to be right. If it was doomed from the start, now was the time to find out.

He didn't spend all his time writing, by any means. He went out in the fields and helped Syd cock hay while the other men pitched it, he played with Petey and such of the Colton children as were interested, and he made several trips to Worcester to see Jennie and Charlie and the rest of the family. Mother Colton had told him that he could stay at the farm all summer if it became necessary, but he knew that sooner or later he was going to have to get a job, because he had no confidence in his ability to exist by free-lance writing alone. He told Crowninshield to keep him in mind in case some editorial job opened up on *Vanity Fair;* and then, after a certain amount of talking to himself, he wrote to a friend in the Red Cross and volunteered his services, either doing publicity in this country or reconstruction work in France. He never got a reply.

What little confidence he had in his ability as a serious writer was shattered on August 8, when he went down for the mail and found his piece back from the *Atlantic*. He sent it right off to *Harper's*, but with no real hope of success, and he came back to the farm and reread the art-museum piece, to see if there was anything worth while in it. It cheered him enough at least to continue with it, and four days later he finished it, at a total length of 12,000 words. He titled it "The Bishop of Birmingham," because that had nothing to do with the story, and sent it off to Paul Reynolds, an agent. He also wrote to Tom Ybarra, a friend on *The New York Times*, asking if there was a job for him there. Then, about a week later, *Harper's* returned the literary piece and Reynolds returned the art-museum piece, and although Robert sent the museum story off to *The Saturday Evening Post*, he knew that, as a free lance, he was through. He wrote to Dave Wallace, who Adams had told him was looking for someone to replace him as press agent for William A. Brady, the producer, and applied for the job. It was about the last job in the world that he wanted, but he had made exactly $60 in the three months since he was fired from the *Tribune*.

The end of August, he went down to New York and, after being coached by both Adams and Crowninshield, he met Wallace and was introduced to Brady. The meeting lasted for five minutes, and was not particularly cordial. Brady looked Robert over and asked what he wanted; Robert, on Adams's advice, said $75, and Brady said he'd be willing to try it for a couple of weeks. He reminded Robert that there were no clocks on the job, and Robert, who had already taken a dislike to him, just stared at him and said nothing. The interview was over, and Robert was considering refusing the job, when he ran into Brock and Murdock Pemberton at the Hippodrome, and they advised him at least to give it a try. More for the $150 involved than for anything else, he finally agreed to do it for two weeks.

He wound up working for Brady for twelve weeks, and hating every minute of it. The only good thing about it was that it was the first real job (not counting the Boston Museum one) from which he resigned on his own initiative, although the odds are that he would have been fired if he had stayed on much longer. Also, every time he felt like quitting he remembered the $75, which was more money than he had ever made. He reasoned that he could put up with a great deal for $75 a week, but as time passed, his temper grew shorter, and he began to dream of spectacular ways of resigning. Once, when Brady made headlines by getting into a loud, violent brawl at the Ritz, Robert thought of telling him that he didn't need a press agent so much as a wet nurse, and then walking out. Just in time, he remembered what $75 would buy, and he kept quiet.

The main trouble was the difference in temperament between Brady and Robert. Brady was gruff, hearty, and, after a few drinks, either expansive or violent; Robert was quiet and puritanical. Every press release and every ad that Robert wrote had to have Brady's personal approval, and sometimes Robert would hunt through the local bars for an hour or more before finding Brady, and then have his day's work either grudgingly O.K.'d, heavily revised, or thrown out altogether. Brady was furious at him for not staying around after the opening of *The Land of the Free*; to take down whatever commands he might have had, and he luckily didn't know that Robert had deliberately avoided him at the opening as being unfit to talk business. But his anger then was nothing compared to his rage a week later, when the Sunday papers treated the imminent opening of his wife, Grace George, in a play called *Eve's Daughter* with what he considered less than the deference she deserved. He shouted at Robert on the telephone to Crestwood for a half hour, and Robert went into the office the next day fully prepared to carry on the fight, spit in Brady's eye, and slam the door behind him as he walked out. He was even prepared to give Brady his own thoughts about Miss George, which were far from flattering. But when, finally, he came face to face with the producer, Brady seemed to have forgotten all about the day before, and even invited Robert to have a drink. Coldly, Robert said that he didn't drink, and Brady shrugged and went on about his business.

Aside from the personalities involved, the work was tedious and exasperating. Robert had to handle the ads, the features, the road publicity, and the advance billings for three shows, as well as keep the local press happy and the drama editors supplied with pictures and copy. Brady would often change his mind about an ad, or the date of an opening, an hour or so after all the copy had gone to press, and it was Robert's job to rush around to the papers, try to get them to kill the old copy, and substitute what he hoped was the correct information. There were stretches of two weeks at a time when he didn't get home for dinner, and on the night of an opening, or some special occasion, Gertrude would bring his dress clothes to town and he would change in his office at the Playhouse. He accepted a job of writing advertising copy on the side, for the Andruss-Paterson agency, but about all he ever got time to do was a short bit of copy for Dr. Lyon's Tooth Powder. The rest of the time, he was running. And cursing.

He was, therefore, delighted when, on November 1, he received a telegram from Freddy Allen in Washington, urging him to come down and see about taking a job with the Council for National Defense. When Brady called in, Robert told him about the offer and asked if he could look into it, and Brady replied that Robert couldn't work for him and the government too. After he had hung up, Robert told Brady's assistant, who was named Brown, to tell Brady that he would be leaving just as soon as they found someone to replace him. With that off his mind, and feeling ten pounds lighter, he drew his last dollar from the bank and took the midnight train to Washington.

It was his first visit to Washington, and he wandered all over the city before finding a Mr. Clarkson, who told him what the work was like and offered him $50 a week. The work sounded all right, but Mr. Clarkson struck Robert as being "a bit of a twirp," and they left it that they would both think it over. After a trip to the office of the Hoover Food Administration, where they were also looking for a press man and where he got a Mr. Ben Allen to say he would "keep in touch," he took the Congressional Limited back to New York. At the Playhouse, Brown said that he had delivered Robert's message to Brady.

"What did he say?" Robert asked.

"He wasn't prostrated," Brown replied.

With that working understanding, Robert continued to grind out Brady's press notices, keeping an eye out all the while for a successor. *Eve's Daughter* closed, and Grace George went immediately into Bernstein's *L'Élévation*, which opened November 14 and which, although it got good notices, was not a commercial success and closed December 1. On November 24, Brown told Robert that, since Miss George was going to retire for the season after *L'Élévation* closed, there would be no successor to his job and therefore no reason for him to wait around. In fact, he could, Brown said, leave any time he wanted. Robert thanked him, and took the 4:07 for Crestwood. Or, rather, he tried for the 4:07; he squeezed through the gates just as they were closing, and ran full speed down the ramp, but he went so fast his rubbers flew off, and by the time he had hobbled to a stop and retrieved them, the train pulled out. He got the 4:19, with time to spare.

For a week, he sat around Crestwood waiting to hear from Washington, and then the horrible suspicion began to creep over him that something had gone wrong. This was confirmed a few days later, when he got a letter from Allen saying that the Council job no longer existed, but that something else might turn up. Knowing that he couldn't wait much longer, he began to look around for a job in New York, and he also redoubled his efforts to write at home. Lacking the time to do a Really Good story, he started one about travelling with a baby, on which he was a qualified authority. Remembering his trips to and from Worcester and Millbury with Petey, he started off: "In America there are two classes of travel—first class, and with children. Travelling with children corresponds roughly to travelling third class in Bulgaria." Becoming more specific, he went on:

> Those who have taken a very small baby on a train maintain that this ranks as pleasure along with having a nerve killed. On the other hand, those whose wee companions are in the romping stage simply laugh at the claims of the first group. Sometimes you will find a man who has both an infant *and* a romper with him. Such a citizen should receive a salute of twenty-one guns every time he enters the city and should be allowed to wear the insignia of the Pater Dolorosa, giving him the right to solicit alms on the cathedral steps.

He was surprised to find that, although this was not as difficult as the Really Good writing, it seemed to read better when he was through, and it required almost no rewriting. He was pondering the significance of this revelation when another telegram arrived from Allen, calling him to Washington for an interview with Howard Coffin, the chairman of the Aircraft Board.

The second trip to Washington was more encouraging. Coffin was an extremely agreeable gentleman, who outlined to Robert the duties of publicity man for the Board, and said that the meeting of the Board the next day would get the matter settled. The next day, however, the Board adjourned without taking up Robert's case, so he returned to New York to wait.

On January 3, 1918, he received a telegram from Washington, confirming his appointment and ordering him to get down there as soon as possible. He and Gertrude looked around the house, trying to decide what to pack and what to leave. Gertrude and Petey would have to go to Worcester until Robert could find a place for them in Washington—*if* he could find one—and the only economically sound thing they could do would be to try to sublet the house. They got out the trunks, and began to pack with the odd feeling that they were seeing everything for the last time.

Two days later, in the teeth of the coldest weather since 1880, the hot-water boiler sprang a leak, and at 6:30 A.M. Robert was forced to dump the furnace fire—the first time in his life that he had put out a fire intentionally. As the house grew slowly colder, the exercise of packing was no longer sufficient for warmth, and the family bundled up into coats, mufflers, and mittens, and finally moved over to the Stileses', which they used as a base for the final work. At 8:30 that night, after Robert had taken the last package from the house and, with a sentimental feeling of finality, had turned out the yellow light by the bookcase, he closed the door behind him and gave it a small tug to make sure it was locked. Petey was awakened, and bundled into his warmest clothes, and then, with the help of the Stileses and their sled, the Benchley family skidded and slipped down the ringing, icy hill to the station.

Robert had occasion, that night, to realize how well he had written in his travelling-with-children piece. They had a stateroom on the 11:15 for Worcester, and although Petey had been riding trains since he was three months old, this was the first time he had been able to make coherent comment on all the wonders of midnight train travel. At the first soft, magical sensation of movement, he looked out of the window and saw "Muddie's bed going," and no matter how many times he looked out during the night (an estimated hundred and thirty-seven), he made the same astonished, delighted exclamation. He was the official lookout, the guide, and the commentator, and if anything escaped his attention during that night, it was only because it slipped past while he was discoursing on something else. What irritation Robert may have felt was mitigated by the fact that he was already beginning to miss his family, and the thought of an indefinite separation filled him with an aching gloom. It was only by reminding himself that a lot of other men were much more drastically separated from their families that he was able to put up with it at all. He knew he was lucky, but that didn't make him like it. It just made him know better than to complain.

Loring Coes was by this time doing patrol duty as a machinist's mate in the Navy, and Gertrude and Petey were ensconced with Kay Coes and her children in the Coeses' large, grey Worcester house. There was a portcullis, and an iron stag, and the lawn dropped away into a hill that was perfect for sliding, and Robert's mind was eased by the knowledge that Gertrude and Petey would be happy and well taken care of. After a couple of days of doing last-minute odds and ends, he took the train for New York and then on to Washington, arriving four days earlier than he had said he would.

By today's standards, Robert would undoubtedly not have been hired by the government, because his ideas differed so sharply from those of the administration. Luckily, the only questionnaire he had to fill out was one asking him to state his qualifications for the job, which he was required to submit to the Civil Service Commission before he could draw his first pay cheque. He started right to work as the press representative of the Aircraft Board, and was briefed on all the secret data about the production of airplanes and airplane engines. Before long, it was obvious that his job would be more that of a censor than a press agent. There wasn't a great deal to cheer about.

The main trouble was that, a short while back, an enthusiastic but visionary official had loudly promised that this country would deliver 100,000 airplanes during the year 1918. The facts, as Mr. Coffin told them to Robert, were that if we could maintain 5,000 planes at the front, we would be doing better than all the rest of the Allies put together, and that so far all we had produced were training planes. On the cheerful side, the training planes were coming out according to schedule, and the production of fighter planes would begin within the month; also, the famous Liberty engine, contrary to the many rumours of its being a lemon, was a definite success. It turned out 450 horsepower, which, in view of its weight, was considered little short of spectacular.

Robert's first job was to write to all the newspapers that ran stories knocking the Liberty engine, and tell them that it was *so* a success. As an initial step, he subscribed to a clipping service, which he did without waiting for the various official O.K.'s, but when he tried to get a scrapbook to put the clippings in, he ran into a little trouble. He found that he was not allowed to buy less than a half-dozen scrapbooks, and that he could get them only from a certain firm in New York. And, in order to get an Ayer's Newspaper Directory, he had to get three concerns to submit bids. Baffled but amenable, he proceeded according to routine, and accomplished nothing in particular. The military members of the Aircraft Board were against any publicity, and issued a directive that no news should be given out unless under a written order from the Chief Signal Officer (since military aviation had at first been thought of only in terms of observation, it was under the Signal Corps), so Robert had to call Signal Corps officers even for stories about carrier pigeons. He tried this kind of thing for a while, and got nowhere, so he finally started clearing pigeon and propeller stories on his own, and nobody seemed to mind.

Ernest Gruening, his friend from Boston, was on the War Trade Board, and in February he told Robert of an available rental next to the house he had taken in Chevy Chase, in Maryland. It was the ground floor of a house, and it was unfurnished except for a couple of seedy bedsteads and wicker chairs, but the rent was $40 a month, so Robert took it. The Gruenings had two children bracketing Petey's age; Ernest and Robert had a great deal in common and liked to talk far into the night; and life was once again congenial. In his spare time, Robert continued to do pieces for *Vanity Fair*, although some of Crowninshield's suggestions, such as the diary of the future woman President, were a little out of his line. He found that he had better success with the things that he knew, the run-of-the-mill, domestic things that happened every day.

There was, for instance, the matter of the furnace. The furnace in Chevy Chase was a great deal like the one in Crestwood and the one in Watertown, but it had the added feature of a collapsible grate bar, which would occasionally give way and dump the entire fire. This necessitated shovelling out the ashes and hot coals, separating the grate bar from them and letting it cool, and then, after the furnace had cooled down enough to admit a man's head and shoulders without inflicting second-degree burns, wriggling inside and jockeying the grate bar back into place. Robert eventually became so familiar, if not efficient, with the problems of the coal furnace that he wrote an article about it, and later a movie short. The article began:

> Considerable space has been given in the magazines and newspapers this winter to official and expert directions on How to Run Your Furnace and Save Coal—as if the two things were compatible. Some had accompanying diagrams of a furnace in its normal state, showing the exact position of the arteries and vitals, with arrows pointing in interesting directions, indicating the theoretical course of the heat. I have given some time to studying these charts, and have come to the conclusion that when the authors of such articles and I speak the word "furnace," we mean entirely different things. They are referring to some idealized, sublimated creation; perhaps the "furnace" which existed originally in the mind of Horace W. Furnace, the inventor; while, on the other hand, I am referring to the thing that is in my cellar. No wonder that I can't understand their diagrams.

When, eleven years later, he made the movie short about running a furnace, he innocently put in the script that Joe Doakes, the character whom he played, should bump his head on a beam as he went down into the cellar. He knew that the carpenters would make a rubber section in the beam for him to hit his head on, but he didn't know how difficult it would be to make the bumping look accidental; no matter how hard he tried, he flinched just before he hit the beam. The result was that they made retake after retake, all one afternoon, and by the time he finally got it done to the director's satisfaction, he had a lump on his forehead the size of a lemon. That taught him not to write physical violence into any script *he* acted in.

When spring brought a merciful end to his furnace problems, he and Gruening dug a small garden, in which they planted lettuce, chard, radishes, early peas, and parsley. The Crestwood sand dune had yielded a surprising percentage of the vegetables planted, and Robert reasoned that the Maryland clay should bring forth even more. They decided to make the garden small at first, as a test case, and then plant a much bigger one when they saw what kind of vegetables did the best. As it turned out, neither of them got to start the larger garden.

With everything else that it brought, the spring also brought trouble for the Aircraft Board. Just as a starter, a cable arrived from General Pershing in France, saying that all the newspaper talk about the "100,000 airplanes" had succeeded in making the Germans speed up their aircraft production, and he would thank whoever was doing the talking to knock it off. It was Robert's job to answer the cable. Then, in spite of a February announcement by the Secretary of War that the first fighter planes were "on their way," the Providence *Journal* ran a story the end of March, saying that only one battle plane had been shipped to France, and that that was not a fighter plane, but a two-seater De Haviland observation plane. The Associated Press reported that German planes were flying over the American lines with no opposition whatsoever, and everywhere there were stories that the aviation programme was being bungled. In order to refute those stories that were untrue, Robert pleaded with Maj. Stedman Hanks, the Signal Corps liaison officer, to tell him at least *something* concrete, because it was impossible to stall off the reporters with generalities. Hanks took the position that they ought to be able to order the papers not to print such stories, so Robert got little help from that quarter.

Then one day, when Robert was telling reporters the only affirmative story that the Signal Corps would permit—that the production of Curtiss JN-4 training planes was zooming along according to schedule—an air cadet, recently up from training in Texas, passed through the room on his way to see a girl in the office, and he stopped and listened to Robert with growing amazement and anger. The next day the girl, a Miss Harvey, wrote Robert a confidential note, quoting her aviator friend as saying that, at Ellington Field where he was stationed, there were *not* enough planes to learn to fly in, that what few they had were faulty and were killing boys every day, that morale at the field was at rock bottom, and that Robert really ought to learn the facts before he gave anything out to the press. Robert wrote a report on conditions as they had been described to him, and forwarded it to Major Hanks for relay to the interested parties. He never heard from it again.

Then, in April, a Senate investigating committee condemned the aircraft programme as a failure, and on April 24 Mr. Coffin announced that he was being replaced as chairman of the Board by John D. Ryan, the "copper king." Mr. Ryan's policy was to keep from giving out any news whatsoever unless it was absolutely unavoidable, which made Robert's job more or less a phantom one.

Almost the only positive thing he did in his whole Washington career, aside from the futile memorandum about Ellington Field, was to clear a story for the *American Machinist* about the airplane production programme. The writer had spent a long time getting the story, all with official supervision, and Robert knew that if it was submitted through channels for final clearance it might not get printed for months. So, without a shred of authority, he O.K.'d the story, which was, as far as he could tell, both accurate and harmless. He remarked that "I may be shot for it, but at least one man can't complain of red tape."

Ernest Gruening had, in the meantime, gone to New York as managing editor of the *Tribune*. On May 1, at his suggestion, Robert agreed to take a job as editor of the *Tribune Graphic*, the forerunner of the Sunday rotogravure section. His pay would be $75 a week, with the promise of a raise to $100 after a couple of months. Since his work in Washington had dwindled to practically nothing, he felt no compunctions about leaving the job. Also, with Gruening as managing editor of the *Tribune*, he felt that he and the paper might come a little closer to seeing eye to eye about things. It was a naïve thought, but a pleasant one.

His resignation, on May 4, was completely friendly, and he offered to come back any time he was needed, either to unscramble the files or, if it was ever decided to resume active publicity for the aircraft programme, to take up his job again. Then, leaving the family in Chevy Chase until he could find a new temporary home (the house in Crestwood had been sublet until late September), he took off on the midnight for New York and his fourth job in twelve months. With more acumen than he knew, he wrote:

> I have now, after many buffetings, reached a calloused state where I don't look ahead to a permanent holding of any one job for more than six months. And, from what I know of the *Tribune*, I am not in for long. Hi-ho!

Hi-ho indeed. Within ten weeks, he was looking for another job.

Gruening and his family had settled in Bay Shore for the summer, and he put Robert onto a house which, although it was almost a two-hour trip on the Long Island Railroad, had nevertheless such a pleasant salt breeze blowing through it that he decided to take it for the season. He got Gertrude and Petey (now called Nat) and installed them in the house, and began a summer of long-distance commuting.

For the first month, his job at the *Tribune* went deceptively well. The *Graphic* was a twelve-page picture section, several pages of which were taken up by advertisements, and it was Robert's job to buy the pictures, do the layout, and write the captions. The only really difficult part was the so-called "Field of Honour" page, which was devoted to pictures of local boys who had been killed in action, and it was his feeling that it was impossible to do such a page well. He nevertheless did what he could with it, and he was somewhat stunned one day when Rogers, the general manager who had fired him by remote control, complimented him on one of his captions. It was the first time, in all the months he had been with the *Tribune*, that Rogers had spoken to him, and he began to wonder if some subtle change had crept into the paper.

It hadn't. Early in June, he and Gruening had decided to run what they thought was an effective plea for racial tolerance. The idea was as sriking as it was simple: On the top half of a full page, they ran a picture of Negro troops being decorated for bravery in France, and on the bottom half was a long shot (with no unpleasant details) of a lynching in Georgia. The page went to press on June 7, and the first copy hadn't been upstairs more than three minutes when there was a dropping of pencils, a ringing of bells, and then a great, clanking sigh as the presses ground to an emergency stop. Robert was summoned down to the office of Garet Garrett, the assistant editor, and there he found Garrett, Rogers, and Ogden Reid, the editor in chief, standing in a semicircle and looking with frozen horror at the lynching picture. He was told that it was "pro-German," that it was a terrible thing to run "at this time," and that he would damned well get another picture to replace it, because the Alco Company had already been notified to make a new press cylinder. Robert hunted up an innocuous picture of some horses that would fit the space, and then went to see Gruening. He and Ernest were sure that they had been right in trying to run the page, so they didn't feel too badly; but

Robert said he knew, from the way Rogers and Garrett had looked at him, that they were out to get him.

This was apparently confirmed, when Garrett began to criticize Robert's choice of pictures with remarkable vigour. He doubted the validity of a crowd picture in Berlin, saying that there were too many young men out of uniform in it, and that it was therefore an old one, taken before the war. He and Gruening had a long argument about a picture of the Kaiser that Robert had run, Garrett maintaining that to show the Kaiser as a normal human being, walking down the street, tended to weaken the public's hate for him. The policy was that any picture that showed a German who was not cutting off a child's hand was a bad picture. Gruening disagreed violently, and told Garrett exactly what he thought of such a policy, but it had no effect. Three days later, Garrett pounced on a picture that Robert had scheduled for Page 1 of the section, showing a U-boat crew picking up survivors of a ship they had torpedoed. This, it seemed, was as good as a pro-German picture, because they weren't machine-gunning the survivors, so in the interest of what little harmony was left, Robert killed it. He found out that Garrett had written to Washington, asking if the Dutch picture agent named Moussault, from whom Robert had been buying pictures, might not be a German propagandist, so Robert wrote to Capt. Grant Squires, of the local Army Intelligence office, for a little information of his own. Captain Squires called him the next day, and said that he personally passed on all Moussault's pictures, and that, so long as the spirit of the official captions was adhered to, there should be no trouble.

But at a time when people were calling sauerkraut "Liberty cabbage," a man with an implied umlaut in his name had a pretty thin time of it. On July 13, Robert and Gruening took the 8:10 train from Bay Shore together, and Ernest recounted how, the night before, Garrett and Rogers had called him in and told him that his further presence on the paper would be "embarrassing," owing to certain rumours of his pro-German tendencies, and to the fact that he had lived in the next apartment to Dr. Edward A. Rumely, publisher of the *Evening Mail*, who had just been arrested for running a German-owned newspaper. There had been no chance for Gruening to clear himself; he was told that he was through, and that was that.

When he got to the paper, Robert went straight to his office and, with a certain amount of relish, wrote out three copies of the following:

Mr. Ogden Reid
Mr. Rogers
Mr. Garrett

Gentlemen:

Without any rational proof that Dr. Gruening was guilty of the burlesque charges made against him (except the heinous one of living at 324 West 103d St.) you took steps, which on the slightest examination could have been proven unwarranted, to smirch the character and newspaper career of the first man in three years who has been able to make the *Tribune* look like a newspaper.

I haven't the slightest idea who is boss on this sheet, so I am sending this resignation to three whom I suspect.

Robert C. Benchley

He later said that the copy boy carrying his resignation passed the one coming with his discharge, but this was not strictly true; he was undoubtedly slated for a discharge, but he beat them to the draw with his letters. He then packed up a few things, called a friend on the Liberty Loan to see if there was a job for him there, and then left the paper by way of the city room. There he found Dennis Lynch, the reporter who had been assigned to collect the "evidence" against Gruening, and he told Lynch a number of things for his own good. He also had a violent argument with an editorial writer who wanted to bet that Gruening would be in jail within a year. Robert took the bet, and then slammed out of the *Tribune* and went to the Harvard Club.

Far from going to jail, Gruening was publicly cleared the next day by the Department of Justice and by Army Intelligence. After entering a $32,000 slander suit against the *Tribune*, he enlisted in the Field Artillery and went down to Camp Zachary Taylor, in Kentucky, for training, and he was in line for a commission when the war ended. He subsequently rated a four-and-a-half inch biography in *Who's Who*, among his accomplishments being Governor of Alaska for fourteen consecutive years.

As for Robert, he went back to Bay Shore, where he passed Bastille Day wondering what his next job would be like.

8 His next job was with the Liberty Loan, and he stayed with it for almost nine months. The Fourth Liberty Loan raised something over six billion dollars, and it was Robert's duty, as a member of the press section, to solicit articles publicizing the Loan, and to get these articles placed in various national magazines. As a starter, he went through all the current magazines, to see which authors were the favourite of which editors, and thereby know where to go when he got a contribution from a certain author. He also wrote captions for Liberty Bond posters, editorials for camp papers, and signs to be hung on the captured German cannons that were dragged around in Liberty Bond parades. A lot of it was hyperthyroid writing, with little subtlety and no humour, but he swallowed his scruples in the interest of the cause.

He also swallowed, or at least kept under control, his thoughts about war in general. One time, in Washington, he had been dismayed to find that a certain man, whose ideas on the subject were pretty much his own, had sounded remarkably shallow and fuzzy in stating his case, and as he thought back it occurred to him that all the pacifists shared a certain looseness of thought. Rather than sound like the rest of them, which he was afraid he did, he kept quiet. Or relatively quiet. The thing was such a burning obsession with him that he couldn't keep it completely under control, but he no longer tried to convert people to his way of thinking. He knew that he was beaten, and he didn't want to make a fool of himself into the bargain.

Monday, November 11, began at 4 A.M. in Crestwood, when the Stileses and Benchleys were awakened by the sound of whistles, echoing eerily through the darkness. The noise was different from the bull-like groan of the Tuckahoe fire alarm, although that was bellowing in the background too, and suddenly they realized that this was the real Armistice, as distinct from the false, or United Press, Armistice of the previous Thursday. There was no more sleep in either house, and at the first light both families, with the children (David Stiles having been born in August), went across the street to the fire gong. A group of neighbours gathered and stood in line, while each person took his turn at the sledge hammer, crashing it against the steel hoop and producing a furious, vibrating, bonging noise; which filled the air almost like rain. The children, unable to hold the hammer, were lifted in their mothers' arms and touched the smooth wooden handle, while their fathers hit the gong for them. (Twenty-six years later, during World War II, Robert sent Nat a birthday cablegram overseas that said, MAYBE YOU DIDN'T RING THAT GONG HARD ENOUGH, and the Navy cable censor at Coca Sola suspected it might be secret code. Nat's reply: WHAT DID YOU EXPECT FROM A THREE-YEAR-OLD—BELGIAN CHIMES? convinced him, and there was all hell to pay.)

Robert and Gertrude had been married fifty-five days before war broke out in Europe; to celebrate their fifty-sixth day free from the shadow of war, she went in town November 12 and Robert bought her a winter coat and hat at Arnold Constable's, and then they got some presents for Nat's birthday the next day, and after that they had lunch at Henri's. Gertrude took the 2:35 back to Crestwood, and Robert went over to *Vanity Fair* and picked up a cheque that didn't quite cover the day's expenditures. That day, it didn't matter what he spent; there was a clean feeling in the air, and he felt as though there might once more be some point in planning toward the future.

The Armistice threw the Liberty Loan office into a state of confusion amounting to stupor. The Fifth Loan had already been started, but nobody, not even Washington, knew what the plans were going to be for continuing the drive. The result was that nobody did anything except sit around and wait for the word that seemed never to come.

One thing he did was catch cold, and this was considered a serious thing that November, because of the flu epidemic that was raging all around. Gertrude called the doctor, and told him that Robert had been going to the theatre a lot lately, so the doctor diagnosed the cold as "a touch of influenza" and, much to Robert's horror, prescribed a tablespoon of whisky every three hours. He protested that it was just a case of snuffles, but there was no getting out of it, and for two days he moped around the house, gagging down his whisky and insisting that it was only making him feel worse. At the end of two days, the cold was better, but he had developed a rum blossom on the end of his nose, and he continued to maintain that he had been perfectly all right until the doctor came around.

And his health wasn't the only problem. There was always the furnace. The grate bar not only fell out, but broke in two one Saturday night, and Robert had to keep the fire going all Sunday by necromancy, faith, and a great deal of coal, carefully deposited. The next day, he went to the American Radiator Company for a new grate bar, and got home to find the fire raging so fiercely that it took him some time to kill it, and several hours for the furnace to cool down enough for him to crawl inside. And it was, of course, only then that he found that the new grate bar didn't fit. Somehow, he was never quite sure how, he made it fit, probably through the blind power of rage.

Oddly enough, 1918 was Robert's best year, financially speaking. He made a total of $5,125, on which he paid a Federal tax of $160, and 1919 saw him, for the first time, beginning to creep out of debt. Also, Deems Taylor, who had moved over to *Collier's*, had him to lunch with William LeBaron, the managing editor, one day in January, and they suggested that he do a series of pieces to appeal to out-of-town readers, pieces about home-life happenings, with himself as the poor boob. His reply was "Done and done!" and he went to work on the project almost immediately. It was the kind of writing that he knew he could do, and the ideas came easily to him. At the age of twenty-nine, he knew a great deal about domestic life in suburbia.

As far as he was concerned, everything about 1919 was good. The war was over, he had assignments to do the kind of writing he liked, he was almost financially solvent (which was especially good because Gertrude was expecting another baby), and—wonder of wonders—the thirty-sixth state ratified the Eighteenth Amendment to the Constitution, and Prohibition was to go into effect in just one year! Robert confided to his diary that he had never thought that he would "live to see this step taken toward Eutopia" (his spelling), and he worried only that the liquor industry might be successful in challenging the constitutionality of the amendment. "It is almost too good to be true," he concluded.

His only minor dissatisfaction was with his job, and that was because he knew that he wasn't being particularly efficient. The brief spurt of activity that followed the post-Armistice slump levelled off after a couple of months, and soon all that Robert was doing was collecting reports and rustling memoranda. He had a small jolt of alarm the end of January, when he found out that he was under consideration for the job of editor of the *Harvard Alumni Bulletin*, and he suddenly realized that he no longer yearned to go back to Boston. In fact, he dreaded the idea of ever leaving New York again; Boston's State Street, where he had worked for more than a year with the Russell Company, now appeared to him to be "dark and Bourbonic." As it turned out, he needn't have worried; he was turned down because he was (*a*) not a resident of Boston, and (*b*) suspected of having liberal leanings.

For several months, Crowninshield had been making small, chirruping noises about the managing-editorship of *Vanity Fair*, but nothing had ever come of it. Then, in March, Deems Taylor left his job as associate editor of *Collier's*, and LeBaron offered it to Robert. With this as a lever, he went to

Crowninshield, and Crowninshield told him to come back that afternoon for an interview with Condé Nast. At 4:30 Robert returned, and Crowninshield took him into Nast's elegant, softly glistening office. Nast asked him if he would be in sympathy with the idea of injecting a little more serious stuff in the magazine, and he replied, "Sure," and when Nast asked him if all the detail work would be agreeable to him, he said, "Sure," again; so Nast said, "Then I think it would be ideal for you to come in as managing editor," and that was that. They settled on $100 a week as pay, and May 19 as a starting date, and the understanding was that Robert could do two pieces a month for outside publications. The whole thing seemed to be perfect.

On May 19, as he took the 9:07 in for his new job, he reflected that it had more earmarks of permanence than anything he had done since the old *Tribune Magazine*. He realized that *Vanity Fair* did not represent a very substantial contribution toward Progress, but he felt financially safe for the first time in his career, and he saw no reason why he couldn't contribute to Progress on the side. There was a bowl of roses on his desk when he arrived, and everything was very homelike and congenial. He spent the day finishing a piece he had started, called "The Community Masque as a Substitute for War." The opening went:

With War and Licker removed from the list of "What's Going on This Week," how will mankind spend the long summer evenings? Some advocate another war. Others recommend a piece of yeast in a glass of grape-juice. The effect is said to be equally devastating.

He then went on to say that "whenever a neighbourhood, or a country, feels the old craving for blood-letting and gas-bombing coming on, a town meeting is to be called and plans drawn up for the presentation of a masque entitled 'Democracy' or 'From Chrysalis to Butterfly.' " The typical masque, as he outlined it, would be called "The March of Civilization," because "it calls for Boy Scout uniforms and a Goddess of Liberty costume, all of which are on hand, together with lots of Red Cross regalia, left over from the war drives." The more he wrote on the piece, the more he was aware that there were things he could now say that would have been considered too frivolous a year ago, and he had a magnificent time with it. The summary of the masque started out:

> The plot concerns the adventures of the young girl *Civilization* who leaves her home in the *Neolithic Period* accompanied only by her faithful old nurse *Language* and *Language's* little children, the *Vowels* and the *Consonants*. She is followed all the way from the *Neolithic Age* to the Present Time by the evil spirit, *Indigestion*, but, thanks to the helpful offices of *Spirits of Capillary Attraction*, and *Indestructibility of Matter*, she overcomes all obstacles and reaches her goal, *The League of Nations*, at last.

After a lot of involved subplot, the summary concludes:

> She takes counsel with the kind old lady, *Self-determination of Peoples*, and is considerably helped by the low-comedy character, *Obesity*, who always appears at just the right moment. So in the end, there is a big ensemble, involving Boy Scouts, representatives of those Allies who happen to be in good standing in that particular month, seven boys and girls personifying the twelve months of the year, Red Cross workers, the Mayor's Committee of Welcome, a selection of Major Prophets, children typifying the ten different ways of cooking an egg, and the all-pervading *Spirit of the Post-office Department*, seated on a dais in the rear and watching over the assemblage with kindly eyes and an armful of bricks.

He took time out for lunch at the Coffee House with Crowninshield, and finished the piece late in the afternoon.

He then wrote a caption for a picture of Houdini, and got the 5:37 for Crestwood, as happy with a job as he had been in many years.

Two days later, all six feet seven inches of Robert Emmet Sherwood wandered into the office. He was shy and quiet, and when he talked it was very slowly, but he wore his straw hat at a slightly rakish angle, and there was a quality about him that suggested that he might not be quite as timid as he at first appeared. He was twenty-three, and had left Harvard in his junior year to join the Canadian Black Watch, from which he was discharged after being hospitalized for gas poisoning and wounds in both legs. (He never explained how, with so much of him above the ground to shoot at, the Germans managed to hit him where they did, but he hotly denied Robert's theory that he was lying on his back and waving his feet in the air.) *Vanity Fair* hired him, at $25 a week, for a three-month trial period, during which he was technically called drama editor, but actually was a kind of maid-of-all-work around the office.

The drama critic, as opposed to the drama editor, was a Mrs. Edwin Parker, nee Dorothy Rothschild, who had joined the Condé Nast Publications as a staff member at *Vogue*, for $10 a week, and had been transferred to *Vanity Fair* when it became apparent that her ideas about fashion writing were not those of the management. She contributed satirical verse and, in all, about eighty pieces to the magazine, and she succeeded P. G. Wodehouse as critic when he left for an extended trip to Europe. Sometimes she signed herself Helène Rousseau, but more often her by-line was Dorothy Parker. She was small—standing not much, if anything, over five feet even—but her eyes were large and dark, and they peered wistfully out from beneath the drape effect in which her brown hair was parted. When she and Sherwood and Robert went down the street together, their assorted sizes made them look like a walking pipe organ.

It was, as a matter of fact, in their line of duty as a sort of convoy for Sherwood that Robert and Mrs. Parker got to know him well. The *Vanity Fair* office was on 44th Street, not far from the Hippodrome, where a troupe of particularly unpleasant midgets happened to be playing. If any of them chanced to spot Sherwood walking down the street alone, the whole mob of midgets would come scampering after him, nibbling at his knees, jeering at him, and asking him how the weather was up there. As a result, Sherwood wouldn't go out to lunch alone, and he took to asking Robert and Mrs. Parker if they would mind walking on either side of him, at least until they had got past the midgets. This led to the three of them having lunch together every day, either at the Algonquin or at a local Childs or wherever, and long after the midgets had left town, Mr. Sherwood and Mrs. Parker and Mr. Benchley were an inseparable trio. They worked, they played, and they talked long hours together, and they almost without exception referred to each other as Mr. Sherwood, Mrs. Parker, and Mr. Benchley. The only exceptions were that Sherwood and Robert called each other Rob (which nobody else did), and Mrs. Parker called Robert Fred, when she didn't call him Mr. Benchley. And, like so many people who sit around and talk, they decided to write a play together. Since both Robs had worked on Hasty Pudding shows, it seemed logical to make it a musical. That was about as far as it got.

The Robs became close enough friends so that Benchley had no fear of offending Sherwood about his height, and was not above making a joke about it, if the occasion seemed right. And a man who was game for any kind of joke was Marc Connelly, an ex-reporter and budding playwright who had been stranded in New York with the collapse of a show he had brought up from Pittsburgh, and who was waiting around, doing free-lance writing and thinking up another play. Connelly also lunched at the Algonquin, and was around some of the haunts frequented by Benchley and Sherwood, and one day the three of them were walking down the street, with Sherwood in the middle, when a sandwich man on stilts approached them from the opposite direction. Immediately, and on some unspoken cue, Benchley and Connelly squatted down, looked up at Sherwood, and said, "Hey, mister, what are *you* advertising?" The passers-by were convulsed with laughter, but Sherwood didn't think it was particularly funny. He was, however, nice enough not to make an issue of it. Just by falling on them, he could have crushed the two of them flat.

Two years earlier, on his first tour of duty at the *Tribune*, Robert had run across an undertaker's magazine called *The Casket*. It interested him, partially because of his research into the subject for his school and college themes, and partially because the magazine contained, aside from some fetching charts and diagrams, a feature page entitled "Underground Novelties," and a joke column called "From Grave to Gay." He now wrote in and took a subscription, and also wrote for another, similar magazine called *Sunnyside*, in one issue of which was a picture of a corpse, done up in full dress and propped in a corner holding a cane, over the caption: "In life they called him Jim." When the magazines arrived, he clipped selected bits from them and passed them on to Mrs. Parker, and she put them up over her desk. When Crowninshield suggested that this display might startle or offend the occasional visitors to the office, and that a Marie Laurencin original might fill the space more decorously, Mrs. Parker turned away with such withering scorn that he never mentioned the subject again.

With his suggestions to Robert he had a little, although not much, better luck. Robert had done a piece called "The Social Life of the Newt," and in one paragraph had described, as innocuously as possible, the mating habits of that diminutive animal. (It is only fair to point out that no newt could have distinguished it from an account of a rare-book auction; it was Robert's idea, and his alone, of newt courtship.) Crowninshield was afraid that some of *Vanity Fair's* more sensitive readers might be dismayed by a description of any kind of contact between newts, and he therefore asked Robert if there wasn't some way of rewording it—some way that would be sure not to give any kind of offence. Robert gave him a long look, and then went back to his typewriter and came up with the following paragraph:

The peculiar thing about a newt's courtship is its restraint. It is carried on, at all times, with a minimum distance of fifty paces (newt measure) between the male and the female. Some of the bolder males may now and then attempt to overstep the bounds of good sportsmanship and crowd in to forty-five paces, but such tactics are frowned on by the Rules Committee. To the eye of an uninitiated observer, the pair might be dancing a few of the more open figures of the minuet.

Nobody is quite sure what gave Crowninshield and Nast the courage to think that they could go to Europe and leave the entire publication of *Vanity Fair* in Robert's hands, but they did, and two issues were put out by the team of Sherwood, Parker, and Benchley. One of Sherwood's jobs was to fill any space that ran short; for $25 a week, he would add twenty-seven lines to a piece by G. K. Chesterton, or insert a paragraph or two to pad out Grantland Rice's copy. (His first trial period of three months having been successfully weathered, he was started on another trial period at the same salary.) With Crowninshield and Nast away, it seemed like the ideal time for him to start out as a writer of his own material, so he wrote a piece and Benchley bought it, for $75. Not only were the top brass away, but the writer of the "What the Well-dressed Man Will Wear" department went on his vacation with half of the column unwritten, so with fiendish delight Sherwood finished the column for him. Several advertisers kicked up a ruckus, but the only person they could complain to was Benchley, and a fat lot of good *that* did them.

The trio had such a fine time on their own that they were

a little sorry when Crowninshield and Nast returned. This in no way lessened their affection for Crowninshield, and as a welcome-home present for him they went shopping around Broadway and Sixth Avenue, and decorated his tastefully appointed office with the most garish banners, placards, and pictures they could find. For a number of reasons, they left Nast's office alone.

Robert and Gertrude weren't quite sure why, but they knew in advance that the new baby was going to be a girl, and they decided to call her Barbara. Her estimated time of arrival was September 1, but that estimate was sharply revised in the early morning of August 26. At 8:30, Robert took Gertrude in a taxi to the hospital in Bronxville, and then, since she was having no pain, he went in town to take care of a few necessary things at the office. He had lunch at the Harvard Club, where Lincoln MacVeagh, of Henry Holt and Company, talked to him about the possibility of gathering some of his pieces together in book form. At two o'clock, he called the hospital and was told that nothing at all was happening, so he took the 3:24 out, buying flowers and magazines and preparing himself for a long wait. He was not in the coma that a first-time father gets into, and he knew what to expect and how to prepare for it. Gertrude was asleep when he arrived, so he settled down in a chair across the room, and began to read. A nurse looked in, then disappeared and came back a few minutes later, carrying a small baby. She held it out for Robert to inspect, and he, thinking that he was going to have to look at every new baby on the floor, gave it a perfunctory chuck under the chin. "Cute little thing," he whispered. "Whose is it?"

"It's yours," the nurse replied.

"*What?*" Robert shouted.

Gertrude sat up like a jack-in-the-box, and looked at Robert's incredulous face. "Didn't you know you had another son?" she asked.

He shook his head. "I never had a baby so easily in all my life," he said.

That part of it may have been easy, but the matter of a name was something else again. Since Barbara was obviously out, and since they had given no thought at all to boys' names, he was tentatively referred to as Robert Junior. Robert wasn't particularly happy with this, and thought Gale might be a nice middle name, but nobody ever did anything about it, and for the first few months of his life the younger son was referred to as Young Benchley, then as Bub, and then, when he had grown so chunky that he resembled an Irish washerwoman, as Annie. Shortly after his twenty-fourth birthday, he was christened Robert Benchley, Jr. He subsequently had a son, Robert Benchley III, known only as Chub. Nat's first son, christened Bradford, was called Pete so much that his name was legally changed. Before he was called Pete, Bradford was called Paddington Station. Nat's second son, Nathaniel Robert, was known as Whistle Stop. For some reason, no Benchley ever seems to come by his right name easily. Robert Senior dropped the Charles from his name around 1923, for reasons of numerology. This caused considerable trouble when Robert Junior got to college, because Harvard said that they had his father listed as Robert Charles Benchley and it was therefore impossible for him to be Robert Benchley, Jr.; he had to be Robert *Charles* Benchley, Jr. He wrote them a stiff reply and signed it Robert Gale Benchley, Jr., and that was the end of that, except that they put him on probation.

Basically, the Nast organization was not geared to handle a group like Sherwood, Parker, and Benchley, and eventually the strain began to show. It was what Robert described as the ultimate "whited sepulchre," steeped in an aura of unutterable elegance, in which the employees were expected to dress the part, although they were treated like serfs by the business management and, in general, paid that way as well. Crowninshield was kind and gentle and a delight to work for, but he had to follow the dictates of the publisher, and there were certain times where he was powerless to prevent policies that he knew would lead to trouble. There was, for instance, an office efficiency manager, named Francis Lewis Wurzburg, who was forever issuing memorandums, some of which could most accurately be described as Prussian. One, dated October 14, 1919, ran as follows:

POLICY MEMORANDUM

Forbidding Discussion Among Employees of Salary Received

It has been the policy of the organization to base salaries on the value of the service rendered. We have, therefore, a long established rule that the salary question is a confidential matter between the organization and individual.

It is obviously important that employees carefully live up to this rule in order to avoid invidious comparison and dissatisfaction. Recently several cases have come to the notice of the management where employees have discussed the salary question among themselves.

This memorandum should serve as a warning that anyone who breaks this rule in the future will be instantly discharged.

The day that memorandum was distributed, Sherwood and Parker and Benchley went into action. The first thing they did was decide to answer the memorandum with one of their own, which Robert wrote and which went:

POLICY MEMORANDUM

Concerning the Forbidding of Discussion Among Employees

We emphatically resent both the policy and wording of your policy memorandum of October 14. We resent being told what we may and what we may not discuss, and we protest against the spirit of petty regulation which has made possible the sending out of such an edict.

We especially call your attention to the wording of the last paragraph, regarding the "instant" discharge of employees violating this new regulation, and would eagerly inquire if *our* obligations under the contracts we have been asked to sign are as elastic as those of the management are here construed as being.

They then made signs, on which they wrote their salaries, and went through the office wearing the signs around their necks. That was the end of the no-talking-about-your-salary policy.

Then there was the matter of the "tardy" slips. Employees were expected to be in the office at 8:50 A.M., so as to be at their desks, ready to work, by 9, and it was Wurzburg's idea to require anyone who was late to fill out a printed slip, explaining his tardiness. One day, when Robert had been about eleven minutes late, he received a slip and, in his smallest handwriting, covered every square millimetre of space on both sides of the card with his excuse. He had been coming along 44th Street from Grand Central, he said, when he had seen a large crowd in front of the Hippodrome. Inquiring as to what the excitement was, he was told that the Hippodrome elephants had escaped, and that there was a call out for all civic-minded citizens to help round them up, lest they trample helpless women and children in the streets. Obviously, he could not ignore such a call, so he pitched in with a few others to help round up the elephants, a task that took him up Fifth Avenue, once around the Plaza, and then up and through Central Park at 72d Street, after which the elephants crossed over to West End Avenue and seemed headed for the Hudson River. With almost superhuman effort, Robert managed to divert them and get them going south, and they came down Twelfth Avenue and then swung over toward the docks, apparently looking for one of the boats of the Fall River Line. Again, all his knowledge of animals had to be brought into play in order to keep the elephants from getting aboard the ship, which would have been a major marine disaster had they succeeded, but in the end he triumphed, and got them coming back with the traffic along 44th Street, which luckily was eastbound. There was a little trumpeting and stalling before he finally got them into the Hippodrome, and what with everything, he found that he was eleven minutes late getting to the office. He never got a tardy slip again.

Gradually, as the gap between the trio and the management widened, Crowninshield began to find himself in the irritating position of being the go-between. He had to administer the official rebukes when copy was late, and it annoyed him that nobody seemed to take him very seriously. He liked them all personally, but he knew that their irreverent attitude was doing them no good and that sooner or later they would get into trouble. When Sherwood asked for a raise, at the end of his second three-month "trial" period, Crowninshield, in what was later described as "exquisite pussyfooting," told him that a raise was not only out of the question, but that Nast's daughter's music teacher was being considered for his job. Added to that, Mrs. Parker did not get a raise that she had expected, and it became clear that the group was badly out of favour. Instead of trying to get back into the Nast good graces, they became slightly truculent, and Robert and Mrs. Parker decided that this would be as good a time as any to get to work on their play. Letting Sherwood go his own way as a dramatist, they dreamed up a plot about a man who had an affair with a mousy, domestically inclined woman, in preference to his gay wife, and with that ingenious switch established, they settled down to do the work of writing. On their first—and almost last—day of actual work, they attended to a few office chores in the morning, and then, after lunch at the Algonquin, went back to *Vanity Fair* and got things lined up. A guest came in to see

Sherwood, which destroyed the privacy necessary for creation, so Robert and Mrs. Parker went in to Crowninshield's office, and had just closed the door when he came back from lunch. Next, they tried the Drama League library, but it was locked, and they went to the Roosevelt Coffee House, which was too stuffy, and to a friend's room, which was full of people, before Mrs. Parker finally said, "The hell with this —I'm going to buy some bloomers." She went over to Stern's and bought her bloomers, and then met Robert on the sofa in the lobby of the Algonquin, where they outlined the first scene of the play. They couldn't afford to spend much time on it after that, because Mrs. Parker was fired the following day.

It all happened because of the biting candour of her drama reviews. Discussing the acting of Billie Burke in a Maugham play called *Caesar's Wife*, she wrote: "Miss Burke is at her best in her more serious moments; in her desire to convey the girlishness of the character, she plays her lighter scenes rather as if she were giving an impersonation of Eva Tanguay." Not only did Miss Burke object loudly to this; her husband, Florenz Ziegfeld, also wrote to Crowninshield, and their letters arrived in practically the same mail as those from David Belasco, producer of *The Son-Daughter*, and Charles Dillingham, of *Apple Blossoms*, who were registering complaints about the way their plays had been treated. On Sunday, January 11, Crowninshield asked Mrs. Parker to meet him for tea and a little chat about her work, during the course of which he told her that it had been decided that she would not do the drama reviews any more; if she wanted to write little pieces at home and send them in, they'd love to print them, and maybe some agreement as to price could be worked out, and so on and so on. She said no, thank you, and that was that. She called Robert in Crestwood and told him what had happened, and the next day both Robert and Sherwood wrote out their resignations.

When Crowninshield read Robert's resignation, he called

him into his office for a talk. He was very quiet and grieved, but said he supposed it was the best thing for Robert to do, and that someday he would be very famous. He tried to explain that it had all happened because Mrs. Parker came in late mornings, but he didn't even pretend he thought Robert would believe it; it was simply an attempt to gloss the whole thing over as painlessly as possible. He had discussed the matter with Robert before seeing Mrs. Parker, and had gone ahead over Robert's violent objections, so although he tried officially to pretend that the complaints were not responsible, he knew that Robert knew the story. Later, in talking with Sherwood, Crowninshield said that he admired Robert's writing, and was sorry to see him go, but that, in all frankness, his stuff was mostly about suburbia, whereas *Vanity Fair* preferred the debutante's approach. Sherwood, Parker, and Benchley went to the Algonquin, where they announced their impending unemployment to their friends, and then, after a long and boisterous lunch, they returned to the *Vanity Fair* office and spent the afternoon laughing loudly at not much of anything. There had been a great deal of laughter and clowning in their office during the last eight months—Sherwood remembers the time as "one big blur of laughter" —but it was all different from the laughter on that particular day, which was just a shade too loud.

Two newspapers carried the story the next day, and although they printed the official reason, which was that Wodehouse was coming back to resume his duties as drama critic, they left no doubt as to what the real reason was. And three years later, in a review of Booth Tarkington's *Rose Briar* for *Life*, Robert wrote:

A few years ago a young dramatic critic lost her job for saying, among other disrespectful things, that Billie Burke had a tendency to fling herself coyly about like Eva Tanguay. Even in the face of this proof of divine vengeance, we apprehensively endorse the unfortunate young reviewer's judgment and assert that even after having her attention called to it three years ago, Miss Burke *still* flings herself coyly about like Eva Tanguay.

Applications for the job of dramatic reviewer on *Life* should be sent to the Managing Editor.

Sherwood and Mrs. Parker stayed on for two more weeks, and Robert stayed until the end of January, but nobody did much more than go through the motions of working. For a while, each of them wore a red chevron on the left sleeve, the symbol of troops who had been mustered out but were still in uniform, but they tired of that after a while, and just went quietly about their business. The last day they were all together, they ate a subdued luncheon at the Algonquin, and then Sherwood and Mrs. Parker went out to Mamaroneck to see about writing movie captions for D. W. Griffith, and Robert went back to the lonely office and wrote letters.

He had resolved to work for nobody but himself, and to that end he and Mrs. Parker rented a triangular cubbyhole on the third floor of the Metropolitan Opera House studios, at $30 a month. It was heated, and it had a window that looked down on Broadway, but it was so small that, as he later said, "one cubic foot less of space and it would have constituted adultery." They moved their undertakers' pamphlets and posters into the office, and on February 2 he settled down on his second try at serious free-lancing. The furniture consisted of two chairs, two kitchen tables, and a hatrack, and that was all. Contrary to popular supposition, they did *not* letter on the door "Utica Drop Forge and Tool Co., Robert Benchley, President; Dorothy Parker, President," nor did they apply for the cable address "Parkbench," nor did Mrs. Parker, after Robert moved into the office at *Life*, write "Men" on the door in order to see some new faces. Those stories grew up out of jokes and ideas (Mrs. Parker *did* write to a friend once, saying that unless someone came near her office—in Hollywood—she was going to have to write "Men" on the door) and the swirling mists of legend that surround anyone who becomes famous for funny sayings. By the same token, Robert never said, "Let's get out of these wet clothes and into a dry Martini," although there are people who will swear they were there when he said it. It was a joke in somebody's column, and a press agent picked it up and attributed it to Robert, and it stuck.

His free-lancing, in the new "office," consisted of writing advertising copy for the Logan agency on an aniline dye account, and reviewing books for the *New York World*. The *World* column, which he signed up for shortly after resigning from *Vanity Fair*, was called "Books and Other Things," and it paid him $100 a week, and the "other things" element in the title allowed him to branch out a little from straight book reviews. It was there, for instance, that he ran his "Christmas Afternoon," a satire done "in the manner, if not the spirit, of Dickens," which showed how there developed, following Christmas dinner, "an *ennui* which carried with it a retinue of yawns, snarls, and thinly veiled insults, and which ended in ruptures in the clan spirit serious enough to last throughout the glad new year." It wound up: "And, as Tiny Tim might say in speaking of Christmas afternoon as an institution, 'God help us, every one.' "

In the spring of 1920 Robert wrote out another resignation, and although it, like his resignation from *Vanity Fair*, was motivated by personal principles, its value as a gesture was lost because it was not immediately accepted. He had, for several years, been a member of the admissions committee of the Harvard Club, and back in October of 1919 a man named John Macy had been brought up and then held over, pending an investigation of charges of radicalism. He had, it appeared, written a book about socialism, and although he had found a great deal to criticize about socialism, the mere fact that he had written the book was considered suspicious. Also, he had written that violence in labour disputes was a matter of policy, not of ethics. Robert held his temper while Macy's name was brought up time after time, only to be put over for further investigation, and at each meeting there were fewer people against him. Finally, after a mass of letters from such influential alumni as Thomas W. Lamont, Eliot Wadsworth, and Edgar Wells had been received, all urging that a man's opinions be no bar to his membership to the club, there were only two holdouts. But these two were what Robert called the "intellectual pygmies" of the committee, and in a formal vote they could defeat the majority, so the vote was again postponed. After seven months of bickering, when the cause was lost, Robert wrote a violent letter of denunciation, saying that if Macy shouldn't be a member of the Harvard Club then *he* shouldn't, and that he was hereby resigning. Coldly, the Board of Managers pointed out that he owed the club considerable money and therefore couldn't resign, but that he was suspended for a year. They assumed that the suspension would chasten him, but just before the year was up he paid his bill and resigned for good. Twenty years later, one of the surviving members of the committee wrote to Walter Winchell, giving him the tip that Robert had been fired from the Harvard Club for nonpayment of dues. Winchell checked the item with Robert, just as a precaution, and never ran it.

The spring of 1920 brought a couple of other changes. The Crestwood house was sold to some people named Vaughan, who were to take over on May 1, and Thomas Masson, the managing editor of *Life*, offered Robert $100 for a thousand words a week. J. S. Metcalfe, the drama critic, was leaving the magazine, and Masson wanted Robert to take his place. There was only one hitch, and that was that E. S. Martin, the editor, had someone else in mind, so Masson's offer seemed subject to revision. Robert met Charles Dana Gibson, the president of *Life*, with whom he had a congenial evening's talk about the magazine, and then, still more or less on a trial basis, he was assigned to cover a play called *The Bonehead*. It was so bad that he left after the second act, and went back to his cubbyhole and wrote a review of the programme. That was all he wrote about—just the programme. The next day, he took the copy to Martin, who was only mildly pleased with it. But within about three days Masson and Gibson had their way, and Robert was taken on as drama critic. He got $100 a week for the drama page, and 7 cents a word for anything else he did.

With this assurance of extra wealth, he and Gertrude decided to buy a house they had seen being built in Scarsdale, which could be had for $17,500, and only $4,200 of it cash. It seemed so reasonable that Robert signed up right away, without having any clear idea where the $4,200 was coming from. It came from Ernest Gruening, who loaned him six New York City bonds as collateral, and Mrs. Parker, who loaned him $200 for a half hour. With the $200, he opened an account at the Lincoln Trust Company; they then loaned him $4,000 on the bonds; he deposited the $4,000 and gave Mrs. Parker back her $200. It still left him $500 short, what with the first payment on the mortgage, but he figured that he could earn that. On May 1, he and the family and their suitcases squeezed into a taxi and went down the dusty back road to Scarsdale. On May 30, Sherwood came out to spend the night with them in their new home, and at 3 A.M. the ceiling fell on and between Robert's and Gertrude's beds. They were now full-fledged homeowners.

9

The job of drama critic on *Life,* about which he had dreamed when he was groping around in the Curtis Publishing Company, opened up a whole new era for Robert. It also changed his living habits, because in those days six, eight, or even nine plays might open in a week, sometimes three of them in one night. When necessary, Gertrude would bring his dress clothes to town, as she had when he was working with Brady, and he would change in a ten-cent cubicle in the Grand Central men's room. After the show, he would either go back to Scarsdale with her or, if the copy deadline was too close, he would do his review that night and then sleep in Sherwood's apartment, or with the Gruenings, or on the couch of some other friend. During the theatre season, he averaged perhaps one dinner a week at home, and Gertrude was as much of a commuter as he was.

On one of these theatre nights, when Gertrude had not come to town because young Bub was sick, she called Robert and told him to be sure to go into the front bedroom when he got home, since a nurse was sleeping in the room with Bobby. He said O.K., and when he got out to Scarsdale, around 1 A.M., he went straight into Bobby's room, stripped down to his underwear in the dark, then prodded the lump end of the figure that was sprawled across the bed. "Come on," he said. "Move over."

The nurse whirled into a sitting position, clutching the covers around her. "*Mrs.* Benchley," she hissed, "is in the *other* room!" Robert scurried out the door, and as he tottered, weak with laughter, down the hall to the room where Gertrude was sleeping, the nurse got up and locked the door. When he could speak again, Robert asked Gertrude if she hadn't said that she would be sleeping in the room with Bobby. She replied that she had said just the reverse, and they both laughed until the nurse could not help hearing them. She left later that day, and spread the story about wherever she went, making it considerably more flattering to herself than it actually had been.

Aside from his drama criticism, Robert also did side pieces for *Life*, and his work was made much more cheerful by the arrival of Sherwood as an associate editor. Connelly and Mrs. Parker were also occasional contributors, and it was inevitable that this combination would lead, if not to trouble, at least to something wildly out of the ordinary. Robert remembered the talk he had had with Gibson, about injecting a little more humour into the publication, and it occurred to him that it might be a good idea to get out an issue which, like the successful *Lampoon* parody of *Life*, was a parody of some of *Life's* contemporaries. The "Burlesque Issue," as it was called, lampooned *Photoplay*, *The New Republic*, *Everybody's* and the *Daily News*, to name just a few, and the contributors included Connelly, Mrs. Parker, Corey Ford, Herman J. Mankiewicz, John Held, Jr., Rea Irvin, and Rube Goldberg. One of Robert's most memorable captions, in the section parodying the *Daily News*, ran under a picture of the Royal Coach being drawn through the crowded streets of London. It was a view looking down on the ornate, gilded coach, taken from a balcony above the street, and the caption ran: "Convention-crazed Dentists Parade Through Streets of London, Dragging Largest Gold Tooth In the World." Another feature of the issue was an article on bridge building by Connelly, which was illustrated by a cut of a wooded canyon, across which was strung a banner reading: "Your Daughter Is Safe on a Gonnick Bridge." What with one thing and another, the Burlesque Issue of *Life* sold every copy printed and was such a success that the idea was repeated twice in subsequent years.

Probably the most memorable thing that happened to Robert in the nine years he was with *Life* was the five-year run of *Abie's Irish Rose*. This little number opened in May of

1922, the day after a now-forgotten mistake called *The Rotters,* and Robert joined all the other critics in deploring it. His review was comparatively short:

On the night following the presentation of "The Rotters," residents of Broadway, New York City, were startled by the sound of horse's hoofs clattering up the famous thoroughfare. Rushing to their windows they saw a man in Colonial costume riding a bay mare from whose eyes flashed fire. The man was shouting as he rode, and his message was: " 'The Rotters' is no longer the worst play in town! 'Abie's Irish Rose' has just opened!"

"Abie's Irish Rose" is the kind of play in which a Jewish boy, wanting to marry an Irish girl named Rosemary Murphy, tells his orthodox father that her name is Rosie Murphesky, and the wedding proceeds.

Any further information, if such could possibly be necessary, will be furnished at the old office of *Puck,* the comic weekly which flourished in the '90's. Although that paper is no longer in existence, there must be some old retainer still about the premises who could tell you everything that is in "Abie's Irish Rose."

It never occurred to Robert that the play would last, and he was therefore surprised the next week, when he came to make out the "Confidential Guide" page, to see that it was still running. The "Confidential Guide" was a listing of every show in town, with a one-sentence description, which he had to write for each issue. For *Abie's Irish Rose* he put down "Something awful," and let it go at that. The following week, with *Abie* incredibly still doing business, he was more specific; he wrote, "Among the season's worst." But this had no effect on *Abie's* box office, and he found himself faced with the problem of saying the same thing, time and again. The third week, he called it "Eighty-ton fun," then "Comic-supplement stuff," and then he realized that he was in for a protracted siege. His comments, between June of 1922 and November of 1927, included the following:

People laugh at this every night, which explains why democracy can never be a success.

Just about as low as good, clean fun can get.

In another two or three years, we'll have this play driven out of town.

The management sent us some pencils for Christmas; so maybe it isn't so bad after all.

Where do the people come from who keep this going? You don't see them out in the daytime.

A-ha-ha-ha-ha! Oh, well, all right.

All right if you never went beyond the fourth grade.

We were only fooling all the time. It's a great show.

Almost two years old, God forbid.

America's favourite comedy, which accounts for the number of shaved necks on the streets.

Probably the funniest and most stimulating play ever written by an American. (Now let's see what *that* will do.)

For the best comment to go in this space, we will give two tickets to the play.

Contest for line closes at midnight, or at the latest, quarter past midnight, on Jan. 8. At present Mr. Arthur Marx is leading with "No worse than a bad cold."

We've got those old pains in the back coming on us again. Every spring we have them.

The Phoenicians were among the earliest settlers of Britain.

The oldest profession in the world.

There is no letter "w" in the French language.

Four years old this week. Three ounces of drinking-iodine, please.

Viktusnak most már nines maradása otthon. Félti az 6 Jani urfijat, hogy valami Kart tesz magában.

See Hebrews 13:8.*

We might as well say it now as later. We don't like this play.

We see that earthquakes are predicted in these parts some time in the next seven years. Could it be that. . . .

Closing soon. (Only fooling.)

Flying fish are sometimes seen at as great a height as fifteen feet.

The week after *Abie* closed, having run up a record of 2,327 performances, it was listed in the "Confidential Guide" enclosed in a heavy black border and with "In Memoriam," set in Gothic type. Two subsequent attempts to revive the show met with comparative disaster, which may or may not prove something about the maturity of the theatregoing public.

Beyond his tussle with *Abie*, however, Robert did something in 1922 that, whether he liked it or not, proved to be a major turning point in his career. It seemed innocuous enough at the time, but in more ways than one it literally changed the course of his life. This was his delivery of the Treasurer's Report, at a one-night show put on by a lot of writers, critics, and assorted talent who frequented the Algonquin. For a couple of years, he had been having lunch more and more often at the Algonquin, with a group that included—aside from Sherwood and Mrs. Parker—Frank Adams, George Kaufman, Deems Taylor, Alexander Woollcott, Marc Connelly, Heywood Broun, Brock and Murdock Pemberton, Neysa McMein, Margalo Gillmore, Edna Ferber, Peggy Wood, and a few others. They didn't all lunch there every day, but they did meet with enough regularity so that they were finally assigned the same round table in the main dining-room, and although they first called it the Board, it later became known (because of a cartoon by Ed Duffy, showing them all as knights in armour) as the Round Table.

* Jesus Christ the same yesterday, and today, and forever.

The group was, in its inception, completely informal; these people met because they had in common the fact that most of them were young, all of them were talented in one way or another, and they enjoyed each other's company. It was a time when people were almost spontaneously idealistic, and when a great many things were done for no other reason than the fact that they seemed like a good idea at the time. The Algonquin group, who sometimes called themselves the Vicious Circle, thought that it would be nice to put on a revue, sort of a parody of Baliev's *Chauve-Souris*, and to have the attendance by invitation. Since they couldn't guarantee the quality of the entertainment, they themselves bought all the tickets, and passed them out to selected friends. As an added good idea, they asked Laurette Taylor, the actress, to review the show in Woollcott's space in *The New York Times*.

At the first rehearsal of the show, which was called *No Sirree!* (to rhyme with *Chauve-Souris*), it was decided that Broun would be master of ceremonies, more or less impersonating Baliev, and that Jascha Heifetz would provide occasional offstage music—that is, if he could bring himself to play off key. (He could, and did.) Sherwood, who had just come in from out-of-town and didn't know what was going on, was given a song to sing, called "The Everlastin' Ingénue Blues." The song was written by Mrs. Parker, and among the ingénues who dimpled as he sang were Helen Hayes and Tallulah Bankhead. Robert—who had been asked to think up a sketch and hadn't—decided, in the taxi on the way to rehearsal, to pretend he had misunderstood what they wanted, and to give them an accounting of the past year's finances. He jotted down a few figures and then, when he was called on, stood up and read them off, ad-libbing as he went along. Without actually trying to, he was delving back into his own past—imitating the speakers he was forced to listen to as a reporter on the *Tribune*, burlesquing the reports he had to make as welfare secretary of the Russell Company, and mocking some of the eager planners of the advertising department of the Curtis Publishing Company. In ten years, he had been exposed to treasurers and speakers and assistant treasurers and substitute speakers of every known variety, and what came out that night was one, gloriously fumbling, parody of the lot of them. The show committee decided that he should do it just as it was, and in order to fool the audience into thinking that it was a real treasurer's report, he was not listed on the programme. He just came out in front of the curtain, smiled nervously, and began. It was not until eight years later that he wrote the whole thing down, together with the stage directions:

The report is delivered by an Assistant Treasurer who has been called in to substitute for the regular Treasurer who is ill. He is not a very good public-speaker, this assistant, but after a few minutes of confusion is caught up by the spell of his own oratory and is hard to stop.

I shall take but a very few moments of your time this evening, for I realize that you would much rather be listening to this interesting entertainment than to a dry financial statement . . . but I *am* reminded of a story—which you have probably all of you heard.

It seems that there were these two Irishmen walking down the street when they came to a—oh, I should have said in the first place that the parrot which was hanging out in *front* of the store—or rather belonging to one of these two fellows—the *first* Irishman, that is—was—well, *any*way, this parrot—

[*After a slight cogitation, he realizes that, for all practical purposes, the story is as good as lost; so he abandons it entirely and, stepping forward, drops his facile, story-telling manner and assumes a quite spurious businesslike air.*]

Now, in connection with reading this report, there are one or two points which Dr. Murnie wanted brought up in connection with it, and he has asked me to bring them up in connec—to bring them up.

In the first place, there is the question of the work which we are trying to do up there at our little place at Silver Lake, a work which we feel not only fills a very definite need in the community but also fills a very definite need—er—in the community. I don't think that many members of the Society realize just how big the work is that we are trying to do up there. For instance, I don't think that it is generally known that most of our boys are between the age of fourteen. We feel that, by taking the boy at this age, we can get closer to his real nature—for a boy *has* a very real nature, you may be sure—and bring him into closer touch not only with the school, the parents, and with each other, but also with the town in which they live, the country to whose flag they pay allegiance, and to the—ah—[*trailing off*] town in which they live.

Now the fourth point which Dr. Murnie wanted brought up was that in connection with the installation of the new furnace last Fall. There seems to have been considerable talk going around about this not having been done quite as economically as it might—have—been—done, when, as a matter of fact, the whole thing *was* done just as economically as possible—in fact, even *more* so. I have here a report of the Furnace Committee, showing just how the whole thing was handled from start to finish.

[*Reads from report, with considerable initial difficulty with the stiff covers.*]

Bids were submitted by the following firms of furnace contractors, with a clause stating that if we did not engage a firm to do the work for us we should pay them nothing for submitting the bids. This clause alone saved us a great deal of money.

The following firms, then, submitted bids: Merkle, Wybigant Co., the Eureka Dust Bin and Shaker Co., The Elite Furnace Shop, and Harris, Birnbauer and Harris. The bid of Merkle, Wybigant being the lowest, Harris Birnbauer were selected to do the job.

[*Here a page is evidently missing from the report, and a hurried search is carried on through all the pages, without result.*]

Well, that pretty well clears up that end of the work.

Those of you who contributed so generously last year to the floating hospital have probably wondered what became of the money. I was speaking on this subject only last week at our up-town branch, and, after the meeting, a dear little old lady, dressed all in lavender, came up on the platform, and, laying her hand on my arm, said: "Mr. So-and-so (calling me by name) Mr. So-and-so, what the hell did you do with all the money we gave you last year?" Well, I just laughed and pushed her off the platform, but it has occurred to the committee that perhaps some of you, like that little old lady, would be interested in knowing the disposition of the funds.

Now, Mr. Rossiter, unfortunately our treasurer—or rather Mr. Rossiter our *treasurer, unfortunately* is confined at his home tonight with a bad head-cold and I have been asked [*he hears someone whispering at him from the wings, but decides to ignore it*] and I have been asked if I would [*the whisperer will not be denied, so he goes over to the entrance and receives a brief message, returning beaming and laughing to himself*] Well, thc joke seems to be on *me!* Mr. Rossiter has *pneumonia!*

Following, then, is a summary of the Treasurer's Report:

[*Reads, in a very businesslike manner*]

During the year 1922—and by that is meant 1921—the Choral Society received the following in donations:

B.L.G.	$500
G.K.M.	500
Lottie and Nellie W——	500
In memory of a happy summer at Rye Beach	10
Proceeds of a sale of coats and hats left in the boat house	14.55
And then the Junior League gave a performance of "Pinafore" for the benefit of the Fund which, unfortunately, resulted in a deficit of	$300
Then, from dues and charges	2,354.75
And, following the installation of the new furnace,	

a saving in coal amounting to $374.75—which made Dr. Murnie very happy, you may be sure.

Making a total of receipts amounting to $3,645.75

This is all, of course, reckoned as of June.

In the matter of expenditures, the Club has not been so fortunate. There was the unsettled condition of business, and the late Spring, to contend with, resulting in the following—er—rather discouraging figures, I am afraid.

Expenditures	$23,574.85
Then there was a loss, owing to—several things—of	3,326.70
Car-fare	4,452.25
And then, Mrs. Rawlins' expense account, when she went down to see the work they are doing in Baltimore, came to $256.50, but I am sure that you will all agree that it was worth it to find out —er—what they are doing in Baltimore.	
And then, under the general head of Odds and Ends	2,537.50
Making a total disbursement of . . [*hurriedly*]	$416,546.75

or a net deficit of—ah—several thousand dollars.

Now, these figures bring us down only to October. In October my sister was married, and the house was all torn up, and in the general confusion we lost track of the figures for May and August. All those wishing the *approximate* figures for May and August, however, may obtain them from me in the vestry after the dinner, where I will be with pledge cards for those of you who wish to subscribe over and above your annual dues, and I hope that each and every one of you here tonight will look deep into his heart and [*archly*] into his pocketbook, and see if he can not find it there to help us to put this thing over with a bang [*accompanied by a wholly ineffectual gesture representing a bang*] and to help and make this just the biggest and best year the Armenians have ever had. . . . . . . I thank you.

[*Exits, bumping into the proscenium*]

The show was put on the night of Sunday, April 30, in the Forty-ninth Street Theater. The Treasurer's Report represented a new and completely different kind of comedy (in spite of the lack of gags as they are now known, there was a laugh on an average of once every ten seconds), and Robert's stage presence and delivery were perfectly suited to it. People have since described that first performance with a kind of quiet awe, as though they were remembering a mountain avalanche, or the discovery of radium. The only person who wasn't impressed was Laurette Taylor, who wrote that she had always hated figures, and couldn't see anything funny in the reading of a whole mess of them. "Robert Benchley came out and read, as far as I could understand it, the multiplication table, or perhaps it was a timetable," she reported.

Irving Berlin was among those at the show, and he and his partner, Sam H. Harris, offered Robert a spot in their next, or third, *Music Box Revue*. Robert felt that a drama critic had no right going on the stage, where anything he did might lessen his ability to criticize real actors, but he hated to say no to Berlin. So, instead, he asked for $500 a week, which he knew was so outlandish that they would just laugh, and they all could part with mutual expressions of esteem and nobody's feelings would be hurt. Harris thought for a minute, then said, "Well, for five hundred dollars you'd better be awfully good," and Robert was left to think it over and wrestle with his conscience. His conscience lost the decision, when he thought of all the things that $500 a week would do, but it kept nagging at him during the nine months he played in the *Music Box Revue*, and the ten weeks following that that he did it on the Keith's vaudeville circuit. Berlin arranged it so that Robert came on at 8:50, just after Grace Moore and John Steel had sung "An Orange Grove in California," and he was on until 8:58. This gave him time to see the beginning of whatever show he might be reviewing for *Life*, and allowed him to get back in his seat before the first act was over, when Gertrude or whoever was with him could fill him in on what had happened. On the vaudeville circuit, he was on the same bill with Victor Moore and Emma Littlefield, who did a sketch called "Change Your Act or Back to the Woods." It was early in 1925, when he was playing Washington, D.C., that he counted up the money he was getting, and called Gertrude long distance. "Let's take the kids to Europe this summer," he said. They went to the south of France, where he stayed for three months, and Gertrude and the children stayed five.

The Treasurer's Report was also responsible, although more indirectly, for his taking a room in town. In 1923, when he was doing eight performances a week and sometimes reviewing as many shows, he got out to Scarsdale no earlier than 1 A.M., and returned to New York around 8 A.M. One night, he went onstage with a temperature of 103 and aching in every joint. He got through his act, and then saw a doctor, who diagnosed it as a touch of grippe, brought on by exhaustion, and also some latent arthritis. The grippe got better, but the arthritis got worse; it became so acute, in fact, that he had to use crutches to get to the wings, from which he would totter onstage unassisted. Finally, when he was well again, the doctor said that he was going to have to choose between living in the country and working nights in New York; he could not do both and stay in any kind of health. So he took a room on Madison Avenue with Charles MacArthur, a reporter and about-to-be playwright whom he had met around town and with whom he had shared some memorable prowls. Gertrude continued to commute to the theatre, and he went out to Scarsdale for the weekends or, later on, just for Sundays. It eventually worked out that Gertrude and the boys came in for Sunday lunch with him. They became the commuters, both to New York and Hollywood.

The final direct result of the Treasurer's Report was that it established him as a celebrity. The year before, Holt had published his first collection of pieces, called *Of All Things*, and it eventually went into thirteen printings, not counting an

English edition. But appearing in person, on Broadway and on the road, brought him more immediately into the public attention than did his book, and he became, in a less limited way than before, a public figure. He wasn't what could be called famous, but he had at last, after ten years, succeeded in doing something on his own that was good enough to win wide and enthusiastic applause. His friends had never doubted that he would make it, but there had been many nights when he had lain awake, staring into the dark and wondering if he was any good, and if so why he couldn't seem to make a success of anything. He had been nagged by the constant dread that he was losing his grip, and the only things that he felt were worthwhile that he had done were the things that had failed, or turned out badly. And, in spite of making more money than ever before, and itemizing every cent paid out, he had been deeper in debt than ever before, because of having bought the house and also having two growing boys.

It was, therefore, something of a revelation to him, when he began to make $500 and more a week, what a good time a person could have if only he was a success and had money. He had never, even in his lowest periods, let other people know that he was nervous or depressed, but now, when everything seemed to be breaking the right way, he not only loved everybody, but they loved him, which made it even nicer. His self-confidence returned, and although the small voice of his conscience kept nibbling at him and telling him that he was wasting his time in frivolity, he decided to relax and enjoy himself—just for a minute or two. In other words, he let down his guard.

The 1920s were, for the people in Robert's general category (almost all of whom had come to New York from out-of-town), intensely vibrant and exciting. There was an air of daring, and rejoicing, and rebellion, and the main goal was to have as much fun as possible. It was a period of group activity, when people moved in groups, ate and drank in groups, loved more or less in groups, thought in groups, and kept going until they dropped from exhaustion; then they revived in groups, and were off and at it again, and the strongest and the most durable were admired the most. The Round Table group was present, en masse, at every party given by Neysa McMein, and her studio was open house all day and night, day in and night out; while she worked at her pastels, her guests laughed and talked and drank and played word games, and a great many people said a great many witty things, which were repeated around town the next day by those who could remember what had been said. There was never just one wit in any crowd—there were several, who could take an idea or take a joke and bat it back and forth like a shuttlecock until all the feathers had been beaten off. (Or, looking at it another way, they might polish it until it sparkled and gave off light.) The sounds of laughter and of singing echoed throughout the night and even into the bleak, tinny-tasting morning, and there was never any need to worry or feel lonely, because the group was always there and ready to keep on going. The lonely ones were those who fell behind, or fell in hopeless love, and their anguish was all the greater because of the fun that everybody else was having. It was a time of peaks and depths, greater and sharper peaks and depths than are known today, and the excesses were in the realms of fun and heartbreak, with not much happening in between. Even the work was fun, because there was lots of money for everybody, and because of the creative surge that drove people on with new ideas and new plans and new imagination, and the sixty theatres on Broadway were full from early fall till late in spring. Brady opened every season with three or four failures, just to get things rolling, and there was unlimited money for anyone who had a play that stood a chance. Creative talent fed and thrived upon itself, and project led to project and success to more success, and books and verse and plays and songs poured out in ever-increasing volume.

There was only one resentment, and that was against the Act, which many felt had been wangled through while all their backs were turned. So Prohibition was cheerfully and generally flouted, and society linked arms with the bootleggers and the gangsters, and everybody had a glorious time. True, some people were shot or sunk in cement, and others went blind or died from government drink, but those were little risks you ran, like crossing streets against the lights. It was fun to drink, and fun to mock the law, and it was considered rude not to accept a drink that was offered to you. You drank whatever you could get, or what your host had, and you drank it in orange juice or ginger ale, or both, but you drank it. Mostly, you carried your own, so as to be sure of what you got. Or as sure as anyone could be of what he got.

For a while, Robert went to speakeasies with his friends and didn't drink. Sometimes, he would deliver little lectures on how people weren't themselves when they drank, and his friends smiled, and said he was right and wasn't it probably a good thing that they *weren't* themselves. The first social drink he took was an Orange Blossom, and he tried one sip, then put the glass down and looked around the room. "This place ought to be closed by law," he said, and everybody fell off their chairs with laughter. Then, one day, he was leaving Tony's with his friend Donald Ogden Stewart, and when they got outside, a light rain was falling. A little man came hustling down the street, carrying an umbrella, and Stewart ducked underneath the umbrella, took the little man by the arm, and said, "Yale Club, please." Robert thought a long time about that. If you could drink and have quiet, innocent fun like that, he told himself, then maybe there *was* something to it, after all. Maybe he had been a prude, and maybe all his friends were right, and—come to think of it—if the government had gone to all the trouble of passing a law against it, there must be *something* that a lot of people found good about it, or else there wouldn't have to be a law.

And who was the government to tell a man what he could or could not do? The whole thing worried him, and he decided to find out for himself; after all, *he* could take it or leave it alone, but if there really was something that he was missing, he might as well find out about it now as later.

The first glass of rye he lifted to his lips came as a nostalgic, jarring shock. He got it just beneath his nose, smelled it, and put the glass down, his mind swimming back to what the odour had made him think of. "My God," he said, after a moment. "It's Uncle Albert." He remembered his Uncle Albert Prentice, in Worcester, and he remembered what he had always thought was Uncle Albert's personal bouquet; now it turned out that Uncle Albert had been walking around in a cloud of rye-whisky fumes. He remembered, too, that Uncle Albert used often to go out to the barn to curry the horses, or mend the harness, or paint the sleigh, and that scarcely an hour went by but what Uncle Albert thought of something to do around the barn. Robert sipped his rye, and smiled, and thought of Uncle Albert.

10

The team of Benchley and MacArthur was one about which many stories were told, and nobody is sure how many of them are true. But MacArthur had a fertile and a bizarre imagination (which is plumbing the depths of understatement), and Robert would do almost anything a friend suggested, just for the fun of it, so between them they managed to become involved in a number of picturesque situations. And it wasn't always at MacArthur's instigation, either; it was just that, with him, Robert did things that he probably wouldn't have done in the company of, say, James Russell Lowell.

Their apartment was on the fourth floor of the building at 536 Madison Avenue, and they were almost evicted for the noise they made one night, putting fake battle scars on a trench helmet. MacArthur, who had been a private in the artillery during the war, had thoughtlessly promised his old helmet to Robert's boys as a souvenir, forgetting that the first thing he had done when his troop transport arrived in New York was to scale his helmet into the bay. So they bought a helmet at an Army-Navy store, and took it up to the room, where they proceeded to pound it, hammer it, and puncture it, leaving a series of dents and holes that made it look as though the wearer had defended Verdun singlehanded. There was one big dent, which the boys were told was where a shell had struck; there was a smaller dent with a blackened hole in the middle, representing a shrapnel gash; and, as a sure bit of authenticity, there was candle wax dripping down the sides of the helmet, showing how MacArthur had used it as a candlestand while writing letters in the dugout at night. It was many years before either of Robert's sons questioned how a man could have stood under that hat and survived, but the Benchley-MacArthur lease almost expired the night the helmet got the treatment.

Then there was the Sunday morning in spring, when Robert and Charlie woke up with eight dollars between them, and no immediate way of raising any more. To put on a brave front, they went to the Pierre for breakfast, where they dawdled over their food and tried to think of quick ways of raising—or even earning—money, and it occurred to them that the rowboat concession in Central Park was about the easiest, as well as the cheapest way, because the only overhead would be one sneaker, for the man who put one foot in the water to launch the boats. Everything else was gravy, since the customers did their own rowing. By the time they finished breakfast they were as good as millionaires, and they went out onto Fifth Avenue feeling several years younger. Suddenly, walking down the Avenue, they spotted the imposing, top-hatted figure of Charles Evans Hughes, striding along with the wind blowing softly through his beard. "Charles Evans Hughes, the Secretary of State," MacArthur called after him. "Why aren't you in Washington?" The two of them followed Hughes, jeering and whistling, until, with one frantic backward glance, he sprang off the curb, chased down a taxi, and jumped inside.

The time they came much closer to trouble, however, was the time when, through an insane combination of circumstances, MacArthur became temporary public-relations counsel for a mausoleum in New Jersey. He was, at the moment, a reporter on the New York *American*, and although he was an unusually highly paid reporter ($125 a week), he was nevertheless in debt to his bootlegger, and bootleggers didn't like to let debts ride for long. When, incredibly, Charlie convinced a mausoleum in Union, New Jersey, that he was not only a partner of Hearst and Brisbane but that, for $500, he could get them invaluable publicity, they came up with the advance and he was temporarily saved. But he soon needed another $500 and, knowing that he couldn't pose as a public-relations expert for too long, he decided to ask for one more advance and then propose an idea so unbelievable that they would have to fire him. Gently, in order to pry them loose from the second $500, he suggested that they have a Poets' Corner, and change their name to Fairview Abbey, something like Westminster Abbey in England. At first they were sceptical, but Charlie wrote them a few sample letters to poets like Edgar Guest, and said that, as soon as he got his advance, he would show them how to make a going thing out of it. When, reluctantly, they gave him the money, he said that the best way to get publicity for their Poets' Corner would be to have the bones of Henry Wadsworth Longfellow interred there, and that even if they couldn't actually get him, the controversy would provide thousands of dollars' worth of free publicity. To show his good faith, he wrote a letter to Mayor James M. Curley, of Boston, saying that Boston had lost its right to Longfellow's bones by burying them in a simple grave, when any schoolboy knew, from the lines:

> Life is real! Life is earnest!
> And the grave is not its goal

that Longfellow did not want to be buried in a grave, but rather in a crypt or, preferably, in a Poets' Corner such as the one at Fairview Abbey. Furthermore, the letter said, it was common knowledge that Curley had appointed his brother-in-law as caretaker of the grave, and that the Democratic convention would take into account such matters, as well as the possible mitigating circumstance if Curley were to have a part in restoring the poet to his rightful resting place.

The letter was written on mausoleum stationery, and Charlie conned one of the clergymen on the staff into signing it. Mayor Curley's reply was sincere, and troubled. Longfellow was not buried in Boston, he said, but rather in Cambridge, under the jurisdiction of Mayor Flynn; furthermore, he—Curley—had never appointed his brother-in-law to any gravekeeper's job, and that there must be some mistake all around. He closed with his best wishes to all delegates to the Democratic convention.

It was at this point that Robert came into the picture. Charlie showed him Curley's letter one night, shortly after it was received, and they decided that something drastic had to be done. The Boston papers had run Charlie's letter, and accompanied it with screams of rage in the editorial columns, and under the circumstances the best thing seemed to be to give the movement nationwide scope. They got a sheaf of telegram blanks and retired to a corner, where they wrote out a dozen or more messages to Curley, saying such things as: THE COUNTRY DEMANDS THE BODY OF HENRY WADSWORTH LONGFELLOW; IF YOU VALUE YOUR JOB YOU WILL FORWARD IT IMMEDIATELY, and COME CLEAN WITH THAT BODY, and ROLL DEM BONES, and the like. They signed the telegrams The Parochial Students' League for Longfellow, The Longfellow Lovers of America, The Longfellow Society of Union, New Jersey, and, once or twice, Robert Benchley and Charles MacArthur. The next day, Curley applied to get warrants for both of their arrests in New Jersey, and Charlie was finally fired.

They parted as roommates when Charlie's first play, *Lulu Belle*, opened and was a resounding success, allowing him to afford more sumptuous quarters. They were, by that time, living in the Shelton Hotel; Robert stayed on at the Shelton for a while, and then moved to the Algonquin, where he could be in closer touch with things.

It was pleasant to be a celebrity, but Robert regretted the fact that his prominence stemmed from so trivial a source; he still was determined to be a serious writer, or at least a writer of something worthwhile. He did the comedy and the light pieces because that seemed to be the only way he could make money, and at the same time he brooded over the fact that he was making no substantial contribution to

Progress. He didn't care what kind of Progress it was—whether it was social or literary or spiritual—he just wanted to feel that he had done something to make things a little better. The only trouble was that he didn't seem to have the time to do the worthwhile things; almost all his available time was spent writing the things that made money.

In June of 1926, he swallowed his scruples about working with the country's more frivolous people, and accepted an offer from Jesse L. Lasky to go out to Hollywood and do dialogue and subtitles for a picture at Paramount. He told himself that it would be for just a couple of months, and besides, Laurence Stallings, another Round Table member, was out there working on *Old Ironsides*, and Don Stewart, who was working on *Brown of Harvard*, had invited him to come out and be best man at his wedding to Beatrice Ames. Everything considered, Robert didn't see how he could very well refuse. He went out, worked on a picture called *You'd Be Surprised*, which featured Raymond Griffith, and was back by August, having been best man at Stewart's wedding and having contracted water on the knee in the process. At a prewedding party, given at a house on the beach, he went out onto the porch in the dark, and off where a flight of steps should have been but weren't. His duties as best man were carried out on crutches, with his left leg encased in a plaster cast. He was also singed, from having had a fire lighted under his chair at the bachelors' dinner.

In spite of the change that had come over his way of life, his New England conscience was still with him, as was also his New England disapproval of sex as a marketable commodity in the theatre. Back in 1917, when he was substituting for Wodehouse as drama critic of *Vanity Fair*, he saw a play called *'Ception Shoals*, with Nazimova as what he described (although not in print) as "the leading spermatozoa." He concluded that the play was "too obstetric for my simple soul and too tragic for anybody." Many years later, after having sat through innumerable plays that dealt more or less directly with the same subject, he wrote in a review that "I am definitely ready to announce that Sex, as a theatrical property, is as tiresome as the Old Mortgage, and that I don't want to hear it mentioned again." His disapproval was made stronger, and his irritation was increased, by the way some audiences reacted to anything suggestive on the stage, and he found that matinee audiences, consisting as they did primarily of women, were absolutely unbearable. One day, having been to the opening of Eugene O'Neill's *Desire Under the Elms* but wanting to recheck it for a follow-up review, he went back to a matinee, and was acutely embarrassed by the way the audience behaved. But he could have stood it if it hadn't been for two women, sitting directly behind him, who nudged each other and leered and tittered audibly all through the first act, making it difficult to hear what was being said on the stage. At the interval, he rose, took out his wallet, and approached the women.

"I hope you'll excuse me," he said, as he fingered through the wallet, "but if you two ladies would be so kind as to leave the theatre, I shall be more than glad to pay for your seats."

There was not another sound out of them during the rest of the show.

He subsequently wrote a piece about matinee audiences, in which he said that scenes of, for instance, seduction, "which in the evening are taken with at least a modicum of the seriousness intended by the author, become, at matinees, occasions for giggling and obscene hilarity, making the lone male feel that perhaps, in spite of its traditional temporary advantages, the whole institution of Sex has been a mistake. Woman, however lovely she may be in stooping to folly in individual cases, is never so unlovely as when giggling at it in a group over boxes of chocolates."

In the approximately twenty-five years that he reviewed the theatre, he never lost this embarrassment at jokes about sex, and on some occasions the embarrassment took the form of violence. Once, after a comedienne in a beer-and-pretzels show called *She Gave Him All He Wanted* had become so offensive that he could no longer stand it, he and his party got up and left Uncle Sam's Music Hall. Outside, Robert prowled down the line of tuxedoed men around the box office, looking for the producer of the show, and when he found him he cut loose with a tirade of abuse that could be heard down the block. The gist of it was that this was the most abysmal bit of bad taste that he had seen in twenty-five years, that anything good that the producer had done before deserved to be expunged from the records, and he concluded by saying, "Don't you *ever* insult the public again by giving out free seats to a thing like this!" With that, he stamped off down the street, leaving the stunned producer examining some ticket stubs he found in his moist hands. He did not review the show, and thought the whole thing was over with, until, about a week later, a column in the *Daily News* carried an item that ran: "What littérateur, movie actor, radio comic, and whilom dramatic critic was thrown bodily from Uncle Sam's Music Hall the other night for being drunk and disorderly?" Robert wired both the columnist and the producer, asking them if they had anything to say for themselves before he went to press, and the producer wired back, expressing pained surprise that Robert should think he had had anything to do with the item. The columnist, with the charm that had made him famous, replied: "I don't know what you're talking about. The description fits three other people perfectly." So Robert wrote his rebuttal in *The New Yorker*, giving the facts of the case and winding up by saying he would have dropped the whole matter, except that "it was that 'whilom' that hurt."

In general, however, his presence was noticeable only when he approved of a show, and his laughter was the one welcome sign for which all actors waited. It was not a self-conscious or an overly loud laugh, but it was unmistakable and it was wholehearted, and it sometimes came when nobody else was laughing very hard. Small things could break him up completely, such as the comedian who said that he had three children but was afraid to have another because he'd heard that every fourth child in the world was Chinese. Robert's reaction to that was such that the rest of the audience laughed more at him than they did at the joke, and the comedian lost his timing and went up in his lines.

Probably his most famous exit from a theatre was from the Forty-eighth Street Theater, at the opening of a play called *The Squall*, on November 11, 1926. The play featured Blanche Yurka, Romney Brent, and Dorothy Stickney; it was written by Jean Bart and directed by Lionel Atwill, and it dealt with the peasants in the hills around Granada—peasants who all, it seemed, spoke in sultry pidgin English. After there had been a certain amount of to-do in this comic-strip dialect, Robert turned to Gertrude, sitting next to him. "If one more of these wonderful natives shows up speaking pidgin, I leave," he whispered, and gave his attention back to the stage. The scene was in a farmhouse, and the rustics were gathered around for the evening meal. Suddenly, a storm came howling up the valley, sound-effect rain lashed at the farmhouse, and the door burst open and in staggered a tawny, half-clad, wild-eyed, gypsy girl. Robert tensed himself, as the girl crawled to the feet of the mother of the household and kissed the hem of her garment.

"Me Nubi," the gypsy said. "Nubi good girl. Nubi stay here."

"O.K.," Robert whispered, rising. "Me Bobby. Me bad boy. Me go."

Alexander Woollcott, whose first-night seats were usually directly in front of Robert's, heard him, and incorporated the remark, with some revisions and embellishments, in his review the next day. The way Woollcott reported it, Robert said, "In that respect, me different from Nubi. Benchley good boy, but Benchley not stay here. Benchley go away," a mouthful that would have taken him half the way to Broadway to enunciate. Nevertheless, the remark in its various forms became famous, and the general public, who did not share Robert's revulsion of dialect, came to the play in such numbers that it ran for more than a year.

On another occasion, at the opening of *He Who Gets Slapped*, Robert's words to Woollcott had a less happy effect. Robert and Gertrude were sitting behind Woollcott and some anonymous lady, and an elaborate circus scene was being played on the stage. Three beautiful white horses —real ones—came on, and the middle horse had its lips drawn back in a broad, toothy smile. Robert leaned forward and tapped Woollcott on the shoulder. "See that middle horse?" he said. "That's Violet Kemble-Cooper." (Violet Kemble-Cooper was a popular actress of the time, who had a broad smile and a handsome, glistening set of teeth.)

Woollcott gave a barely perceptible start, then turned halfway around, and looked at the woman beside him. "Miss Kemble-Cooper, may I present Mr. Benchley?" he said, to the actress's younger sister.

Robert swallowed, then smiled. "But it's such a beautiful horse," he said. Woollcott and Miss Kemble-Cooper returned their attention to the show, and Robert sat back in his seat.

Occasionally, when he had left an unbearable show or when he found himself in the theatre district with nothing much to do, he would make a round of the various plays, standing up in back just long enough to catch the high points, or certain good scenes, in each play, the timing of which he knew by heart. He could organize a tour that might include six or eight shows, seeing some particularly good part of each one, and it was a memorable experience for whoever accompanied him. One time, however, he and George Oppenheimer left *Run, Lil' Chillun* because there had been one too many revival scenes—like the dialect characters in *The Squall*—and started on a tour, but their timing was off, and they hit every show on the circuit on an average of two minutes after the good scenes were over. Robert became desperate, and tried to reorganize his timing by cutting corners, but the whole evening was off synchronization, and they didn't see one outstanding scene. They finally gave up trying, and went to Tony's.

In spite of the fact that he was more whimsical about leaving a show than the daily newspaper critics were allowed to be, Robert always felt bad about giving an unfavourable notice, and he tried to let a play or a person down as gently as possible. (There were exceptions, of course, as in *Abie's Irish Rose*, where he felt the public had been insulted, but in general he tried to be as kind as he could.) He once took some actor to task for a really terrible performance, and then, after the review came out, he worried for days that he might have been instrumental in hurting the actor's career. It didn't matter that this particular actor probably *had* no career; Robert simply didn't want to feel that he was in any way responsible. Early in the depression, when things were still falling apart with sickening speed, he published his fifth book, titled *The Treasurer's Report, and Other Aspects of Community Singing*, and in a letter to Frank Gillmore, president of Actors Equity, he said that "I don't seem to be able to do much for the Actors' Unemployment Relief Fund except possibly help to throw more actors out of work," and that he would therefore donate 10 per cent of his royalties to Equity. Harper & Brothers, the publishers, added 10 per cent of the sale price, and the first cheque to Equity, two months after the agreement went into effect, was for $378.50. The book subsequently went into twelve editions.

Briefly, in 1927, he had a chance to do something that he considered worthwhile, but the end result was that it created a lot of publicity and strained a friendship, and that was all. Back in June of 1921, when Robert and Gertrude were visiting friends in Worcester, they had gone to the Worcester Golf Club to pick up their host. The trial of Nicola Sacco and Bartolomeo Vanzetti, two acknowledged anarchists who were accused of a payroll murder in South Braintree, was on at the time, and Judge Webster Thayer, who was presiding at the trial, was also a member of the Worcester club. When Robert's friend came out of the locker room, he said that he had just been talking with Judge Thayer, who had referred to Sacco and Vanzetti as "those bastards down there," and had said that he was going to "get them good and proper." Furthermore, the friend reported, Thayer had said that the "radicals" were trying to pressure him, and that he "would show them and get those guys hanged," and that he "would also like to hang a few dozen of the radicals." Robert listened to this account of what seemed like acute judicial misbehaviour, and said nothing.

On July 14, Sacco and Vanzetti were found guilty, and there started more than six years of legal wrangling in an attempt to get them a new trial. The case received worldwide attention, because there was the strong evidence that the men had been convicted for being anarchists and not for the crime of which they had been accused, and from what Robert had heard, this seemed more than likely. On May 4, 1927, Vanzetti sent an appeal for a new trial to Governor Alvan T. Fuller of Massachusetts, and it was accompanied by five affidavits of prejudice, one of them volunteered by Robert. He testified, in a legal deposition, to what he remembered his friend had told him, and when the deposition was made public the friend flatly denied having said a word of it. He'd known Web Thayer for years, the friend said, and was sure he would have remembered it if Web had ever said things like that.

Finally, the case became so controversial, and the accusations so loudly and widely expressed, that Governor Fuller appointed a so-called advisory committee, consisting of Abbott Lawrence Lowell, Samuel Wesley Stratton, and Robert Grant, to study the whole conduct of the trial and related aspects of the case, and to report on it to him. Robert went steaming up to Boston, and repeated his testimony before the advisory committee, but the minute he walked into the room he knew that he might just as well have stayed at home. He told them everything that he could remember that his friend had said, and they nodded and thanked him and looked through him as they did. So he went to Fuller himself, and repeated his story, and Fuller leaned back and smiled, and said, "Mr. Benchley . . . when I hear a good story, and then when I go back and tell it to my wife, Mrs. Fuller often says to me, 'Alvan, haven't you fixed it up just a little?' And sometimes I have, just to make it better telling." He looked at Robert, and smiled again. "Now, doesn't that sometimes happen with you, too, Mr. Benchley?" he asked. "Don't you think we all sometimes improve a story with the telling?"

He then suggested that if Robert thought Judge Thayer had been prejudiced, he go through the testimony and show exactly where the prejudice appeared. In this he was fairly safe, since the state supreme court had already found all of Thayer's in-court remarks to be legally correct, but Robert took the copy of the testimony Fuller gave him, and went back to New York with it. He later wrote Fuller a three-page letter in which he began by conceding that if the supreme court said so, then the judge's *in-court* conduct was probably defensible by the cold letter of the law. He added:

> But, as neither you nor I are lawyers, I trust that I may dispense with technicalities in this matter and ask you to consider it as a layman who wants to see justice done, even justice at the expense of the judiciary—if such a paradox is possible, and I am afraid that it is.
>
> And, as a first step toward this frame of mind, please consider that the judge who is being quoted now is the same man who *one week before*, had told his golf-mates in the locker room of the Worcester Golf Club that he would "get these reds good and proper."

He then went on to show, from the record, how Thayer had sided with the prosecution in heckling Sacco, overruling objections when Sacco's words were taken out of context and distorted, and in general living up to his prediction of the week before. Robert concluded the letter:

I am afraid that this has been a pretty long letter. I hope that it has not been so long but that you have been able to read some of it. I have no personal interest in this case, and, in fact, have tried not to think about it any more than I could help, because I find that I get too sore about it if I do. But Massachusetts is my home state . . . and I have enough pride left to get excited whenever the good name of Massachusetts is concerned. And I feel very strongly—just as you do—that it is concerned here.

When the Advisory Committee finally published its report, stating that the trial had been perfectly fair and legal, Robert was surprised to see that they had gone so far as to say that "the Judge was indiscreet in his conversation with outsiders during the trial." Hurriedly, however, the report continued: "But we do not believe that he used some of the expressions attributed to him, and we think that there is exaggeration in what the persons to whom he spoke remember."

Less than a month later, Sacco and Vanzetti were executed. There were riots, demonstrations, and strikes in cities all over the world, and one British periodical said that "for the first time in 150 years, the flag of the United States has been treated in every land as the symbol of a great wrong."

Robert's testimony was written into all the histories of the case, along with the testimony of the other people who thought they had evidence of prejudice, and that was all the good it did.

11

The year 1927 was a busy one for Robert. He started a column for *The New Yorker* called "The Wayward Press," which commented on the vagaries of the local newspapers every three weeks and which he signed Guy Fawkes; he agreed to film the Treasurer's Report as the first all-talking motion picture; and he collaborated on a Broadway musical comedy—all in addition to his regular duties as drama critic for *Life*. His "Books and Other Things" column for the *World* had lasted only about a year; that had been superseded by a weekly syndicate feature for David Lawrence, and from that he had gained little except a seat at the inauguration of President Harding, whom he described as "a good man, who ought to be Lieutenant Governor of Rhode Island." He sold free-lance pieces to *The Bookman*, *The Detroit Athletic Club News*, *College Humor*, and, after 1925, *The New Yorker*, with occasional stabs at erudition for *The Atlantic Monthly* and *The Yale Review*.

But his main love was the theatre. Ever since his days as a Sothern and Marlowe extra in Worcester, and then the Hasty Pudding and D.U. shows, he had had that sneaking affection for the theatre that most people will violently deny, in the same breath with which they talk about the smell of grease paint. He never thought of himself as an actor, and he didn't feel that he was good enough to call himself a writer (he listed himself in *Who's Who* as a journalist, and when someone once asked him about his style, he replied, "I don't know enough words to have a style; I know, at the most, fifteen adjectives"), but he knew that somewhere, preferably around the theatre, there was a place where he should be. And every opening night, at that moment when the house lights go down and the actors close their eyes in hurried prayer and the playwright feels that he's going under ether, when the gabble in the audience stops and all eyes are turned to the lighted curtain—every night that he sat in his seat and felt that mass expectancy, Robert hoped that what he was about to see might be the great one, that this might be the outstanding play of the season.

He and Mrs. Parker had more or less given up their idea of writing a play, and Sherwood had gone off on his own and written a little piece called *The Road to Rome*, which put him out of their class immediately. But Robert was still in a playwrighting frame of mind when Alex A. Aarons and Vinton Freedley suggested that he collaborate on the book of a musical comedy with Fred Thompson. The music and lyrics were to be by George and Ira Gershwin, with Fred and Adele Astaire in the leads, and the setup was so good that the play could almost write itself. Possibly it could have, but it didn't, and by the time they got on the road, prior to the Broadway opening, they were up to their hips in revisions, cuts, inserts, and juggling. The name changed, from *Smarty* to *Funny Face*, and the book credit changed, from Robert Benchley and Fred Thompson to Fred Thompson and Paul Gerard Smith. One of Robert's last official acts, before he returned to the comparatively rational business of drama criticism, was to look at a scene that had been rewritten four times in the last week, and was being rehearsed while the stage hands set up the scenery. Throughout the playing of the scene, a rope dangled from the flies, first in the centre of the stage, then over to the left, and then across right, and there were times when the actors had to duck to get out of its way. Ladders were moved about, men called to each other from the wings, and idle actors spilled coffee and crumpled sandwich bags. Finally, when the scene was over, Freedley asked Robert what he thought of the new version.

"I like it best with the rope in the middle," Robert said, and drifted out of the theatre. But his experience with *Funny Face*, brief though it was, was valuable and sobering to him as a critic. He later wrote:

The more I learn about the inside working of the theatre, the less qualified I feel to write about it. Unless a critic has sat in at rehearsals and seen what has happened to the author's script (for better or worse), has heard what the director has told the actors—and what the actors have told the director—unless he knows who is to blame for what and who is to be acclaimed for what—then how can he assign blame or praise for any given effect? All he can do is to say how he himself liked the show, which results in what is scornfully known as "personal journalism."

His movie of the Treasurer's Report was the result of suggestions from Thomas Chalmers, of Fox Films, who claimed that he ought to act in movies as well as write for them. Not wanting to be known as an actor, because he still felt that it would jeopardize his position as a critic, he put Chalmers off with one excuse after another, but finally, when he went out for a quick, three-week writing job in the summer of 1927, Chalmers got him to agree, more or less as an experiment, to try it. There had been pictures with musical background, and pictures with sound effects, but there had never been sustained speech of more than a minute on the screen, and the Fox people wanted to play around with it. So, in January of 1928, Robert went over to the Fox studios in Astoria and recited the Treasurer's Report in front of the camera and microphone, and when the result was run off in the preview room, one producer stated flatly that there was no future for talking pictures. Nevertheless, the film was released that spring, and the movie critic for the *World* said that

Mr. Benchley leads us all to suspect that if he really cared to do it he might go to Hollywood and be funny most conspicuously and most successfully. The young man tones and keys his humour; he knows when and where to toss off a gag; his acting is smart and intelligent, and he is vastly pleasing to his audience.

And that, loosely speaking, did it. He made a short of *The Sex Life of the Polyp* that same year; in 1929 he did three more shorts, and by 1932 the movie people had bullied him into appearing in a full-length picture. It was called *Sport Parade*, and he played a radio announcer in a short bit that he had written. His notices were better than those of the picture, and from then on he couldn't stop. It wasn't the notices, or the producers, that kept him going; it was the fact that he suddenly couldn't afford *not* to be in pictures. In all, he made forty-eight shorts, and appeared in and/or collaborated on forty-seven feature pictures. In 1929, he moved from *Life* to *The New Yorker*, succeeding Charles Brackett as drama critic there, but he couldn't get by on the $300 a week alone, and it seemed that the more money he made, the more he was required to spend. In contrast to the days when he itemized every penny that went in or out, and when his month's surplus or deficit might run to $1.87, he now found it hard to keep track of five-dollar bills, which lay around in little crumpled balls and then disappeared. He developed a phobia about letting anyone pay the bill in a restaurant, and if anything seemed like a good idea he would do it, forgetting about the cost until much later. His theory was that money was intended to be spent, and if you had it you ought to put it to the best uses possible. And the best uses possible did not, for him, include burying it away in stocks or bonds, where *nobody* knew what might happen to it. This theory put him in a position, around 1930, to jeer at the financiers and businessmen who had previously scorned him for being impractical. As he wrote it:

I am known as a bad business man from one end of the country to just a little beyond the same end . . . [but] if I wanted to, I might point out that out of a possible $5000 which I have made since I left school I have had $3000 worth of good food (all of which has gone into making bone and muscle and some nice fat), $1500 worth of theatre tickets, and $500 worth of candy; whereas many of my business friends have simply had $5000 worth of whatever that stock was which got so yellow along about last November. . . . Those of us who have nothing but fripperies to show for our money have had a good laugh. At least we've got the fripperies.

Just how bad a businessman he was was illustrated a few years later, when he was sharing a cottage in Beverly Hills with John McClain. McClain had a combination chauffeur-valet-butler, as did Robert, although Robert's man was a bad driver and not much of a valet. But Robert didn't feel that he ought to let his man go, because once, when the car was overturned in an accident, he had had to step on the man's neck in order to get out the wreckage, and he still felt bad about it. So they had two menservants around the house and nothing for them to do, because Robert and McClain had their meals out, and took taxis wherever they went. The result was that the two valets spent most of every day cooking exotic dishes for themselves, and the first month's grocery bill came to $600. McClain said he thought something should be done about it.

"Oh, I don't know," Robert replied. "Do you think that's excessive, really?"

What he did about it was accede to his valet's request for an adding machine for the pantry, so that they could be sure they weren't being cheated. He paid a considerable sum for the adding machine, but figured that in the long run it would pay for itself. He finally got rid of his valet by helping him set up in business with a waxworks museum.

One thing that did not work out so well in New York was his room at the Algonquin. As a room it was all right, but as a place to work it was out of the question, because too many of his friends were in or near it too much of the time. It was physically impossible for him to ask anyone to leave, and the knowledge of a friendly gathering nearby was often enough to make him leave the typewriter and go and investigate, just in case he might be missing something important. Once, he had been trying to start a piece but couldn't get it under way, so he went down the corridor to where a poker game was in progress, just to jolt his mind into starting up. Some time later, he returned to his room, sat down to the clean sheet of paper in the typewriter, and pecked out the word "The." This, he reasoned, was as safe a start as any, and might possibly break the block. But nothing else came, so he went downstairs and ran into a group of Round Table people, with whom he passed a cheerful hour or so. Then, protesting that he had to work, he went back upstairs, where the small, bleak "The" was looking at him out of the expanse of yellow paper. He sat down and stared at it for several minutes, then a sudden idea came to him, and he finished the sentence, making it read "The hell with it," and got up and went happily out for the evening.

Obviously, this kind of thing could not keep up for very long, and he finally decided to move across the street, to the Royalton, which was then a bachelors' hotel and which would give him just enough, but not too much, privacy. He told Frank Case, the Algonquin owner, of his plans, and Case was distressed and volunteered to see to it that nobody would be allowed in his room during working hours. "No, thanks," Robert replied. "You might keep them from coming up, but you can't keep me from coming down."

So he moved across the street, where there was no dining-room, no lobby to speak of, and nothing to make him want to peek out of his room. Almost before he knew it, he had a room that was as famous as, and in some ways resembled, the Smithsonian Institution.

It all started when he first saw the place, which, even in the glaring nudity of a semifurnished hotel room, looked Victorian. The walls were a deep cream colour, with dark mahogany baseboards and trim, and the windows were cross-latticed, so that each pane was diamond-shaped.

"Oh, so they think they're Victorian," he said. "*I'll* show them something Victorian, if that's the way they want to play."

His first move was to get a dark red rug, and red curtains

to cover the windows and shut out all the light. Then he put a red-velvet, tasselled cover on the fumed-oak table in the middle of the living room (it was a two-room suite), and placed brass student lamps, with green shades, around at various strategic spots. Bookcases were installed on all four walls, and three pictures of Queen Victoria, one of them framed in red velvet, were hung between the windows. He covered the walls with every kind of picture he could find, and as time passed, his family and friends contributed enough so that there was practically no bare space showing.

You entered the room through a small hall, so small as to be almost square, which soon became filled with trunks, stacks of old newspapers and foreign magazines, bound volumes of *The New Yorker*, overcoats, canes, a sword, and other items not often used. A shelf in this hall contained bills, telephone messages, and a deer skull.

The primary colour of the room itself was red, although the green student lamps gave it an atmosphere of well-lighted darkness like that in a sleeping car at night. To the left, as you entered, was a blue couch, sometimes called "The Track," because when he wanted to take a nap on it he would say, "Well, I guess I'll do a couple of laps around the track," and then lie down. The other name for it was the "Wirephoto Couch," because it had a rough, corduroylike covering, and when a person woke up from a nap his face was streaked in horizontal lines, like the early wirephotos.

Beyond the couch was a small desk, on which was an old, battered typewriter, and over the desk was a five-foot shelf of books that were collected for their titles alone. Over the years, he acquired such items as *Forty Thousand Sublime and Beautiful Thoughts*, *Success with Small Fruits*, *Talks on Manure*, *Keeping a Single Cow*, *Bicycling for Ladies*, *The Culture and Diseases of the Sweet Potato*, *Ailments of the Leg*, *In and Out with Mary Ann*, *Perverse Pussy*, and several others. Over this shelf was a glassed-in model of an Erie steamboat, donated by Paul Hollister. In the same corner were a cello and a music stand, gifts of a friend to whom he once remarked that he would like to play the cello. The music on the stand was dedicated to him, but he never got around to playing it. He tuned the cello once, though.

Between the curtained windows was a bookcase which stood about chest-high, and this was the cause of the collection that later all but got out of hand, and made the room the cleaning-woman's hell that it was. Robert wanted some knickknacks to put on top of this bookcase, and he started off with miniature geese, globes that made snowstorms when shaken, and gruesome little figures carved out of roots. He invited contributions from his friends, and suddenly there was a new game, called Dig It Up, Dust It Off, and Give It to Benchley. To make matters worse, the Royalton abandoned its for-men-only policy, and women joined in the headlong rush to donate something horrible to the room. In almost no time, the bookcase was overflowing onto the tables and desks, and Robert found himself swamped with, as he described it, "old busts of Sir Walter Scott, four-foot statues of men whose shirtfronts lit up when attached to an electric connection, stuffed owls, and fox terriers that had lain too long at the taxidermist's." He got rid of many of the larger and more sordid items, admitting that it was his fault for having brought the subject up, but adding, plaintively, "What I meant was contributions I could use. I didn't mean that I was starting a whaling museum or that I planned to build new rooms. . . . I have a horrible premonition that some day soon they are going to drag around a Pullman car named 'Gleeber's Falls' or 'Angostura' and ask me to give it a home."

In the corner beyond the windows were two more bookcases, which reached to the ceiling, and in one of which were drama books and the programmes for most of the plays he had seen. The next wall was taken up pretty much by his desk, over which were reference books, four small Breughel prints, and two signs, one reading, "We All Speak English," and the other, "Why Can't You Write?" To the right of the desk was the door to the bedroom, covered by a set of bead curtains which were acquired by Don Stewart in a Marseilles bordello. Over the door hung four beer mugs; a blue-green bird, under the tail of which "1903" was written in beads; and a sign saying "MR. Benchley, please." The "Mr." was in red, and the sign was a gift from Frank Adams, in return for a thoughtful favour Robert had done him. When the *World* closed and F.P.A. went to the *Herald Tribune* (having, ten years before, left the old *Tribune* for the *World*), Robert went down to the empty *World* office at night, stole the frosted-glass doorpane with Adams's name still on it, and took it to Adams's new office, just to make him feel more at home.

One entire wall, which ran from the bedroom door to the hall door, was covered with bookcases and, where there was any space left, framed pictures from the old *Life*. A closet was sandwiched between the bookcases, and it contained, among other things, clothes, a banjo mandolin, glasses, a fire chief's hat from Worcester (he was made honorary chief of the Worcester Fire Department, after he once gave an interviewer to believe that his boyhood ambition had been to be a fireman), a hot plate, several empty flasks and decanters, a box of crackers, a jar of peanut butter, paper-covered sugar lumps appropriated from restaurants, a three-foot cocktail shaker in the form of a lighthouse, a couple of suitcases, and the large jar of New England boiled dressing with which Gertrude always kept him supplied. Also, hidden away in the closet were his more erudite books—books in German, books on philosophy, books on obscure subjects, books on music —which he didn't especially want people to know that he was reading. He read all the time, sometimes being into four or five books at once, but he was so afraid of appearing pretentious that he would occasionally, particularly in Hollywood, cover a volume of Proust with the dust jacket from a murder mystery.

The whole room was about twelve by twenty feet. On the

table in the middle were a dozen or so books and magazines, the current week's crop of mail and telephone messages, a small, black-framed picture of a couple taken about 1870, and a piece of jade which he kept around because it had a nice tactile quality. Between the table and the couch was a red chair with white antimacassars that were always coming unpinned, and in front of the chair was a card table on which he read the papers and played solitaire. The chair was just low enough and comfortable enough so that it was hard to get out of, and he sometimes spent most of the day there.

He did his writing on a portable typewriter table, which was small and low and could be pushed out of the way when anything more important came up. It was in one corner, near his desk and out of the general stream of traffic.

The bar, if such it could be called, was just what was necessary to meet the needs of the moment, and was usually located on top of a set of the *Encyclopaedia Britannica*, near the closet. It consisted of a large vacuum jug for ice, some assorted glasses (a few of them the trick kind, donated by friends), and three or four bottles. There were also three glass decanters, marked "Scotch," "Rye," and "Sherry." The Scotch and rye decanters could usually be trusted, but the sherry one was something of a catchall, and might contain anything from muscatel to mouthwash. A small bottle, labelled "Hot Drops," held what sherry there was.

Through the bead curtains, toward the bedroom, were more bookcases and a filing cabinet, in which all the fifteen hundred or more books were cross-indexed. The bedroom was about big enough to hold the bed, the dresser, and a clothes cabinet, with room for a person to walk between them. Its size became important one year, when the Internal Revenue inspectors challenged Robert's deduction of the entire Royalton rent as office expense, and they got down and measured the square feet in the bedroom and then disallowed a proportionate amount of his deduction, on the ground that nobody was ever going to get any work done in *that* room. Robert tried to convince them that a writer is always working, but they wouldn't listen.

The main drawback to the bedroom, however, was the fact that it faced onto 43d Street, and was almost directly over a fire station. At all hours of the day and night, the room would suddenly be filled with the howling, clanging sounds of the fire trucks getting underway, and then, later on, the throaty, disagreeable noises of their return. He became more or less accustomed to it, but not to the subtler, more irritating noises of the pigeons that roosted on the window ledge. Early in the morning, they would fly down and perch near his window, gargling and muttering, and when he chased them off by snapping a towel at them, they went across the street and continued their depraved business, only louder, on the ledges of Stern's department store. He had a violent, almost pathological, hatred of pigeons, and the pigeons behaved as though they knew it. At one point, he even toyed with the idea of getting an air rifle of some sort, but he gave that up when a friend pointed out that the police were dead set against civilians' shooting in the city streets.

To a newcomer, the room had a baffling, almost overwhelming effect. There was too much to be taken in all at once, and yet out of the disorder there came a kind of relaxing sense of order, because there was no emphasis on any particular item. The first time Noel Coward visited the room, he came in, looked quickly about him, and said, "So *this* is your little rose bower. . . . I must say, it looks *lived* in." Another English visitor became fascinated by a trick cigarette box, the kind in which the bottom rises when the lid is lifted, thereby bringing the cigarettes in reach through little holes near the top. There were never any cigarettes in it, and this Britisher lifted the lid a couple of times and silently watched the bottom rise, and all the time he was in the room it was obvious that his mind kept wandering back to the box, trying to figure out its purpose. Finally, just as he was leaving, he lifted the lid once more, stared at the way the bottom worked, then snapped the lid down and turned away. "I dare say it has its advantages," he said, briskly and to nobody in particular, as he walked out the door.

Occasionally, Ernest Hemingway dropped into the room, on his way to or from France, Spain, Africa, or Cuba, and one night he was browsing through the bookshelves and came upon a set of his own works. Robert had bought Hemingway's first book, a slender volume of sketches called *In Our Time*, and had a first edition of every book since. Hemingway took down *In Our Time* and opened it.

"So you were going to save this, and then sell it when it got to be worth a lot of money," he said. "All right. I'll fix *you*." He took out a pencil, and inscribed the book to Robert in a way that made it immediately unfit for travel through the United States mail, and then he took down *A Farewell to Arms* and, in diminutive handwriting, filled in every blank that the publisher had been forced to substitute in the original dialogue. "Corrected edition with filled-in blanks," he wrote on the flyleaf. "Very valuable—sell quick."

The room would have driven a woman crazy, because things were put in their functional rather than their usual places. The bottle opener, for instance, was not on the bar but was just around the corner from it, on a shelf in the closet. It was easier to reach that way, and might have been lost on the bar, or fallen down behind something. The clean towels were not in a drawer, but were on a pile of books at the foot of the bed, where it was easier for a person with wet hands to get at them. And the Band-Aid box, far from being in an out-of-the-way place like the medicine cabinet, was on the table in the living room, because that was where it would most probably be needed. Pictures of the family were kept in drawers, and pictures of himself were under the ragged shirts that he kept meaning to throw away.

There were other things about the room which any stranger, male or female, needed a long time to get used to. When

Robert was in Hollywood, he gave the room to whoever happened to want it, and he could always tell if a comparative stranger had taken a bath recently, because the water would still be in the tub. The drain plunger for the tub was on the floor behind the shower curtain, and the uninitiated could almost never find it. The lamp shade in the bedroom was too big and would always fall askew, and you had to balance it just right to keep it from smouldering. The dial on the radio was off synchronization, so if you wanted a station at, say, 770, you turned it to about 830 and then fiddled to find it. And you never, *never* opened the curtains in the living room.

One of the tall bookcases in the living room held his growing collection of books about the Queen Anne period, of which he finally gathered about a hundred. At one point he decided, as a salve to his consicence and as proof that he could do some serious writing, to write a history of the humorists in the time of Queen Anne. He left a standing order at the Holliday Bookshop that any book about that period, or any book relating to it in any way, should be sent to him, and he read them all as they came in and then filed his notes in a card file with a secret coding system. After he had done a monumental amount of reading, beginning with all the works of all the humorists, he came to the reluctant conclusion that not one of them was funny. After a period of brooding, during which books continued to pour in from Holliday, he settled on the idea of writing a general history of the time, but writing it in the form of a play, with the characters and settings explained in advance and the story told through dialogue and stage directions. He continued to read, and to make notes, and to amass background material. He never once made a definite start on the writing.

His method of reading was one that sometimes came close to defeating its own purpose. He maintained very strict self-discipline on certain matters, and when reading, for instance, a newspaper, he read from Column 1 to Column 8, Page 1 to Page 36, always in their proper sequence. No matter if there was a story on Column 8 that carried a five-column headline; he would not read a line of it until he had finished Columns 1 through 7. And he would never follow the jump when a story continued inside the paper; he would finish reading the intervening pages, and pick up the story when he came to it. He didn't read all of every story, but he never read out of sequence. With this same kind of discipline, he was able to read five or so books at one time, reading parts of them and putting them down without losing track of where he was in any one of them.

But the thing that almost undid him was footnotes. Just as he would never pass over a word of which he was not sure without looking it up in the dictionary, so he could not pass over a footnote without, if it referred to some other page or some other book, looking up what it referred to. One night, he was reading one of his Queen Anne books in bed, and he came to a footnote that read "cf, p. 378, Dimmick *Wars of Succession.*" With a sigh, he got out of bed, went into the living room, took down Dimmick's *Wars of Succession,* and opened it to Page 378. He had read only one paragraph, when he came to a footnote referring him to another book, so he flicked on an extra light and started to look for *that* one. By this time, he was determined not to be thrown by a mere "cf.," and when the third book also had a cross-referring footnote, he cleared his throat, said, "All right, you son of a bitch," and went back to the bookcase. Dawn found him sitting in the middle of the floor, surrounded by books, grimly reading something that had nothing whatsoever to do with Queen Anne.

One nice thing about the place was that, if you were in the living room, you didn't notice the advent of dawn, because the curtains were always tightly closed and there was a constant level of light in the room. Of course, if you were seated facing the bedroom you could sometimes see the night colour change to cold blue-grey, but the character of the room itself—its inherent warmth and colour—never changed. It was a room that was good to come back to, and there were many nights, when Robert had been out with one or more friends and had closed most of the regular places, that they would all come back to the room for just a little more talk, because talk came very easily there. Sometimes the talk was funny, and sometimes it wasn't; very often, after perhaps 4 A.M., when all the jokes had been told and they all had laughed as much as they could, the talk would be serious and, notwithstanding the lateness of the hour, profound. It was then that some people found out, much to their surprise, that Robert was deeply religious. It was a surprise because his normal gaiety and ebullience sometimes took an almost raffish form, and also because he was such a determined anti-formalist as to appear practically agnostic. But what looked on the surface like a hatred of religion was actually a resentment of any interpretative authority; his belief in God and the hereafter was so strong as to communicate itself to others, and if not actually to convert them, at least to reaffirm their own faith. Not many people saw this side of him, although there were quite a few who saw the superficial aspects.

There was, for instance, his feeling about Christmas. He wrote two biting satires on how the spirit of Christmas gets lost through the dogged determination of the celebrants to preserve it, and he once made a remark, on leaving a restaurant the afternoon of Christmas Eve, that summed up his idea of what often goes wrong with the whole holiday. He and a group of friends had been having a Christmas Eve luncheon at "21," and around four o'clock he looked at his watch and rose from the table, saying that he had to get out to Scarsdale. The others urged him to stay just a little longer, but he was adamant.

"After all, I owe it to the children," he said softly, as he straightened his shoulders and turned toward the door. "They've never seen me drunk."

If he actually *had* been drunk, the remark wouldn't have been so funny; as it was, it made a perfect exit line.

His deeper feeling about Christmas was shown by the fact

that he and Gertrude read Dickens's *A Christmas Carol* every Christmas Eve, year after year, and on one occasion he recorded in his diary that they had "read the morning-after scene in the *Christmas Carol*, crying, as usual; not at the sad parts, but at the parts that are so glad that they shut off your wind."

And he usually did all his shopping Christmas Eve, waiting until the stores had cleared out and relaxation had begun to set in, and then he and whatever members of the family had had lunch with him would go from store to store, laughing and buying things as though it were just a shopping spree instead of a formal occasion. He would do anything to keep a celebration from being formal or routine.

Sometimes a fine insanity crept into these shopping expeditions, as in the time when he was leaving Wadley & Smythe, the florists, after having suddenly decided to buy flowers for everyone, and when he got on the street, he said, almost wistfully, "You know, I wish I worked there. Then when people asked me what I did for a living, I could say, 'Oh, I waddly . . . and I Smythe.' "

It was the informality of the Royalton room that made it a good place to come back to, but by the same token it was a bad place to start out from, because sometimes you never left. Robert had a theory that drinking in the home was dangerous, because he could never make just a single Martini; mixing them at five to one, he was bound by simple arithmetic to make six, and six Martinis when you intended one could radically alter an evening's schedule. So he preferred to meet his companions out for dinner (this was not an unalterable rule; the cases varied with the circumstances), and save the room as a retreat for later. And "later" could mean the next day or the next week, or, if the trail had led to Europe, two or three weeks afterward. You never could be sure just what was going to happen.

This air of suspense—or anticipation—was heightened, during Prohibition, by the fact that Robert appeared to have no fear of gangsters, and would give anyone a dressing-down whom he considered out of order, including the police. One time, when he and Gertrude were eating at the Algonquin, they heard a mounted policeman cantering his horse up and down the block, and after several minutes of this Robert left the table, went outside, and stopped the policeman on his next time past. He said the policeman knew good and damned well that that was bad for the horse's hoofs, and that he should stop it immediately. The policeman offered to run Robert in, and Robert offered to run *him* in, and they glowered at each other for a moment and then the policeman walked his horse away, muttering as he did. Robert went back inside, and finished his meal. On the more dangerous side, he once went back to a speakeasy, the proprietors of which had given a friend of his a Mickey Finn, and told them all, individually and collectively, what he thought of them, and the speakeasy people stood on one foot and then the other and took it, although there were plenty of guns and blackjacks at their disposal if they had wanted to use them. Another time, in a loft in the mid-Forties called Chez Florence, there was a loud-mouthed oaf who turned out to be a prosperous gangster, and he became so offensive that Robert mocked him to his face by giving a particularly brutal imitation of him. Robert's friends were numb with fright as the gangster looked over and saw the parody of himself, and they did their best to get Robert to stop, but he wouldn't. With a delighted leer, the gangster came over to the party, put his arms around Robert's shoulders, and insisted that they all go on a tour of the town with him. They had a terrible time getting rid of him.

Another time, in California, Robert and Myron Selznick were in a gambling casino, and it was Robert's turn to be frightened. They had both lost a good deal of money, Selznick considerably more than Robert, when suddenly Selznick picked up the dice and put them in his pocket. "Come on," he said. "Let's go." Robert was sweating as they walked out of the casino, and he swore he could feel the guns aimed at his back, but Selznick was unperturbed. Around noon the next day, Selznick called on the phone. "How much money did you lose last night?" he asked.

"Oh, about $200," Robert replied.

"Did you say $2,000?" Selznick asked. "Or was it $20,-000?"

"I said $200," said Robert. "Two oh oh. Give or take a nickel, that is. Why?"

"There's a man here to buy back the dice for what we lost," Selznick replied. "I'd been kind of hoping you'd lost more."

No matter how far afield he got, he always came back to the room at the Royalton, often bringing with him some friend acquired during the expedition. It didn't make any difference who the person was; if he met someone who he thought was funny, or interesting, or in trouble, or just friendly, he would bring that person back to the Royalton and provide food, conversation, money, or whatever was needed. Strangely enough, these casual encounters almost always worked out well. Once, to be sure, he loaned $20 to a man who turned out to be a notorious pickpocket, con man, and general grifter; and another time a lady guest, who had appeared to be in desperate trouble when he met her, announced on entering the room that unless she got $5,000 immediately she would scream the place down, but in the main the guests were well behaved and appreciative. He took care of the lady by slipping into the bedroom and calling a friend, and within a matter of minutes people began to converge on the Royalton, singly and in groups of from three to seven, all prepared to swear that they had been with Robert since sundown. It was the only time he ever had to call for help, and the response was overwhelming. It was also almost unstoppable, because once the word got started that he was in trouble, everybody east of Teaneck, New Jersey, wanted to come to the Royalton and lend a hand. It was several days before the last of them left.

Generally, however, it was Robert who did the helping.

One evening, before "Prince" Michael Romanoff had become a famous restaurateur, he came up to the room and announced, almost casually, that he was sailing for Europe that evening. Romanoff's main fame at that point was as a traveller-without-passport; he had two shirts to his name, one of which was always at the laundry as deposit, and on this particular evening he was obviously hungry. Robert suggested that they have a *bon voyage* dinner, but Prince Mike replied that he had already had an excellent dinner at the Colony, thank you, and was just dropping by to pay his respects before going down to the *Île de France*, where he intended to stow away in Lifeboat No. 11. In as offhand a manner as he could, Robert took the peanut butter and the crackers from the closet, left them on the table, and then drifted around the corner into the bedroom. He looked back through the bead curtains, and saw Prince Mike wolfing down the crackers with both hands, so he went quietly to the bedroom phone and made a few calls. The *bon voyage* party that followed was of staggering proportions. There were baskets of fruit, baskets of food, and baskets of liquor, and in the small hours of the night (some people say it was the following night) Prince Mike's well-wishers took him down and tucked him and his provisions into Lifeboat No. 11. There are those who claim that he never made the *Île de France* at all, that it was Lifeboat No. 11 of the *Lafayette* into which they lashed him; whatever the ship, he had a pleasant crossing, and evaded the authorities at Le Havre by wearing a baggage porter's apron and carrying a few loads of luggage onto the dock before walking off.

But the help that Robert provided was not always in money or gifts. Most often, it was the subtler help of making a person feel wanted, or important, or even competent, and people would leave him feeling a glow of well-being that stayed with them a long time, and often developed into a kind of love. There was a young actress, for instance, who was maladjusted and unhappy and unsure of herself, and

Robert spent a great deal of time teaching her poise and control, and almost as an afterthought he taught her how to speak French, just as an added boost to her confidence. He could accomplish somewhat the same thing in a word or two, as he did with Wolcott Gibbs, who substituted for him on *The New Yorker* when he was in Hollywood and who was depressed about the inadequacy of his copy. Once, shortly after Robert returned, Gibbs told him that he was going to give up theatre reviewing, because no matter how hard he tried, his prose sounded awful. Robert took him out and bought him a drink, and told him not to worry, that his stuff was fine. "I wish I could write as well," he concluded. It was what Gibbs described as a grotesque thing to say, but he almost believed that Robert meant it, and that borderline belief was enough to encourage him to continue.

He assisted people in many other ways, too; he seemed always to want to help people to improve themselves, and he would supply advice, encouragement, money, and support wherever he thought they were needed. Sometimes it was only moral support, sometimes it was financial, and sometimes it was both, and his knack lay in instinctively knowing what kind of help was needed most. The exact number of people he helped or tried to help is unknown, but their range and variety are incredibly wide, and they turn up in the most unlikely places, from Rotterdam to Seattle and points north and south between.

So the room at the Royalton was a number of things besides a workroom. It was a meeting place, a confessional, and a schoolroom; it exuded Robert's personality and it absorbed all others that entered it, and it was impossible to stay long in the room without feeling warm and content.

12

The pigeons that heckled him from the window ledges of the Royalton were conducting only minor skirmishes in the larger, and unceasing, war that went on between Robert and all birds. He had an uneasy feeling that animals knew more than they were telling, and for that reason he was guarded in his approach to all of them, but for birds he had an outright, raging hostility, and the birds retaliated. It is hard at this point to say who started the war, but it was one of extraordinary bitterness.

No matter who started it, the birds were the more constant aggressors, and their tactics varied from heckling to outright assault to public mockery. Robert once hit a bird on the jaw, and another time was privileged to see a blackbird skid and lose its balance on a wet pavement—a sight that cheered him so that he not only razzed the blackbird loudly on the spot, but also wrote an article about it—but for the most part he could retaliate only by shouting and throwing things. And what hurt him most was that the birds used their worst weapon—public mockery—the one time he tried to make peace and be nice to them.

It happened in the Piazza San Marco, in Venice, where tourists traditionally have their pictures taken feeding the pigeons. A small bag of corn is all you need to attract the pigeons in swooping, fluttering clouds; they come at you like rain down a funnel; they perch on your hat, your shoulders, and your wrists, and it is considered a poor picture that doesn't have at least half of the tourist obscured by the wings, bodies, and blurs of pigeons. For some now-forgotten reason, Robert decided that he wanted to have his picture taken feeding the pigeons, so he bought a bag of corn and alerted the photographer. He opened the corn, and held it out in his hands and waited. One or two pigeons flew past him, landed, and began to grub around the street, looking for leftovers. He tossed a little corn to them, and one of them hopped out of the way but otherwise paid no attention. Of all the thousands of pigeons in the Piazza San Marco, not one of them came near him; and worse, they didn't even do him the honour of flying away. They just turned their backs and *walked* off, leaving him alone in the empty Piazza, making clucking noises and tossing little handfuls of corn into the street. It was the last time he ever tried to be nice to a bird.

A more aggressive attitude was adopted by a flock of catbirds in Beverly Hills, where he once rented a house that came complete with a patio and a Japanese butler. Every morning, the catbirds would hide in a eucalyptus tree, near the patio, while the butler set the breakfast out under covered dishes. Then, the minute the covers were removed, they would peel off and dive down from the tree, zinging past the table from all angles and taking first the toast, then returning for whatever else they could carry. The fact that Robert was sitting at the table made no difference; if he so much as leaned back to refold the newspaper, there would be a quick whir across the plate and a catbird would be off with a piece of sausage or bacon. This constant swooping and fluttering and darting, plus the loss of his food, finally drove him to having breakfast indoors, where he sat in the shadows and cursed the catbirds.

Pelicans, on the other hand, were more subtle. One evening, he and Edward Sutherland, the director, decided that it was important to drive up to Santa Barbara, a matter of some ninety-seven miles, in order to surprise their friends the Nick Ludingtons. They set off in the early hours of the morning, and sunrise found them humming along the coast road several miles short of their objective. In the clear, pink light of dawn, the sea was calm and silvery, and the tide washed coolly around the jagged rocks of the shore line. The salt smell in the air was clean and invigorating, and as Robert rolled down the window to breathe more deeply of it, he saw what appeared to be a group of fishermen, sitting quietly on the rocks by the sea.

"What an insane time to go fishing," he said, scornfully.

"I wouldn't get up at this hour for anything," said Sutherland. "Do you think they're having a good time?"

"They can't be," Robert said. "Look at the way they're hunched over. Nobody can have a good time all scrunched down like that."

"Still, we might ask them," said Sutherland. "They might have an interesting story to tell."

He leaned out and hailed the fishermen, who rose from the rocks and flew slowly away. It was a subdued pair who finally arrived in Santa Barbara, and it was remarked that they always seemed to look twice at people before speaking.

But it was the terns who were the assault troops in this Birds-versus-Benchley war. They were the ones who made the outright, personal attack with intent to maim or kill, and like the pigeons in Venice, they made their move when Robert was so nonbelligerent as to be almost friendly. He had gone swimming on the south shore of Nantucket; or, more accurately, he had gone to watch the rest of his family swim. Although he was technically dressed for swimming, in that he was wearing a bathing suit, he was also wearing a large peignoir, moccasins, a yachting cap, and dark glasses, and had a piece of paper stuck under the glasses to protect his nose. He was rubbing sun-tan lotion on his hands and ankles, which were the only parts of him exposed to the direct rays of the sun. Farther down the beach, one of the bathers came out of the water and by accident stumbled on a terns' nesting area. The birds rose in a great, squeaking cloud, and began to zoom and dive on the bather, and Robert was doubled over with laughter when one tern separated itself from the group, flew to a spot directly above him, then folded its wings and dropped like a bomb onto the top of his head, driving its beak through his yachting cap and inflicting a jagged scalp wound. He rolled over and started digging, but before he could throw up any kind of shelter, several more terns had left the nesting area and had joined the first in attacking him. It was completely unprovoked aggression; their nests were at least fifty yards away, and they had left the real intruder to assault Robert, who wouldn't have cared if he never saw a tern's egg from one year to the next.

It was a long time before he was able to retaliate, but when his chance came he made the most of it. He was staying at the Garden of Allah, a hotel-*cum*-bungalows-*cum*-swimming-pool arrangement on Sunset Boulevard in Hollywood, and on this particular morning he was awakened by a rustling and crunching in the mock-orange tree outside his window. At first it just sounded like a drunk who had lost his way, then it began to sound more as though a team of horses had become entangled in the tree, and finally the sounds of thrashing were so loud and so insistent that Robert got out of bed and went crossly to the window and looked out. There, banging around among the branches, was a monstrous bird, which he later described as a cross between a flamingo and a seagull. With a hoarse shout, Robert flung out of his room and ran to the tree, and before the startled bird could get clear of the branches he hit it a good, solid right to the side of the beak. The bird squawked and flapped into the air, just avoiding the left hook that cut past its tail feathers. Panting but triumphant, Robert watched it lumber away, then turned and went back to bed.

His only other revenge was against the blackbird, and this triumph was so sweet that part of the subsequent article could probably stand reprinting. It goes:

There is a great satisfaction to us clumsy humans when we see an animal that is supposed to surpass us in skill making a monkey of itself.

I am still gloating over a blackbird that I saw, with my own eyes, in as disgraceful a bit of flying as any novice ever put on.

I was sitting in an automobile by the side of the curb when this bird swooped down. With some idea, evidently, of making a two-point landing, just to show off. Well, just as his feet hit the sidewalk, one of them slipped out from under him, and I was witness to the remarkable sight of a full-grown, adult bird falling on its tail. A vaudeville comic couldn't have taken a neater spill.

The chagrin and humiliation of that blackbird were gratifying to see. He got back his balance immediately and tried to act as if nothing had happened, but he knew I had seen him and he was furious. He was off in the air again right away, but not before I had sneered: "Nyaya!" at him and called "Get a horse!"

Everyone ought to see a bird slip on its tail at least once. It is a gratifying experience and one good for the soul.

The only birds that he could abide were penguins, because penguins look even more clumsy than humans and there is broad comedy in the way their dignity is constantly being destroyed. He once worked in a movie with a penguin named Eddie, and Eddie couldn't walk ten feet without tripping over a cable or something, always going flat on his face but always picking himself up and carrying on as though he had just been clowning. Robert and Eddie became good friends, to the point where Robert tried to get Eddie into one of his shorts, just to walk across in front of the camera while Robert was giving a lecture about income-tax returns. The sequence was filmed, and was generally conceded to be hilarious, and then was cut out on the grounds that it was too off-beat for general distribution.

Aside from birds, however, he was generally reserved in his feelings for animals, although he once wrote:

I am such a friend of animals that I am practically penniless. I have been known to take in dogs who were obviously imposters and put them through college. I am a sucker for kittens, even though I know that one day they will grow into cats who will betray and traduce me. I have even been known to pat a tiger cub, which accounts for my writing this with my left hand.

His affection was not quite as unrestrained as he pictured it, and as for the wild animals in his life, he had only one experience with them. It was, however, something of a shock to his system. In 1933, William Randolph Hearst got him to agree to do three syndicated columns a week, and the arrangement was formalized on a weekend at San Simeon, Hearst's sprawling, ornate, California ranch. When the time for athletics was announced, the guests divided into tennis, golf, or croquet groups according to their moods, and Robert slipped quickly out of sight and started off for a walk. He hiked briskly along for a while, remembering the days when he used to walk from Crestwood down to Tuckahoe or Bronxville to get his train into town, and without paying much attention to it he crossed a large iron fence. He had not gone a great deal farther when suddenly, off to his left, a herd of antelope bounded over a hill and across the plain. Interested, he watched them for a while, and then continued his walk, although at a slower pace. The feeling began to creep over him that he was being watched, and looking at a clump of trees he saw, but did not identify, a wildebeest standing in the shade and regarding him with mild curiosity. Slowly, he began to circle back toward the ranch, and then with growing panic he set his course between a herd of zebra and two elephants, which had wandered into sight over the top of a hill. Out of the corner of his eye he saw a giraffe peering at him across the top of a tree, and he broke into a run. Finally, wet and panting, he reached the fence, and only when he was on the other side did he see the sign: "Beware of Wild Animals." The roaring of some lions kept him awake most of that night.

Of all the animals, dogs seemed to like him best, and he reciprocated when he could. He never had a dog of his own, but he was always pleasant to friends' dogs, and he would talk to them and feed them peanut butter and pickles when they appeared around his bungalow. He was therefore a little hurt by the contempt shown by a fox terrier that he had never seen before. He was shaving one morning, when this dog walked into the bathroom, went directly to the soap dish in the tub, ate the cake of soap, threw up on the floor, and walked out, all without looking at him once. He never saw the dog again, but he worried about it for quite a while. He began to suspect that it had been deliberately sent to do what it did, and probably sent by the pigeons.

An incident symbolic of the lack of rapport between him and most animals occurred one time in Cambridge, when he was in college. Or possibly it shows great rapport; it is open to a wide variety of interpretations. At any rate, he and Paul Hollister were standing in front of Max Keezer's clothing store, in Harvard Square, and they happened to be discussing Lillian Russell, when Robert began to have the sensation of an extra presence in the conversation. Turning around, he saw that a policeman's horse, which had been standing at the curb, had edged up onto the sidewalk and had its head practically on his shoulder. It was quietly breathing down his neck, apparently intent on catching every word he said.

"Excuse me a minute," Robert said to Hollister, and he turned and faced the horse. "I was just saying," he said, "that Lillian Russell's opera company did more to make the American male conscious of music than any other single factor since Stephen Foster. Do you agree?"

The horse slowly shook its head.

"Good Lord, man, you must be mad," said Robert, just as an elderly lady walked past, stared, and then hurried on. "She possessed the rare combination of beauty and a good voice, the first of which drew men to see her and the second of which gave them musical pleasure to match their visual pleasure. Nobody in recent years has an appeal that anywhere near matches hers. Or perhaps you know of someone?"

The horse shook its head again, disregarding the small crowd that had begun to gather.

"Well, then," said Robert, "I see no point in continuing

the argument. I'm perfectly willing to listen to a man who has the facts, but in the absence of them I think I am just wasting your time and mine. Come, Paul, let's get a malted."

He and Hollister walked away, and the horse stepped back into the street.

13

Everything considered, it's a wonder he travelled as much as he did. He *liked* to travel, God knows, but whenever he left home plate he left what might laughingly be called his ordered way of life, and entered a world where the individual must continually be prepared to cope with the unexpected. In his case, he himself was often the unexpected element, but this in no way lessened the confusion.

For one thing, anything mechanical reduced him to a welter of helplessness, and for this reason he preferred not to travel by plane. He was worried not so much by the possible danger of flying as by his feeling that all inanimate objects, especially those designed to do something, were in a sinister conspiracy to deprive him of his reason. Even an ordinary buckle irritated him; he once watched his friend Gerald Murphy buckling and unbuckling a leather folder, and he concluded that the buckle must be Murphy's personal hair shirt, put on the folder (Murphy, as president of Mark Cross, can have his leather goods more or less as he wants them) as an act of penance. He could not understand how anybody would have anything to do with a buckle if he could possibly avoid it. By the same token, he could never figure out how to fasten the seat belt in an airplane; I have seen him, on take-off and landing, stuff the ends of the belt under his coat and hold them there, chuckling at the thought that he had at least momentarily outwitted the machine. I tried to show him how the belt worked but he waved me off, saying that his way was just as good. One time, when I was not with him, he was in a plane that was attempting a landing in a severe storm; it came down, touched its wheels to the ground, and then the pilot opened the throttles wide and it roared back up into the night.

The stewardess came out and smiled thinly at the passengers. "He's going to try it again," she said.

"Not with me, he isn't," said Robert, and dropped his seat belt and headed for the door.

But even on a train, where things are comparatively predictable, he also had his troubles. One time, before the advent of air conditioning, he was on a train crossing the Arizona desert, and the heat in his compartment was suffocating. The books which he always carried with him were too hot to touch, and he decided that the only way out of his misery was to take off all his clothes, lie down on the couch, and go to sleep. He did, and awoke a few hours later to find that the train had stopped. When his eyes came into focus he saw a grinning face peering in the window at him; some enterprising native had put a packing case alongside the train, and was charging people to stand on it and gaze in at him. It was clearly impossible for him to rush across and pull down the shade; all he could do was roll over and pretend to go back to sleep, while the unknown promoter outside kept taking in the money.

On another, although less spectacular, occasion, he caused a certain amount of flurry in a Pullman car. My brother had been married in Detroit, and the nucleus of the wedding party was returning to New York on a train that had only one sleeping car. It was during World War II; the trains were crowded, and Robert—or Gramps, as he was known to us—wound up in a lower berth. The next morning, after everybody else in the car had returned from breakfast, only his berth was still occupied, and the lone green curtain was as conspicuous as a flag on a balcony. Suddenly, I saw the curtain twitch and bulge. It was still for a moment, then came more signs of thrashing behind it, and finally a long, bare arm reached out and groped blindly about underneath the berth. The other passengers stared in mute fascination while the hand probed back and forth. Then the hand withdrew behind the curtain, and there was another pause. All at once,

Gramps's head appeared, wearing a battered, brown felt hat. He kept the curtains clutched tightly under his chin, and smiled. "It's a good joke on my socks," he said. "They got off at Schenectady."

There have been those who, for one reason or another, have been ejected from trains, but he was probably the only person ever to eject himself. During the latter part of the war he was coming East from California, and in the club car he met a young lady who was married to a Marine, and who had just seen her husband off for duty in the Pacific. She was understandably depressed, and he did his best to lessen her gloom. When the conductor came around, Robert produced his ticket, and the young lady opened her purse. She hadn't had time to get a reservation, she explained, but she had the money to pay for whatever space was available. Curtly, the conductor told her that there was no space, and that she would have to get off at the next stop. (At that time, when every train was full to the washrooms, railroad employees could afford to have slovenly manners.) Robert, nettled by the conductor's tone of voice, spoke up.

"Wait a minute," he said. "The lady can use my compartment. I'll sleep in here."

"Oh no you don't, Buster," replied the conductor, and the next instant he found himself the centre of a typhoon of outraged chivalry. He was told that he was a narrow-minded, pettifogging, middle-aged Storm Trooper; that if it weren't for the war nobody would be riding his bloody railroad; and that if he didn't trust Robert to sleep in the club car, then he and the entire railroad could step straight to hell. By unfortunate coincidence, the train was at that minute pulling into Victorville, or Barstow, or some such place, and Robert climaxed his remarks by jamming on his hat, picking up his brief case, and stamping off the train and into the desert. It occurred to him, as he watched the observation car dwindle into the distance, that there might have been a better way of handling the argument, but by then it was a little late for second guessing. He chartered a plane to the nearest commercial airport, then flew to Chicago, where he waited for the train to arrive with his baggage. He never found out what happened to the Marine's wife.

He had one other experience in the desert during the war, when he was with a USO entertainment troupe that was supposed to assemble in Albuquerque, and then fan out through the camps in the Southwest. He was the only person who was not notified that the tour had been cancelled, so he went to Albuquerque and was trying to fan out through the Southwest on his own, when they finally got the word to him. It had been pretty fruitless fanning, because wherever he had gone people had been unprepared for him, and in one place they had several thousand troops and not even a microphone. Under such circumstances, the Treasurer's Report contributed almost nothing to GI morale.

Of all the methods of travel, he liked boats the best, and once he went to Europe just because somebody at a party blew into an empty soda-water bottle, which made a noise so like a ship's whistle that everybody went down to the docks and got on the first boat for France. Another time, he was seeing a friend off on a North German Lloyd liner, and the friend suggested that he come along, just for the ride. The next day, Gertrude got a radiogram saying, EXCUSE IT PLEASE BACK ON THE NEXT BOAT. He had seven dollars in his pocket, no passport, and no change of clothes worth mentioning, and he had to stay in bed every morning until the stewardess returned the items she had washed overnight. Because of the lack of passport, the American consul in Bremen advised him to stay close to the ship until it started the return trip, but the friend with whom he had sailed was Nick Ludington, of the Ludington Air Lines, and the *Lufthansa* did Ludington the courtesy of inviting him and his party up for a joy ride. The joy ride ended in Paris, where Robert and the Ludingtons stayed until time for him to catch the boat at Cherbourg. This was in 1932, and the consul in Bremen, who happened to be a classmate of Robert's, had filled him in on the political situation during the brief time they had together. Robert returned to the United States with the inside information that nobody should get too worked up about this fellow Hitler; the Germans were just giving him enough rope to hang himself. It would all be over in a matter of months.

In 1925, the first year we all went abroad together, Marc Connelly came on the same ship, the S.S. *Resolute*. Connelly and Robert had a standing bet of a dollar, to be paid to the first man to spot another ship on the ocean, and for the first few days they were about even. Then, one afternoon, Connelly came into the stateroom and found Robert lying on his bunk, all bundled up in a life preserver and yachting cap, reading the instructions for abandoning ship. A flashlight lay on the bunk beside him.

"I'm not even going to look at you," Connelly said, walking over to the porthole. "You're just trying to make me panicky." He stared out the port, and in the middle distance saw an indistinguishable kind of craft; it was small, and low in the water, and although it had a smokestack, there was also some kind of sail arrangement, which seemed to have wrapped itself around the pilot house. Connelly regarded it for a moment, and then said, "I don't know whether you owe me a dollar or not. Come here and see what I see."

Robert got off the bunk, joined Connelly at the porthole, and was quiet while he studied the contraption. "Small towns don't count in this bet, you know," he said at last. "Only ships."

They finally decided that Robert should pay thirty-nine cents, on the premise that what Connelly had spotted was the *Mary W. Pollack*, bound for Albany with a load of hay.

It may be that Robert liked boats best because he had less trouble with them than with other forms of transportation, but there was one time, in 1929, when it would have been better if he had been dropped into Europe by parachute.

We had all gone over to spend the summer in France, and since he smoked a pipe while working and couldn't stand French tobacco, he had brought along twenty tins of his favourite American brand. For some reason, he had the idea it was forbidden to bring any American tobacco into France —that it would all be confiscated if found—and he had therefore secreted fifteen of the tins throughout our luggage, and given my brother and me two each to hide in our overcoat pockets. The twentieth tin he showed to the *douanier*, with some vague idea of disarming him with his honesty. That, he said, was all he had to declare. The *douanier*, a small man with a red, bristly moustache, felt the tin for a moment, then started rummaging through the luggage. In almost no time, he unearthed another. He showed it to Gramps, who said, "*Tiens*," as though he couldn't believe it, and that tin joined the first on the table. Slowly, the pile mounted, and the *douanier's* moustache crackled with excitement. He came to a small suitcase of Gertrude's, which she had packed and closed herself, and she swore to him that there was no tobacco in it. There were two tins. Afraid that we were going to be jailed and searched, she whispered to my brother and me to jettison what tobacco we had before it was too late. We sidled over to the edge of the pier and dropped the tins into the water, and to our horror they floated, while sailors gathered at the rail of a tug and debated diving in after them. The other passengers cleared the customs and departed; the train for Paris tooted twice and chugged away, and the idle members of the customs force stood in an admiring circle around our *douanier* and watched him pile tin after tin onto the table in front of him. He found them all, except those that were in the water, and the total fine was a thousand francs, which in those days was forty dollars. Then, with an imperceptible click of his heels, he returned them all. Dazedly, we stuffed them back into our rumpled luggage, and sloped off to a nearby hotel to spend the night.

That was his only attempt at smuggling, although on another trip he managed to smuggle liquor past Jennie—and literally under her nose. Five days before sailing for a short trip, he decided to take Jennie, who was then seventy-nine, over to see Dot and Fred Goddard, her niece and nephew-in-law who were living in Paris. Gertrude managed, in those five days, to get Jennie's passport issued to her; Robert cabled the Goddards: MOTHER WANTS TO KNOW WHETHER TO BRING HER BICYCLE; and Jennie was bustled from Nantucket to Boston to New York in time for a midnight sailing. The next night, after dinner, Robert ordered a white crème de menthe, and explained to Jennie that it was peppermint, for his digestion. He let her smell it, and asked her if she would like a glass. She declined, but said it smelled quite nice. Every evening after that, he had any colourless drink he wanted: schnapps, Cointreau, kirsch, gin, vodka, or whatever. And one evening, when he hadn't felt like having anything, Jennie reminded him that he'd forgotten his peppermint, so he snapped his fingers and thanked her and had a shot of vodka. That the whole thing worked out well seemed obvious, and yet, about a year later, Jennie asked Gertrude if Robert ever took a drink.

"Why don't you ask *him?*" Gertrude replied.

"I wouldn't insult him with the question," said Jennie, and the subject was dropped.

It was on the trip with Jennie, after he had got her safely billeted at the Goddards' summer home in Chantilly, that Robert went out in Paris with a group of friends, and told them of a certain restaurant where he had eaten a memorable pressed duck the year before. He couldn't recall the name of the restaurant, but he said he'd be sure to recognize it if he saw it again. It was somewhere in Montmartre, and after a considerable time he found it; everybody piled happily out of the cab and into the restaurant, and only when six orders of pressed duck arrived on the table did he recall what had made it so memorable—it was the worst pressed duck he had ever tasted.

As far as food in general was concerned, he was always willing to try something new, although he didn't much care for frilly dishes. He liked basic New England food, and basic French food, and basic Italian food, but he also liked certain specialties if they weren't too sweet or too gummy. Once, he was at the Grand Hotel in Venice with Gerald and Sara Murphy and Mrs. Parker, and his room adjoined that of the Murphys. The Murphys called through the open door and said they were ready to go down for dinner, and when they got no response after two more such announcements, they looked into his room and found him lying on the bed, his head near the wall, listening. It took some effort for them to pry him away from the wall, and he finally explained that he had found that his room was directly over the kitchen, and he had been listening, through an air shaft, to the reactions of the kitchen staff as the waiters came in with the various orders. The cooks were apparently loud in their derision of certain dishes, and equally loud in their approval of others, and the waiters would sing out the orders and then be greeted by a chorus of the cooks' reactions. From his listening post, Robert was in a position to get the honest, inside information as to what and what not to order in the dining-room.

It was also with the Murphys and Mrs. Parker, in a Swiss alpine town called Montana Vermala, that he got an irresistible urge to sing Harvard football songs. There was a tuberculosis sanatorium at Montana Vermala, and one night it occurred to Robert that somewhere in the village there might be a Harvard man, lonely and sick and far from home. If he were that man, he said, he could imagine nothing more wonderful than to hear "With the Crimson in Triumph Flashing" echoing in the cold night air, so he and Mrs. Parker bundled up and went out and sang the song up and down the darkened streets. There were no reports as to how many, if any, Harvard men heard them.

There was one trip he took to Europe on which he didn't

get into any trouble, but there is no logical reason to explain why. In 1931, he and Douglas Fairbanks and Lewis Milestone went over with the dim idea of making a group of travel pictures in Siberia, the Gobi Desert, Manchuria, Africa, and Switzerland. They weren't too sure of what form the pictures would take, but they reasoned that with Fairbanks to do the acting—or leaping—and Milestone to do the directing, and Robert to do the dialogue, they couldn't very well lose. They got no closer to Siberia than Italy, where someone suggested that they interview Mussolini, just for laughs.

At that time Fairbanks's name was good for an entree anywhere, and an audience was arranged. They showed up at the Palazzo at the appointed hour, and a lackey informed them that they would have to wait a half hour before *Il Duce* would see them. They told the lackey that they were too busy to wait, and while he stared at them goggle-eyed, they turned and stalked out.

Before they left Italy, Robert became intrigued with, and memorized, the "passengers will please refrain" sign on a train, which went something like "*I passaggieri son vivamente pregati de non viatori la canneta della toiletta durante la visitate della stazione*." When they got to Paris, they were assigned a room in the Hotel Crillon with a balcony overlooking the Place de la Concorde, and one afternoon, somewhere around the cocktail hour, Robert appeared on the balcony, flanked by Fairbanks and Milestone, and declaimed this sentence with Mussolini-like gestures. He ran through it several times, with different inflections and different pauses, larding it with what little other Italian he knew; Fairbanks and Milestone applauded at what they considered the appropriate times, and a small crowd gathered below. A few people cheered, some booed, and as the crowd grew larger one or two people broke out small Italian flags and waved them.

Finally, when he had shouted himself hoarse, Robert bowed and retired from the balcony; Fairbanks and Milestone bowed and followed him, and there was minor commotion in the street below. The next day, one Paris paper carried a vague story about some Italian dignitary who was staying at the Crillon.

As I said, I cannot understand how he managed to keep out of trouble on that trip.

Only once did I ever see him consciously ask for trouble, and that was in Chicago on February 14, 1929—the day of the so-called St. Valentine's Day Massacre. We were all on the way to California, and during the stop over in Chicago he decided to take his portable radio, which was not operating properly, to a repair shop. The cab driver told us of a store that would service it in a couple of hours; he took us there, and as Robert stepped out of the cab, a truck backed up toward us and two short-necked, flat-faced goons got out. They approached our cab, walking as though their thighs hurt.

"Ya can't park here," the larger of the two said quietly.

"I'll just be a minute," Robert replied. "I'm just going to leave this inside."

"I said ya can't park here," the goon repeated. "Now, get going."

"Look," said Robert, showing him the radio. "All I'm going to do is *leave* this. I won't be a minute."

"Maybe ya don't understand English," said the goon. "I said ya can't park here."

"*And I said for Christ's sake I'll only be a minute!*" Robert bellowed, and he turned and walked into the radio store. The goons were stricken dumb, and my mother and brother and I held our breaths and closed our eyes. After a couple of minutes he reappeared, and the larger goon opened the cab door for him.

"Did you get what you wanted, sir?" he asked.

Robert nodded, and stepped into the cab; the goon closed the door gently behind him, and we drove off. It later turned out that there was nothing wrong with the radio; it just wouldn't work on trains.

He never left himself more than three minutes to catch a train, and one time this margin was reduced to almost nothing when he got hung up, like a snared woodcock, while packing. He had a trick knee, left over from his accident at Don Stewart's wedding, and it used to flip out of joint every now and then. As he was walking across the room with an armful of shirts, he stepped into an open suitcase; the knee buckled, and he fell forward and closed his fingers in a dresser drawer. It was several minutes before he was able to extricate himself, and he made the train with only seconds to spare, but his real regret was that nobody had been there to witness his fall. He figured that he must have looked unbearably funny.

14

His fight against machines and inanimate objects was one that began in grade school in Worcester, and lasted the rest of his life. From the time that he first tried to sharpen a pencil with a dull penknife, he knew that, as he later put it, "the hundred and one little bits of wood and metal that go to make up the impedimenta of our daily life—the shoes and pins, the picture books and door keys, the bits of fluff and sheets of newspaper—each and every one with just as much vicious ill will toward me personally as the meanest footpad who roams the streets, each and every one [is] bent on my humiliation and working together, as on one great team, to bedevil and confuse me and to get me into a neurasthenics' home before I am sixty. I can't fight these boys. They've got me licked."

And this wasn't said in any spirit of comic exaggeration—they had him licked, and he knew it. Manual training was a required subject at South High School, but in the three years that he took it he never learned to drive a nail neatly and cleanly into a piece of wood. He had an early theory that force was the answer; when a nail started to bend, he simply hit it harder, and then harder, until either it was flattened out on its side or, what was more likely, he had hit his thumb with the hammer. And he described his method when a pen refused to work as being to "press down on it so hard that the points spread open like a fork and then to rip the paper in a frenzied imitation of writing." After a few years of this, he gave up force and tried subtlety, with no more luck than before.

Most of his inanimate enemies were small things, the insignificant things that become important only when they turn mean (like a knotted typewriter ribbon, or a splayed shoelace tip), but once, when he still had some of the confidence of youth, he tried to learn to drive a car. I suppose it could be said that he actually did learn, in that he got from one place to another without an accident, but that is about all that could be said.

His first driving lesson was at Lillian's, shortly after he got out of college, when the chauffeur explained to him the intricacies of the Stevens-Duryea. He made a couple of experimental runs, with the chauffeur helping him, but he was in no way qualified to take over complete command of the car, as he did the day the chauffeur broke his arm cranking it on the Nyack ferry, and Robert was forced to drive it all the way home. It was a precarious and a meandering ride, but the fact that he accomplished it without harm to himself or the car gave him the faint gleam of hope that he might, in time, be able to master the machine.

His next lesson was at Mother Colton's farm in Millbury, in the summer of 1917. Henry, the chauffeur, showed him how the pedal-operated, planetary transmission on the Ford worked, and also tried to explain the spark and throttle levers on the steering post, but he attempted too much at one time, and Robert lost him. Red Farm was at the top of a long hill, and the first time Robert tried to get the Ford up the hill he stalled it as soon as it began to buck. When the car spluttered, it was his instinct to take his foot off the gas; as soon as it stalled, he would clutch tight to the wheel in terror and let it coast backward down the hill. Finally the day arrived when, with the car full of people shouting encouragement and advice to him, he succeeded in keeping pressure on the accelerator, and the Ford lurched up to the top of the hill without stalling once. He was so overcome with confidence that, two days later, he volunteered to drive Gertrude and Syd in to Worcester, a trip of perhaps six or seven miles.

This time it was different. Gertrude and Syd were tight-lipped and silent; there was nobody to help him (the main reason he had volunteered was that he was the only possible person available at the time), and for just one thing, he couldn't seem to get the Ford started. He had never straightened out the spark and throttle levers in his mind, and it was only after cranking the car with the levers in every conceivable position that he finally coaxed the engine into life. Then he climbed in and they rattled off, and for a while it looked as though the trip might be an unqualified success. They breezed into the outskirts of Worcester, but when they got near Rice Square, where Gertrude wanted to get off, Robert found that he had to make a sharp turn; he had, in fact, to turn the car around. He tried to dodge the issue by going up a side street, hoping that it might bring him back facing in the opposite direction, but this led him only into a morass of sharp turns and blind alleys, and he was well on the way to Springfield before he gave in and conceded that he was going to have to use the reverse pedal, which he had thitherto been able to avoid. It was a minor triumph that he stalled the car only twice while turning it around, and when, eventually, he and Syd got back to Red Farm, he resolved to practise up on his reverse pedal before taking the Ford to Worcester again.

His practice was interrupted by the failure of the Ford's ignition system, which left him sitting like a crow on a cornstalk in the middle of the town of Grafton, and during the time it took Henry to come and get him in the Packard, and tow the Ford to the local machinist, he began to wonder if he really had mastered the machine after all. The thing that annoyed him was that the ignition switch *looked* the same, whether it worked or not, and he saw no way of telling when a thing was operating and when it wasn't. As far as he knew, it could have been the windshield that had caused the car to stop, and if the ignition switch didn't glow red or shout "Mother!" he saw no way of knowing that it was at fault. With this sobering thought in mind, he practised his use of the reverse gear on a flat space near the barn at Red Farm, away from all slopes and without too much danger of stalling.

When, finally, he had pedalled neutral-first-neutral-stop-reverse-stop-neutral-first-neutral-high-neutral-stop-reverse-stop-reverse-stop-first-stop-stall-stop until he felt confident he could use the reverse pedal as well as the next man, he invited his family and friends into the car to go for a drive with him. There was a great deal of giggling and laughing as they all piled in, but Robert was confident as he said, "All aboard!" and, having already cranked the car and got the engine running, he stepped on the reverse pedal and put on full throttle. The car lunged backward across the drive and slammed into a chestnut tree; there were sharp screams and then a horrible silence. Nobody was hurt—even the Ford survived without major damage—but he never drove again.

Just how out of tune he was with machines was demonstrated on a flight across the English Channel, in an old Handley-Page biplane that John Hay Whitney had chartered, when one of the two engines began to miss badly. Whitney and the others, who knew at least what an airplane engine should *sound* like, jumped to their feet in momentary fright, but Robert, who had been running up and down the aisle to keep warm, thought only that they wanted to join him in a romp. When he saw the expressions on their faces he was terrified, but by then the engine had resumed its normal noise and everybody sat down again, including him. Without the interpreters, he wouldn't have known a thing was wrong.

Aside from these few experiences with machines, however, his main struggle was against the small but stubborn inanimate objects, like the pieces of paper towel that tear off in your wet fingers, four-in-hand ties that jam under a stiff collar, bedroom slippers that creep out from under the bed at night and turn so that you get into them backwards, and packages of mints that refuse to open without being dashed on the sidewalk (this was before the little tape was invented, which doesn't always work either). As he said of the mint package: "It may be a perfectly dandy wrapper, air-tight, water-tight and germ-proof, but if the buyer has to send it to a garage to get it off, something is wrong somewhere."

Now, many people have trouble with these items, but he was unique in that he even had trouble with such uncomplicated things as hairbrushes. He had a pair of military brushes, about which he once wrote: "I have taken [them] from the bureau and held them in a position to brush my hair, without an unkind thought in my mind, and have had them actually fly out of my hands, execute a pretty take-off of perhaps a foot and a half, and then crash into my forehead with as deft a 'one-two' as any heavyweight ever pulled on a groggy opponent." He went on to say that "It is this element of physical danger which has entered into my struggle with these things which has got me worried. I will match myself in an unequal fight to open a can of sardines or a bottle of water, if the issue is to be merely whether I get it open or not. But I can't face the inevitable gashing and bleeding which always follow my failure. I will tackle the closing of a trunk or suitcase, but I am already licked by the knowledge that, no matter how the fight turns out, the metal snaps are going to reach out and nip my fingers."

I feel I ought to repeat again that this was not exaggeration for the purpose of being funny; this was literally true. He would send out for ice, and wait a half hour for it to arrive, rather than try to cope with an ice tray from his own refrigerator. He was unable to carve anything more complicated than a steak. (Gertrude, who had been required to carve for her table when she was a senior at Smith, did all the carving for the family.) If he tried to drive a picture nail in the wall, he wound up with a gaping hole in the plaster. And yet, incredibly, his fingers were agile enough so that he could play the guitar, the banjo, the mandolin, the violin, and the cello, and he was an expert at the three-finger manipulation of the Punch-and-Judy puppets. It was simply mechanical, or useful, things that had him completely and hopelessly hog-tied.

But there was one great advantage to this monumental

lack of dexterity; it showed up in the way he acted in the movies, and even watching him walk across a room, you could tell by the way he walked that he was going to fail at whatever it was he had set out to do. It was a slightly stooped-forward, stern-out kind of walk that he used when intent on accomplishing something, and it gave him a bumbling appearance that was highly comical but also completely natural. If he was just walking, he was erect and spry, but if he was walking with the idea of doing something constructive around the house, the puttering crouch came over him, as though he were already on the defensive against the inanimate objects that were about to lash out at him. A carpenter on the movie set where he was making a short once watched him fumble and drop something, and said, with quiet awe, "My God, he's a born one—he does it without thinking!"

How useful this was was demonstrated when he was making a short in which he, as a weekend guest, was supposed to get up before his host, and therefore had to entertain himself alone in a strange house. The set represented a suburban living room, and there was a square-rigged ship model on the mantelpiece. He came into the room, strolled over and examined the model, and experimentally touched one of the spars, breaking it. This was supposed to happen; it was a breakaway spar that came loose almost as soon as he touched it, but his reaction was one of real fright when it came apart in his hands, and for a moment he forgot that he was acting and tried to put it back together as though he had actually broken it. As a matter of fact, he *had* broken it a little more than had originally been intended. There were no retakes on the scene, nor could there ever have been; it was perfect the first time, because he was honestly afraid that he had ruined something valuable.

His movie shorts, which began with *The Treasurer's Report* in 1928, were made only spasmodically until 1935, when his *How to Sleep* started a whole train of "how to" pictures.

And, oddly enough, *How to Sleep* was made almost by mistake. Pete Smith, a humorous commentator of documentary and educational shorts, was taken sick, and Robert, who was writing on a picture called *Pursuit*, was called in to do the script for a Pete Smith short on Simmons mattresses. Two or three other people had been given the assignment, but M-G-M hadn't thought that their material was up to Pete Smith's standard, so they asked Robert to take a try at writing the commentary. His original assignment was simply to write the words, which would later be spoken by Smith, but then somebody had the idea that, instead of having an anonymous actor go through the business (Smith was always just a voice; he almost never appeared in front of the camera), it might be funny to have Robert do the commentary and also act in it himself. It was accordingly shot that way, over the gloomy objections of one assistant producer, who prophesied that the whole idea was doomed to disaster. It won the Academy Award in its division for that year, and the assistant producer said he'd known all along that it was going to be great.

The "how to" series came at an extremely opportune time, because in 1935 Robert had one son in college and one in prep school, and suddenly found that he was working his own way through college. Lillian reminded him of the note he had signed to her in 1908, and said that she was sure he could now afford to help her support her favourite charities to the tune of, say, $5,000, so he had to knuckle down and produce an extra $5,000. MacGregor had died of a sudden heart attack that spring, and the finances were in a more turbulent state than ever, but what with one thing and another Robert finally managed to get up enough money to buy back the note.

Aside from the disruption it caused in the office routine, MacGregor's death was a deep personal loss. In the five or so years that MacGregor had been working for him, MacGregor had become not only a good friend, but also something of a literary fixture, in that Robert often used him as a character in the syndicate pieces. The three-a-week articles were a grinding chore, based mostly on trivia from the newspapers, and it strengthened them somewhat to build them around the figure of MacGregor. Thus, one piece might begin:

"I have never really given the matter much thought," said Mr. MacGregor. (I had asked him how he would like to climb the Matterhorn.)

"Well, here we are in Switzerland on business," I said, "and there's the Matterhorn. What are you doing—daydreaming?"

Or, another:

The first day we had our frog farm, Mr. MacGregor put on a pair of overalls and went in to do the chores. In a minute he came out, dispirited.

"I can't make them hold still," he said, in a hurt tone.

Or even:

"What is the news this morning, Mr. MacGregor?" I asked, peering around from behind a hangover. "Just give me the key words."

"It says here," replied MacGregor, catering to my whim, "that the Don Cossacks who have been exiled in this country since the Russian revolution are going to elect a new Ataman this month."

And then there was:

The day that Mr. MacGregor lost the locomotive was a confusing one for our accountants. They didn't know whom to charge it to.

"We have an account here called 'Alterations,'" said the head accountant (Mr. MacGregor). "We might charge it to that. Losing a locomotive is certainly an alteration in something."

That last was inspired by the story that MacGregor, who had been an ensign in the Navy during World War I, had been held accountable for an engine of some sort that had disappeared, and his discharge had been held up until he could explain where it had gone.

Robert had wanted to keep on writing MacGregor stories, and was even going to call his next book *Mr. MacGregor*, but MacGregor's death put an end to that. His death, although sudden, had been foreshadowed two or three times before, when he had had spasms that left him weak and trembling, but neither he nor Robert had thought too much about them at the time. MacGregor had even joked about himself, as he did one time on the train going to California, when he was taken sick and spent almost three days in his berth in the compartment, taking no food and lying perfectly still. Finally Robert, who thought that MacGregor might be faking it just a little, decided to test his appetite by ordering his own dinner to be served in the compartment, in full view of the invalid, and as an added enticement he ordered strawberry shortcake for dessert. He was halfway through the strawberry shortcake when MacGregor lifted himself on one elbow and said, "You know, I might try a little of that cake, just to see how it goes down."

Smiling to himself, Robert ordered another portion of shortcake, and when it arrived MacGregor sat up on the bunk, put the plate on his knees, and cut himself a large mouthful. He chewed it, swallowed it, and was quiet for a moment. Then he said, "You know what my stomach just said?"

"No," said Robert. "What?"

"It just said, 'Well, I'll be a son of a bitch.' "

In many ways, MacGregor was a remarkable man, and in many ways he was a man of mystery. Every year, at the first snowfall, a faraway look would come into his eyes, and he would mutter something about mailing a letter. He would then bundle up in his muffler, his derby, and his Chesterfield coat, and he would go out into the snow and not be seen again for three days. Nobody knew where he went; he wasn't seen in any of the places around town, and none of his or Robert's friends ever heard from him, but eventually he would return to the Royalton, take off his hat, muffler, and overcoat, and sit down to work. He would be fresh and clean-shaven, dressed approximately as he had been when he had left, and he would act as though nothing out of the ordinary had happened.

There were other times when he disappeared, too, as he did when Robert went to see the Ludingtons off to Europe and sailed with them. Robert had planned to go to the Harvard-Yale game, in New Haven, with Gertrude, and he radioed her from the boat and told her that MacGregor had the tickets, in case she wanted to see the game alone or with someone else. Gertrude called the room at the Royalton, but MacGregor wasn't there, nor was he there at any time during the next three days. Finally, as a last resort, she called MacGregor's wife, and it turned out that *she* hadn't seen him for three days, and was even more anxious than was Gertrude to get hold of him. When Saturday came, and Gertrude still hadn't been able to locate him, she went in to New York and, just on a chance, stood at the gate of the special train for New Haven. A minute or two before the train was due to start, MacGregor appeared out of the crowd, handed Gertrude the football tickets, and said quietly, "I have no more home than a rabbit." He turned and left, muttering, "No more home than a rabbit."

In the early spring of 1932, Gertrude and young Bob went to Bermuda for a short vacation, and when they were ready to come home, Robert and MacGregor took the *Monarch of Bermuda* down, just to have the boat ride back with them. There were heavy skies and slashing rain squalls as the ship steamed out of Bermuda, and MacGregor cocked his seaman's eye at the weather and said, "I hope we have a real storm, like some of those we used to have in the Navy."

They not only had a real storm; they sailed right into the teeth of a fifty-two-mile-an-hour gale, and the ship had to heave to and ride out the mountainous seas, which smashed through the superstructure, flooded a few of the cabins, and had loose gear and clothing awash as high up as the sun deck. Some of the passengers, whose cabins had become untenable, slept in the main lounge, and one man, who had been clinging miserably to a couch, opened his eyes just in time to see his shoes sail away in a swirl of water, like canoes in the rapids. Robert and MacGregor were among the very few people aboard who weren't seasick, and they were the only ones who thought that the gale was fun. They tramped about the ship, laughing and shouting, "Aye, aye, sir," and smoking big, black cigars, and they left a wake of ill will and cigar smoke behind them wherever they went. They wound up in the main salon, where a group of passengers were sprawled amongst the overturned, careening bits of furniture, praying for quick and merciful death, and they mounted the empty orchestra platform and did a buck-and-wing, shuffle-off-to-Buffalo dance routine, which they completed without having anything thrown at them. Several people had the desire, but nobody had the strength.

Undeniably, MacGregor was a remarkable man, but his mother was, in some respects, even more remarkable. One autumn, after she had spent the summer at a hotel in the Adirondacks, he met her at Grand Central on her way home (I don't know where she lived, but I have a feeling it was in the Middle West), and took her to lunch before she caught her next train. She chatted away about her summer, telling him who was at the hotel and what they had done, and he wasn't paying too close attention until she told him of a nice Miss Borden, with whom she used to take long walks through the woods and fields and who had behaved rather strangely when they first introduced themselves. Apparently Miss Borden, who came from someplace in New England, felt that Mrs. MacGregor should have recognized her name, because after she told it to her she looked at her kind of queerly, as though waiting for some reaction. Aside from that, though, she had been very nice, and the two ladies had become close friends. But Mrs. MacGregor was still worried as to why she should have recognized Miss Borden's name.

"What did you say her first name was?" MacGregor asked, an odd feeling beginning to creep over him.

"Elizabeth," his mother replied. "Elizabeth Borden, and she came from New Bedford, or Providence, or one of those places."

"Could it have been Fall River?" MacGregor asked.

"That's it," said Mrs. MacGregor. "Fall River. Of course. Why? Have you heard of her?"

"Yes," said MacGregor. He asked her if she remembered the poem, which ran:

> Lizzie Borden took an ax
> And gave her mother forty whacks;
> When she saw what she had done,
> She gave her father forty-one.

No, said Mrs. MacGregor, she had never heard it. So MacGregor gave her a brief outline of the Borden murder case, in which Miss Borden's parents were hacked to death in their Fall River home on August 4, 1892, and for which Miss Borden was never convicted, although she was the only person who could have done it. The murder weapon was never found, and in spite of the fact that Miss Borden was seen burning bloodstained clothing, the jury acquitted her for lack of definite evidence. Well! said Mrs. MacGregor. Just imagine.

The next summer, Mrs. MacGregor went back to the same hotel, and after a while MacGregor got a letter from her which said, in part:

> That Miss Borden from Fall River is here again this summer, and although we are still friendly and go for our walks together, I now let her go through the gateways first. After what you told me, there's no point taking any chances.

MacGregor's legacy to the room at the Royalton was the library of books collected for their titles (*Bicycling for Ladies*, etc.), which he had started and on which he spent some little time, and also a knotted rope, which attached to a radiator and which was supposed to be thrown out the window as an escape in case of fire. It was kept coiled in constant readiness, although the room was on the tenth floor and the rope was no more than twenty feet long. As an old Navy man, MacGregor might conceivably have been able to use it if he had had to, but Robert never paid any attention to it, because he knew that if he were to try even to throw it out the window, it would coil around his foot like a snake and dangle him upside down against the side of the building. If the choice was between fire and an inanimate object, he would take the fire any day.

15

In the spring of 1941, he got a little time off from the movies, and we all went out to share a brief vacation with him. We spent a weekend on Catalina Island, where there is a certain amount of deep-sea fishing, and at one point someone suggested that we charter a boat and try our luck.

"It's all right with me," said Gramps. Then a crafty look came into his eyes, and he added, "Or better yet, we might just row out in the harbour and hurl bait at each other."

As it turned out, we should have followed his suggestion, because we spent the whole day trolling for tuna and nobody else caught anything. What he caught was a triple hooked plug, which sprang unaccountably out of the water and landed in his lap, thereby confirming his suspicion that he had strayed too far from the safety of his room. It was the closest he had come to any exercise in a dozen years, and it proved to be a good warning. We spent the rest of the time at Catalina in the hotel or near some sort of shelter, and had a splendid time.

It wasn't that he wasn't strong, or reasonably healthy; it was just that he had an aversion to any unnecessary motion. He claimed that he was saving his energy against the time when he might need it suddenly for something really important, and that any form of athletics would only stir up all the body poisons and be a drain on this precious, someday-to-be-needed reserve of power. He had, as a matter of fact, great power, but the grace and coordination necessary for an athlete were completely absent, so any application of his power was almost unavoidably accompanied by laughter, both from him and from the bystanders.

His attitude toward exercise was summed up in a piece in which he wrote:

About once a year I come to the realization that unless I get some form of exercise pretty soon I will have little ferns and things growing out on me; so I make out a schedule of quick darting movements to be made at various times of the day, usually just before getting into the tub in the morning. Now, other men seem to be able to find space enough in their room to do a daily dozen or two without banging their elbows against furniture, but I am not so fortunate. No matter how big my room is and no matter how simple my drill, I always bang my elbows against a wall or a bureau at one time or another. I believe that I could stand in the middle of the floor of the room in which they signed the Versailles Treaty, and within a minute and a half be whacking an arm or knee against a wall or one of those big glass chandeliers.

Aside from the walking he used to do in Crestwood, the only exercise he ever indulged in was swimming. At the Cap d'Antibes, where we spent two summers, he used to like to go for a leisurely, two-mile swim, alternating the side stroke with the breast stroke, and chatting with whoever was either swimming with him or rowing beside him. His companion was usually Gerald Murphy, another long-distance swimmer who once distinguished himself on a marathon swim in Venice, when two straw-hatted lifeguards rowed out to warn him that some clouds on the horizon spelled danger. "In love, too, there is danger," Murphy replied in Italian, and he continued his swim while the guards rowed thoughtfully back to the beach.

In 1929 Robert's swimming career ended, when he and Murphy swam for more than an hour on a blindingly hot day and he contracted sunstroke. He was delirious that night, and swore he saw Roman centurions on the walls of the old town of Saint Paul, but everybody thought he was just being funny until, the next morning, we were unable to wake him. A doctor was called, and Robert was finally roused from his coma, after which the doctor applied the French cure-all known as *ventouses*. It's a fairly simple operation, in which four or more jelly glasses are cupped to the patient's bare back by suction. A wad of cotton is put in each glass, the doctor lights the cotton with a match, and then slams the glass into place, leaving the fire inside it to burn up all the air and form the vacuum. It also burns a little skin, and the suction leaves monstrous blood blisters, but the treatment is supposed to cure everything from a hangover to pneumonia. Robert, who had understood the doctor to say he was going to apply some *vendeuses*, or salesladies, was loud in his disapproval of the whole procedure.

He stayed out of the sun after that, and the only other time I saw him on a beach was at Nantucket, when the terns got him.

That and his trick knee gave him a fine excuse to avoid doing almost anything that looked like exercise, although he did, for appearance's sake, buy a rowing machine. He put it under his bed the day it was delivered, and never took it out again. He also rented a sun lamp (and eventually paid more than the purchase price in rent), and with the sun lamp and his couch he settled down to enjoy a sedentary urban existence.

He became, in short, a full-fledged spectator sportsman, and remarked that *jai alai* was his most strenuous game, because of the steepness of the Hippodrome stairs. When he was in Montana Vermala with the Murphys, Gerald lured him outside to see the Rhône glacier, without telling him that it was some little distance away from the house. Every hundred yards Robert would say, "Is this it?" like a child on an automobile trip, and Murphy would say no, it was just a little farther on. When, finally, they reached the glacier, Robert was panting and unimpressed, and Murphy felt he had to do something to justify the trip.

"Just think how far that has to go before it reaches the sea," he said. "That ice melts, and flows all the way down and into Lake Geneva, then it goes through Geneva, Lyons,

Valence, Avignon, and Port Saint-Louis, way down by Marseilles." Robert was still unmoved, and Murphy looked once more at the glacier and said, "Poor dear," and Robert laughed so hard he fell down.

Cavalier though he may have been about his own exercise, he was nevertheless quite interested in other people's sports, especially football and horse racing. He had no interest in baseball, and almost the only baseball game he ever attended was a girls' softball game in Los Angeles. John McClain, who went with him, remarked at one point that it was the first time in his life he had ever wanted to kiss a third baseman, which so paralyzed Robert that the game, as a game, lost all its interest.

Without question, his favourite sport was football. After he moved away from Boston, he continued to go back to as many Harvard-Yale games as he could, and he followed the fortunes of the Harvard team either in person, or on the radio, or in the papers. When listening to a Harvard game on the radio, he always wore his fireman's helmet, which he considered a good-luck token of considerable potency; but when, as often happened, the cause was irretrievably lost, he put it away in the closet, not wanting to strain its powers against obviously hopeless odds. Once or twice he put it away prematurely, and then had to race to the closet and jam the helmet back on his head when Harvard made a momentary surge.

When attending a game in person, he watched the field with fierce intensity, working little-known forms of necromancy and magic in support of the team. If he was sitting in a certain position, or doing anything in particular, when Harvard made a good play, he would continue to do whatever it was throughout the rest of the game. Thus he once sat through a whole half with one foot tucked uncomfortably under the other, because it had happened to be that way when Harvard made a touchdown, and another time he had to chew on a dead pipe for over an hour, because it had gone out just as a Harvard man made a long run. He inherited this form of superstition from Jennie, who once was eating horehound candy when Harvard beat Yale. From then until the year she died she ate horehound candy on the day of the Harvard-Yale game, often sickening herself in a useless cause but never giving up hope that it might be the thing to turn the trick. She had originally bought the candy on a trip to her milliner, so every year she repeated the trip, going over the same route and seeing the milliner on some trumped-up excuse, then taking the candy home and forcing Charlie to join her in eating it. Charlie developed a distaste for horehound candy that amounted to loathing, but it did him no good. When Harvard played Yale, Charlie ate horehound candy.

Probably the greatest thrill Robert had in any football game was at the Harvard-Yale game of 1929, when, in the first quarter with the score 0–0, Yale got to Harvard's sixteen-yard-line and then, with considerable fanfare, brought in Albie Booth to try for a field goal. The kick was blocked, and Robert rose like a rocket from his seat, screaming, "Why don't you put in *Booth?*"

Harvard then took the ball and scored the only touchdown of the game, but the sports writers, who had made Booth their particular hero for the season, all but ignored the fact that Harvard won. Harvard men are normally numb to the jokes and the deprecatory remarks of the press, but in this case, Robert felt, a little retaliation was called for. In his "Wayward Press" column in *The New Yorker,* he wrote:

The sports writers ran in rather bad luck this fall with their football heroes. . . . Albie Booth, built up in the sporting pages as the Superman among Supermen, played them a dirty trick in the Harvard-Yale game by staging one of football's most spectacular flops. The boys in the press stand were left with no Great Name around which to weave their stories, except a few Harvard players whom they had never mentioned before. So they wove them around Booth anyway.

Nothing could have been stage-managed better for the press than the entrance of Mr. Booth into the fray. Many of them must have started writing their leads right there on the spot: "A small, hooded figure trotted onto Soldiers' Field today and stood under the shadow of Harvard's goal-posts. With unerring accuracy he removed a pair of mittens, a becoming raglan, and finally a sweater which covered the magic numbers on his back. Seventy thousand pairs of eyes strained to see. And seventy thousand pairs of lips formed the name 'Booth!' as a great roar went up from the Yale stands. 'It's Booth! It's Albie Booth!' And Booth it was.

"Up until now the game had been anybody's. But with Yale in position for a drop-kick, and Albie Booth standing with hands outstretched, the hearts of Harvard's hosts sank and the sons of Old Eli rose to their feet in confident acclaim of their Midget Marvel . . ."

Unfortunately for the sports writers such a lead had to be discarded, for, after an entrance such as is usually reserved for Mussolini or Mrs. Fiske, and after a tense moment of dramatic expectancy, the Midget Marvel was able to get the ball only as far as a Harvard man's chest. Furthermore, owing to a mix-up of some sort, instead of his presence exerting the customary galvanizing influence on the Yale team, it turned the Harvard team into a small-sized army which proceeded immediately to march eighty-four yards to a touchdown, over, through, and around Mr. Booth personally.

The various alibis offered by the newspapermen on Sunday and Monday for their fallen idol were ingenious if unconvincing. His sweater was too large at the neck, allowing a strange Harvard man named Ticknor to grab him and prevent a touchdown. "Booth missed being a hero by two inches of sweater," was the favourite phrase among the scribes. Then, too, he had been injured, and limped as he came on to the field. (He did not seem to be limping during the first thirty yards of what was intended to be an eighty-yard run, but probably his leg got well.) The field was slippery. It was too cold. Everything was thought of except the fact that Mr. Booth was playing against some boys who had played against him before and knew that he was something less than divine. . . . The impression given was that Albie Booth really won the game for Yale but that, owing to Harvard indifference, the real score wasn't recognized. . . . You must say this for the newspapermen: when they make a god, they *keep* him one, or at least until the end of the season.*

But it wasn't only the Harvard team that he liked to follow; he would listen to any football game, revelling in the crowd noises, the general air of excitement, and, more or less incidentally, the game itself. When he was in California, he would turn on his radio at 10:30 or 11 on Saturday morning and listen to the games being broadcast from the East, and then, when they were over, there was time to catch the better part of the Middle Western and, finally, the Western games. He acknowledged that seven hours of football could play hell with a man's wine cellar, but in California you don't know it's autumn unless you're listening to a football game. And autumn was something he hated to miss.

The other sport that he enjoyed was horse racing, although he had no particular knowledge of horses, and a horse, as such, left him pretty much unmoved. There was, however, a strange kind of luck that followed him, and he was often able to violate the established rules of horse playing and come away with a profit. It was his custom to bet on any horse that had a name reminiscent of Harvard—either by colour, or by some similar clue—and so, one day at the Del Mar track, he selected a horse named Puddin, suggestive of the Hasty Pudding Club. The form sheet showed this to be a ludicrous choice, but he nevertheless went to the five-dollar window and asked for one ticket on Puddin to win. It turned out that he was at the five-dollars-across-the-board window, but he was too embarrassed to admit his mistake, so he put up another ten dollars and then slunk away from the window,

*Copyright 1929, The New Yorker Magazine, Inc.

not daring to tell anybody what he had done. Puddin came in, and paid twenty-four to one on the win ticket alone.

It was Roy Rowland, the director of some of his movie shorts, who whetted his interest in the commercial side of horses, because Rowland was able to pick nine out of ten winners just by the sound of their names. Like Irwin in *Three Men on a Horse*, he was infallible if no pressure was on him, and one afternoon, in the bungalow at the Garden of Allah, he picked eight winners out of seven races, calling his choice as the radio announced the names at the post. In the last race, he was undecided between two horses, and they finished in a dead heat. (There were several reliable witnesses to this, by the way.) With a man like Rowland at his side, it is small wonder that Robert set out for the tracks with confidence, and he might have been able to retire at an early age if Rowland hadn't developed the quirk of getting nervous whenever a lot of money was riding on his decision. For five dollars, Rowland was always right; for five thousand, he would question his hunches, and lose. But he showed that it was possible to beat the horses, even if you had to delve into the supernatural to do it.

Jock Whitney was another person with whom Robert went to the track a lot, although Whitney, as the co-owner of the Greentree Stables, had no such occult connections as Rowland had. He was just a man who owned horses, some of which won and some of which didn't. It was Whitney, fifteen years Robert's junior, who first referred to him as Gramps, and he subsequently named a horse Gramps, in his honour. The honour was dimmed by the suspicion that Gramps, the horse, had a broad streak of yellow in him, and the only time he won was one race when Gramps, the man, had no money on him.

But until his association with Rowland, Robert was more interested in the sociable aspect of horse racing than in which horse won what race. He once went to Saratoga for the weekend with various members of the Whitney family, and one of the Greentree horses was running in an important race. The Whitneys gave Robert a good-luck talisman to hold during the race, and he promised to work what magic he could. He even wore a bowler hat and a loud vest, in order better to get into the spirit of the thing. But he had arranged to meet his friend Frank Sullivan before the race, and he and Sullivan retired to the bar in the clubhouse for a bracer, where they found that there was a bartender who not only was named Sullivan, but also came from Worcester—and had served with Robert's brother Edmund during the Spanish-American War. The race was run; the Whitney horse finished out of the money, and when the Whitneys finally located Robert and Sullivan, they were deep in conversation with the Worcester Sullivan, and the talisman lay neglected on the bar.

Once, and very briefly, Robert owned a horse—or, rather, he co-owned one, with John McClain. It was in 1940, when he and McClain were rooming together at the Garden of Allah. One day at the Hollywood track they ran into Whitney, who had brought his trainer and a few of his horses along with him. One of the horses, a beast named Sharpy, showed so little promise that Whitney told the trainer to get rid of him. Suddenly, both McClain and Robert saw something in Sharpy that appealed to them; they were never able afterward to define it, but they knew that the horse was for them.

"How much will you take for Sharpy?" Robert asked Whitney.

"Why?" Whitney parried, not ready to believe what was coming.

"Because McClain and I want to buy him," Robert replied.

Whitney said he guessed $1,000 should be about right, and before long Robert and McClain had dredged up $500 apiece, had signed the bill of sale, and found that they were full-fledged horse owners, complete with one horse and no place to put it. Furthermore, the horse was entered in a

$1,500 claiming race three days from then, and they were unregistered, they had no jockey, and they had nothing for the jockey to wear even if they had one. During the next two days they worked furiously, first arranging to have Sharpy stabled temporarily at the track, then joining the California Racing Association, then deciding on colours, registering the colours, having the silks made, and employing a jockey to wear them. For colours, they chose a mixture of crimson (for Harvard), brown (McClain's alma mater), and blue (Whitney went to Yale), and over the phone they told the tailor to work these out as best he saw fit. In the racing programme, the horse was listed as belonging to the Garden of Allah Stud Farms. On the day of the claiming race, McClain and Robert arrived at the track in a rented limousine, with owners' stickers on the windshield, paddock passes in their lapels, and a brave smile on each of their faces. Their smiles lasted until Sharpy's race, when they got their first look at the silks the tailor had fashioned for them. The poor jockey was cringing under a cap of off-brindle brown, and his jacket was a jumble of crimson and blue stripes, the over-all effect being to make him look like a stained-glass window in a funeral parlour. The horse didn't look much better, and it was then that McClain had his first premonitions of disaster. "My God," he said suddenly. "What if he doesn't win? He won't be claimed, and we'll have to put him up and feed him."

"So what?" Robert replied. "He can have my bedroom, and I'll sleep on the couch in the living room."

Incredibly, Sharpy won the race, paid four to one, and was claimed. McClain and Robert were almost sorry to see him go, but not sorry enough ever to buy another one. They knew when they were well off.

Looking back on it, I can see now that every brush he had with sports or athletics was more or less a warning to keep his distance, and not to come any closer. Even when he made out well, it was under circumstances that told him plainly not to crowd his luck, and if he persisted in trying to be athletic there were always things like the sunstroke in reserve, to convince him of the folly of such a course.

The whole thing was epitomized very nicely one time at Antibes, when he was swimming from the rocks at the end of the Cap. There was a raft about twenty yards out, and to reach it he would usually go down a small flight of steps cut out of the rock, get in the water up to his waist, and then bend his knees and topple slowly forward, becoming water-borne without so much as a splash. He could, in fact, navigate out to the raft and back without disturbing his hair-comb, and it was therefore a considerable shock to see him, on this particular day, walk out to the end of a diving board, bounce experimentally a couple of times, and then look down into the water, as though estimating how deep he could go in one plunge. All movement among the other bathers ceased, and people held their breaths as he made the motions preliminary to diving, then stopped suddenly, staring at the water directly beneath the diving board. Slowly, and very carefully, he backed off the board, and went to a beach attendant, whom he brought to the water's edge and to whom he pointed out something beneath the surface. The man nodded, and turned and ran up across the rocks, and when the rest of us gathered around and looked we saw, clinging to the rocks past which he had been about to dive, a large and fatly repulsive octopus.

It was caught, and taken to the hotel kitchen, but for the next little while nobody did any diving from that board. With no fanfare and no talk, Robert went back to using the steps, from which it was obvious that he never should have strayed.

16

Although he was not an athlete, he was a man of remarkable stamina. The thirty-two years of righteous living had built up in him an impressive reservoir of strength, and he was able to remain spry and clear-headed long after his more dissolute friends had dropped shuddering by the wayside.

Frank Sullivan found this out one night, when he met Robert at Tony's, and Robert was obviously worried and depressed. The mere fact that he showed his depression was so unusual that Sullivan was concerned, and he asked if there was anything he could do. Robert admitted that he was worried about something, and then added the frightening words: "If you're my friend, you'll stick by me tonight."

Sullivan, consumed by the white-hot fire of loyalty, vowed not to leave his side come hell, high water, or the police, and they started off on a tour of the town that took them to many places, some of which Sullivan had never even heard of, much less been to. Around four in the morning, Sullivan realized that they were approaching his home at Central Park and 105th Street, and he was proud and happy to know that he had not failed his friend. He got out of the cab, said a fond and paternal good night, and fell flat on his face. Robert and the taxi driver helped him up to his apartment, where he was more or less automatically relieved of his duties as chaperone.

Robert later told him that his depression had been caused by the fact that a large note was due the next day, and he had no funds with which to meet it.

Robert himself got a nasty jolt one night, although it later turned out not to be quite as serious as he had thought. Late one winter evening, he and a friend were leaving Tony's, and when they got outside a soft, silent snow was falling. Then suddenly, under the Sixth Avenue Elevated, they saw a line of elephants, trunk in tail, padding through the snow, and on the tail of the last elephant hung a red light. Quietly, Robert and his friend turned and went back inside, clutched the edge of the bar, and ordered two double brandies. For a while, neither of them spoke. Then Robert cleared his throat.

"Did you—ah—see anything?" he asked. "Anything out of the ordinary?"

"You mean outside?" his friend said, hopefully.

"Yes," said Robert. "Over toward Sixth Avenue, sort of."

It turned out that what they had seen were the Hippodrome elephants, on their way downtown for a new show, but it wasn't until the Elevated was torn down, many years later, that he could look in that direction at night without a twinge of worry.

I found out about his stamina in 1939, when I got married and moved to New York. On an average of three nights a week, when he was in town, he would call and suggest that my wife and I have dinner with him. These dinners would follow a precise, almost ritualistic pattern. Marjorie or I would accept the invitation, and then, because we would always have been to "21" the time before, he would say that we ought to try someplace new, just for the sake of variety. We would think of several places, all of which would be discarded for one reason or another, and then he would say, "The hell with it. I'll meet you at '21.'" It seldom varied, although the places we went to afterward varied widely. But no matter where we went, it always got late, because there seemed no rational reason to go to bed when staying up with him was so much more pleasant. Also, both he and I shared the fear that we might miss something good if we went to bed. He once explained why he was always the last to leave a party by saying, "I can't seem to bring myself to say, 'Well, I guess I'll be toddling along.' . . . It isn't that I *can't* toddle. It's that I can't *guess* I'll toddle." And that was the way it was when we were together—until sleep was an absolute necessity, if not an accomplished fact, nobody could guess they'd toddle along. And he had immediately won Marjorie's heart by introducing her as "my daughter" instead of "my daughter-in-law," so she didn't care if she never went to bed.

It was at "21," one night after we had finished dinner, that we saw Humphrey Bogart standing at the bar. At the time, Bogart had played nothing but gangster roles; I had never met him, and knew about him only through his pictures, so I was somewhat surprised when Gramps said, "Watch this," and left the table and moved quietly in behind Bogart. He tapped him on the shoulder. "All right," he said. "Finish your drink and get out. We don't want your kind in here."

Bogart turned and looked at him, then dropped his cigarette on the floor, spat out a thin stream of smoke, and reached slowly into an inner pocket. Two customers next to him sidled away nervously, and the bartender began to grope under the bar for a weapon. "Who's going to make me, pal?" Bogart asked, moving in closer.

"Don't you worry about that," said my father, coldly. "Just get going." He put one finger on Bogart's chest, and gave a small push. I thought he had gone crazy.

"If that's the way you want to play, O.K.," Bogart said, showing his fangs. There was a quick flurry; a woman screamed, and then Bogart began to laugh. "That face," he said, doubling over. "I can't look at that face without laughing."

I later found out that they had staged some fairly spectacular mock fights, but that they always wound up with Bogart helpless with laughter. That face, trying to look like a gangster, was more than he could bear.

There is no way to categorize the prowls we went on or the places we visited, because each night was different in its particulars, and there was in common only the fact that the air was charged with a sense of warmth and well-being. Sometimes we wound up at a small, late-closing place on

53d Street, where the ladies' room attendant, a diminutive, wispy old lady named Fanny, would sit at our table and sing Brahms's "Lullaby" in a high, birdlike German voice that was barely audible. And sometimes we would wind up near Grant's Tomb where, in the shrubbery off the side of the road, there is a small gravestone on which is written:

ERECTED TO THE MEMORY OF AN AMIABLE CHILD
ST CLAIRE POLLOCK
DIED 15 JULY 1797
IN THE FIFTH YEAR OF HIS AGE

That was a place he would visit quite regularly, usually around dawn, just to look at the epitaph and repeat the words to himself. And it often put him in a quiet, introspective mood that was in sharp contrast to the rest of the evening. He developed a proprietary kind of love for the Amiable Child, and would show it to newcomers with a soft, parental pride.

In Hollywood, where we would visit him on my vacations, our routine depended somewhat on whether he was working on a picture at the time. If he was, we would have dinner at some restaurant and then retire early to the Garden of Allah, where Marjorie would read a magazine while he and I wrestled quietly on the floor to work off excess energy. (He was quite strong, and the only time I ever pinned him was once when my brother helped me. Even then, he refused to acknowledge defeat, claiming that he had been laughing so hard that he had pinned himself by mistake.) Then he would put through a call to Gertrude in Scarsdale, or Whitney in England, or any number of people in New York, and one thing would lead to another until, perhaps, three o'clock. If he was not working on a picture, anything might happen.

It was on one of the early, or working, nights that we went to a Russian restaurant for dinner, and all the tables were full. The captain was suave and apologetic.

"I'm sorry, Mr. Oakie," he said, "but if you'd care to wait at the bar, I'll have a table for you shortly."

"Never mind," was all my father said, and we turned and left.

We went to the Trocadero, and he kept looking at himself in every available mirror. When, in the course of events, we left to go home, he went to a uniformed man at the door and said, "Would you get us a taxi, please?"

The man turned, and regarded him icily. "I'm very sorry," he said. "I happen to be a rear admiral in the United States Navy."

"All right, then," said my father. "Get us a battleship."

He felt much better after that.

Most of the time, it was not necessary to leave the Garden of Allah to find entertainment. His bungalow was a meeting place for everybody he knew on the Coast, and also for a lot of people he didn't know. The bungalows at the Garden of Allah are so close together that one night a man, who went sleepily to get a glass of water at a woman's request, didn't realize until he got back into the empty bedroom that it was a woman in the next bungalow who had asked for the water. This proximity made it inevitable that every party, or small gathering, was known to everybody in the area, and people would often drop in just because it sounded as though somebody was having a good time. Generally speaking, guests were welcome to stay as long as they liked, but he became slightly restless one night, when a couple got buried deep in their chairs and showed no intention of moving. Around 4:30 A.M., when the conversation had slowed to an almost complete stop and this couple kept saying just one more drink and then they'd be off, my father got up suddenly and went into the bedroom. I heard him say something on the telephone and hang up, then pick up the instrument and say much more loudly, "Mr. McClain, please. . . . Hello, John. What did you want? . . . Oh. . . . All right, then. You come around by the side gate, and I'll pretend I know you. . . . Good." He hung up, closed the door, and went to bed.

About five minutes later, the doorbell rang. I opened it,

and saw the night watchman standing there, with a flashlight in one hand and a large police dog on a leash. He asked for my father, and when I said he had gone to bed the man looked puzzled, then turned and drifted off into the night. The guests left eventually, and the next morning I asked my father what all the telephoning was about. He said that he had asked the night watchman down just to get a little action going, and had made the dummy call to McClain for the same reason; he felt that if things got any more stagnant the guests would have spent the night, and he was trying to stir things up just enough to get them on their feet.

But the holder of the all-time record for staying was a little man he met one night in a bar, who came up to him and said, "I've just written a song that I think might interest you. The name of my song is 'Stars Fell on Orchi Chornya.'" This struck him as staggeringly funny, and he insisted that the man come back to the Garden of Allah. He then got on the telephone, and told his friends that he had a comic songwriter who might very easily be the new Abe Burrows. A few people came by that night, but the little man had nothing else to offer—in fact, he said nothing at all. He spent the next day, having changed into a dressing gown, and he sat in a chair, reading the paper and sipping drinks as they were offered to him. He would nod when people came into the room, but that was all. He seemed perfectly content to sit and listen to the conversation, smiling every now and then, but not saying anything. Finally, on the second day, my father said he didn't want to keep the man from anything that might be important, and the man agreed that he ought to be off. He went into the bedroom and changed back into his street clothes, and then, as he went to the door, he stopped, looked at my father, and said, "I guess I shot my bolt Thursday night."

Sometimes the late evenings were of his own doing, and other times some supernatural power seemed to step in, determined that, no matter how good his intentions, he should not get to bed before midnight. There is, almost directly across Sunset Boulevard from the Garden of Allah, a restaurant called The Players, and he had lunch there quite often and dinner occasionally. One night, he had had an early dinner and was starting back for the bungalow, looking forward to an evening of reading in bed, when it became apparent that crossing Sunset was going to be a major problem. The boulevard takes a long S curve right at The Players, and since there is no traffic light, cars come howling around the curve in full flight. He was no sprinter, he was extremely nervous about any kind of traffic, and on this evening it was heavy enough so that crossing the street was a complete impossibility. So he hailed a cab, but didn't have the courage to tell the driver that he just wanted to make a U turn and be let out on the other side of the street. Instead, he told him to drive up the Strip a way, and he'd tell him where he wanted to go in a minute. He was about to say to turn around and go back to the Garden of Allah, when Ciro's loomed up ahead on the right, and to save face he told the driver to stop there. He got out, and went inside, where he ran into a group of friends. He returned to the Garden shortly after three o'clock, having picked up a bill for $137.50.

It was, as a matter of fact, unusual for him to be able to get a cab anywhere near the Garden of Allah. There was a cab stand in front of Schwab's drugstore, about fifty yards away, but he had what he called his own personal radar, which scattered the cabs the minute he set foot out of the Garden. He tested this several times, and found the exact spot he could reach before his radar took over, and the taxis were off like a covey of quail. So he wound up by buying a car of his own, but since he never learned how to drive, it didn't do him a great deal of good. It was an Oldsmobile, but for all he knew it could have been a Chris-Craft. When Gertrude asked him what kind of car it was, he answered, "Red." Actually, it was green.

His life in Hollywood followed no particular pattern,

although he avoided the big parties and the elaborate to-dos as much as possible. He liked to sit around and talk, with people like Charles Butterworth, Roland Young, McClain, or whoever, and as time passed he found less and less reason to leave the Garden of Allah.

His main bête noire was games. The mere mention of after-dinner games was enough to chill his blood, and he would feign almost any infirmity in order to get out of playing. Once, when he was on a house party and for dietary reasons was drinking only ginger ale, he passed through a room where a group of celebrants were playing Going to Jerusalem. With the superior scorn of the cold sober, he watched the people as they circled the chairs and then, on signal, scrambled to sit down, laughing and screaming and toppling off one another's laps. He went on about his business, and when he returned to the room, a few minutes later, his clear eye saw what everybody else had overlooked—that these people were not taking one chair out of the line-up after each round; they were simply running around the chairs and then fighting to sit down. It was with some satisfaction that he pointed this out to them, and this spoiled the game for them. Once they started doing it right, all the fun was gone.

The last game he ever played—or was ever invited to play—was a game of charades, commonly called The Game, into which he had unaccountably been trapped. There was a group in Hollywood that used to practise their signals for The Game the way football teams hold secret drills, and they played The Game with the deadly seriousness of people who Have to Be Good at Everything. Nobody was exempt when these people wanted to play, and thus it was that he found himself rushing about the room on his hands and knees, trying to act out *Of Mice and Men.* The idiocy of the whole thing became suddenly unbearable and, still on his hands and knees, he said, "To hell with you all," and crawled through a pair of French doors and out into the night. And there was a great deal more than his dislike of games behind that action; there was an upsurge of his New England conscience that tortured him like a hot iron, and made him want to shake loose from a whole way of life.

He had a theory that everyone tends to become the type of person he hates most, and when he gave up writing he gave up the one thing in which he had honest pride. He had never been able to write all he wanted, he felt that he had burned himself out on the mass production of trivia when he should have been doing something better, and he knew that his fame was more because of the movies than because of his writing; but he would still have preferred to be fairly well known as a writer rather than very well known as a movie and radio comedian. The only trouble was that the movie and radio work paid much more money, and wasn't anywhere near as hard as writing had become. In one respect, his only limitations were those of desire, but his desire was often tempered by more lighthearted factors. He once read, in a family letter, that the Benchleys before him had been remarkable mainly for their good-natured laziness, and he knew that he was no different from the rest of them. But then, when he looked back over the twelve books he had written, and all the bound volumes of *Life* and *The New Yorker*, it occurred to him that he must at one point have had a lot of energy, and it depressed him that he no longer seemed to care. The sleeping pills that he took at night kept him awake, and the Benzedrine that he took on the movie lot made him drowsy, and he finally gave up taking the Benzedrine because he could think of no particular reason for wanting to stay awake anyway.

Only once did he ever shout at Marjorie, and that was when she, warmed by the sunshine around the pool at the Garden of Allah, remarked that this was the way she would like to live—that she would like to bring up the children in the warmth and greenery that flourished there.

"Don't you ever let me hear you say that again!" he snapped. "Ever! This is nothing for you, and nothing for

Nat, and nothing for your children! You keep away from it!"

I was in the Navy during the war, and in the spring of 1945 I was transferred to duty in the Pacific. Marjorie and I spent about a week with him at the Garden of Allah and then, the night it came time for me to leave for San Francisco, he took two small glasses, poured a shot of whisky in each, and gave me one. Then he looked at me, said, "*Gute Reise*," and we downed our drinks and shook hands, and I left.

It would have made a good parting, except that when I got to San Francisco I was told to delay a week and then report to San Diego, so Marjorie and I went back and spent the week at the Garden of Allah. Then, when I left for San Diego, we had the same "*Gute Reise*" drink, and this time it was obviously the last. Or it would have been, if there hadn't been a further delay in my orders, which allowed me to get back to Hollywood for one more weekend. The third "*Gute Reise*" did it, and I was off. Under any other circumstances, it would by that time have been a joke.

It was during that last session at the Garden of Allah that he took Marjorie and me out to dinner and, having thought about asking someone else to come along, finally decided not to. "Nobody else is good enough for us," he said, snapping his fingers.

Allowing for the obvious differences, it was just like one of our nights in New York; we went one place for dinner, and then some other place after that, and then, because of the curfew, we went back to the Garden. It must have reminded him of New York, too, because when we got into the bungalow he took off his coat, settled down, and said, "I like it better in the room, here. . . . You know, the only reason I used to take you out and around to all those places was so that, when you couldn't afford to do it on your own, you'd realize that you weren't missing anything."

17

I got back from the Pacific on November 15, 1945, and those of us who were headed for East Coast separation centres were put in barracks in Oceanside, California, until transportation could be found. The first thing we all did was to call home, and Marjorie reported that everything was well and that Gramps was in New York. I had been thinking of trying to get up to Hollywood to see him, but this saved me the trouble.

Two days later, we boarded a train for Los Angeles where, we were told, a special train was waiting to take us East. We reached Los Angeles about noon, and for some reason the whole place looked different from the last time I had been there; it was drab and dirty in the harsh November sunshine, and there was a kind of flat shabbiness about it that was faintly depressing. We waited in line for about eight hours to get on the special train, and when we got aboard, we found that thirty of us were assigned to an observation car with space for twenty. Lieutenant commanders and above slept alone in upper berths; the rest doubled up in the lowers. Since everybody had colds, it didn't much matter who slept where.

The trip took five days. There was no diner, so three times a day the train stopped and everybody raced into whatever the town was and swarmed through the lunchrooms and cafeterias and saloons, and then the engineer blew the whistle and, like a movie film being run backwards, the town was emptied of running figures and the train filled up and moved on. By the time we reached the home stretch, between Pittsburgh and New York, the train had been shunted and switched around so often that the observation car was just behind the tender, and the coal that blew off the tender was piled knee-deep on the observation platform.

The train's ultimate destination was Boston, but I got off

at Pennsylvania Station, in New York, at 2 A.M. November 22. The station was dark and empty; the escalators had stopped running, and I carried my luggage up the long, echoing staircases into the high-domed concourse. One faint light burned by a telephone booth, and I slid my bags along the floor and then, panting, dropped into the booth and called Marjorie. She answered after one ring.

"I suppose you've heard the news," she said.

I stared at the holes in the telephone mouthpiece, and knew exactly what she was going to say. "No," I said. "What?"

"Gramps died this morning," she said. "Or yesterday morning, I mean."

He had had a series of nosebleeds, each more severe than the one before, and then, about four days previously, he had had one that wouldn't stop. He was taken to the hospital, but the hæmorrhaging had become general and finally he had gone into a coma and, at 6 A.M. November 21, had died of, technically, a cerebral hæmorrhage. There had been a quick, frantic calling and scurrying among his friends, forty people volunteered to give blood, and he had eight transfusions, but the whole thing happened so quickly that many people didn't even hear about it until it was on the radio.

He took with him to the hospital a book of philosophical essays called *The Practical Cogitator, or, The Thinker's Anthology*, and he made marginal notations on the five pages that he read. The last essay he read was called "Am I Thinking?" by James Harvey Robinson, and the marginal notation beside the title reads: "NO. (and supposing you were?)"

His ashes were kept at the crematorium until we decided on a burial place. He had suggested several times that we get a family plot at Nantucket, so in the early spring my mother went up there and bought a lot in the Prospect Hill cemetery, and we then arranged a date when she and my brother and I would go up. She had, in the meantime, ordered a so-called urn, which was actually a small bronze box with his name and dates on the side.

The day we left for Nantucket, she and my brother drove in to pick me up at my apartment, and when I got into the car I threw my bag in back and slid into the driver's seat, at the same time looking for the urn.

"Are we all packed?" I asked.

"Yes," said my mother. "I've got the urn in the Noah bag in the luggage compartment." The Noah bag was a small leather satchel which he had used for carrying books and miscellaneous gear.

We went out the West Side highway and then up the Merritt Parkway, my brother and I alternating at the wheel every hour. It was near the middle of April and the trees were not yet out, but there was a clean, wet smell of spring in the air and it was good driving. My mother kept looking at the map of the route between New York and New Bedford, in spite of the fact that we all knew every mile of the drive by heart. There is a strange kind of fascination about a route map, and you can stare at one for a long time with your mind almost a complete blank.

You can usually see Nantucket shortly after you pass Cross Rip lightship, about an hour out. This time, however, the fog was so thick that we could see nothing until we neared the jetties at the entrance to the harbour. We peered over the side as the first dim outlines of the shore seeped through the fog, and felt a reminiscent pleasure when we finally saw the clean, boxlike houses of the town. We passed by the spot where we had once gone fishing, and Marjorie had caught so many fish that Gramps suggested that she was sitting over an insane asylum. Then the steamer gave a long, hollow blast as it rounded Brant Point and slid into the harbour, and I went below and waited in the car. More or less to kill time, I unlocked the luggage compartment and checked on the Noah bag. It hadn't moved.

When we got ashore, we bumped across the cobblestones

on Main Street, and wound around a loop of one-way streets until we reached the undertaker's. His office, a one-story brown building that was half garage, was closed, so my mother mounted the neat white steps of his house and rang the bell, while I unlocked the luggage compartment and took out the Noah bag.

Mr. Lewis was a small, thin, pleasant man. He had just finished lunch and was apparently expecting us. I was introduced to him and stood, holding the Noah bag, while my mother and he discussed the details of the next day's business. I looked around the room and idly inspected the whaling prints, the Island Service Company calendar, and the Victorian New England drapes. Finally, I put the Noah bag on the reading table.

"Here's this," I said. "Do you want to keep the bag for now?"

"No, that won't be necessary," he said. "I'll just take the urn." He reached in and got the urn, looked at the name on it, and set it down on the table. "That's a nice one," he said.

"All right, then," my mother said, abruptly. "We'll see you at eleven o'clock tomorrow."

"I'll be there," he said, holding the door open for us. "Don't worry."

We went out to the car, and I dropped the empty Noah bag into the back seat. My mother picked up a sweater and handed it to me.

"Here," she said. "Put this in the bag. I want to use it for something else right away." I put the sweater and my hat into the Noah bag, and we started off.

We drove around the moors for a while, and then came back into town and stopped by the paper store to buy some magazines. As I turned off the engine, a car pulled up behind us and Mr. Lewis got out. He came up to the door next to me.

"I've been looking for you for two hours," he said, quietly. "That urn was empty."

"It was—*what?*" said my mother slowly.

"It was empty. Nothing in it. Never had been."

Nobody spoke for a minute, and Mr. Lewis looked uneasy.

My mother leaned forward and put her face in her hands for just a couple of seconds, then straightened up. "Well," she said, "we'll have to call New York. They must have made a mistake."

"I guess they did," said Mr. Lewis. "You can use my phone if you'd like."

We called, and the people nervously admitted their error. The only trouble was that they couldn't do anything about it before we had to leave. Taking the urn from Mr. Lewis, we put it in the Noah bag, and drove back onto the moors.

My mother was quiet for a while, and then slowly she began to smile.

"You know," she said, "I can hear him laughing now."

BOOKS BY ROBERT BENCHLEY

1921 Of All Things
1922 Love Conquers All
1925 Pluck and Luck
1927 The Early Worm
1928 20,000 Leagues Under the Sea, or, David Copperfield
1930 The Treasurer's Report & Other Aspects of Community Singing
1932 No Poems, or, Around the World Backwards and Sideways
1934 From Bed to Worse, or, Comforting Thoughts About the Bison
1936 My Ten Years In a Quandary, and How They Grew
1938 After 1903—What?
1942 Inside Benchley
1943 Benchley Beside Himself
1947 *Benchley—Or Else!
1949 *Chips Off the Old Benchley
1954 *The Benchley Roundup

MOVIE SHORTS IN WHICH ROBERT BENCHLEY APPEARED

1928 The Treasurer's Report (Fox)
1928 The Sex Life of the Polyp (Fox)
1929 Lesson No. 1 (Fox)
1929 Stewed, Fried & Boiled (Fox)

* Posthumous collection.

1929 Furnace Trouble (Fox)
1933 Your Technocracy and Mine (RKO)
1935 How to Sleep (M-G-M)
1936 How to Behave (M-G-M)
1936 How to Train a Dog (M-G-M)
1936 How to Vote (M-G-M)
1936 How to Be a Detective (M-G-M)
1937 The Romance of Digestion (M-G-M)
1937 How to Start the Day (M-G-M)
1937 A Night at the Movies (M-G-M)
1938 How to Figure Income Tax (M-G-M)
1938 Music Made Simple (M-G-M)
1938 An Evening Alone (M-G-M)
1938 How to Raise a Baby (M-G-M)
1938 The Courtship of the Newt (M-G-M)
1938 How to Read (M-G-M)
1938 How to Watch Football (M-G-M)
1938 The Opening Day (M-G-M)
1938 Mental Poise (M-G-M)
1939 How to Sub-Let (M-G-M)
1939 An Hour for Lunch (M-G-M)
1939 Dark Magic (M-G-M)
1939 Home Early (M-G-M)
1939 How to Eat (M-G-M)
1939 The Day of Rest (M-G-M)
1939 See Your Doctor (M-G-M)
1940 Inferiority Complex (M-G-M)
1940 Home Movies (M-G-M)
1940 The Trouble with Husbands (Paramount)
1941 Waiting for Baby (Paramount)
1941 Crime Control (Paramount)
1941 The Forgotten Man (Paramount)
1941 How to Take a Vacation (Paramount)
1942 Nothing But Nerves (Paramount)
1942 The Witness (Paramount)
1942 Keeping in Shape (Paramount)

1942 The Man's Angle (Paramount)
1943 My Tomato (M-G-M)
1943 No News Is Good News (M-G-M)
1944 Important Business (M-G-M)
1944 Why, Daddy? (M-G-M)
1945 I'm a Civilian Here Myself (U.S. Navy)

ABOUT THE AUTHOR Nathaniel Benchley, the elder son of Robert Benchley, was born in Newton, Massachusetts, educated at Phillips Exeter Academy and Harvard College. Aside from service in the Navy in World War II, he has spent most of his adult life in New York City. In New York he has been a reporter on the *New York Herald Tribune*, has done editorial work for the magazine *Newsweek*, but for the most part has been a free-lance writer whose works have appeared in most of the well-known magazines. He has had many short stories in *The New Yorker*, *Collier's*, *Ladies' Home Journal*, *Holiday*, and *Esquire*. He has written a play, *The Frogs of Spring*, which was produced on Broadway in 1953. The author of *Side Street*, published in 1950, he was also the editor of *The Benchley Roundup*, a selection of his father's stories published in 1954.